Defending America

Defending America

America

The Case for Limited National Missile Defense

JAMES M. LINDSAY
MICHAEL E. O'HANLON

BROOKINGS INSTITUTION PRESS
Washington, D.C.

Copyright © 2001
THE BROOKINGS INSTITUTION
1775 Massachusetts Avenue, N.W., Washington, D.C. 20036
www.brookings.edu

Library of Congress Cataloging-in-Publication data
Lindsay, James M., 1959-
Defending America : the case for limited national missile defense /
James M. Lindsay and Michael E. O'Hanlon.
    p.   cm.
Includes bibliographical references and index.
  ISBN 0-8157-0008-3 (cloth : alk. paper)
  1. Ballistic missile defenses—United States. I. O'Hanlon, Michael E.
II. Title.
UG743 .L39 2001
358.1'74'0973—dc21   2001001713

9 8 7 6 5 4 3 2 1

The paper used in this publication meets minimum requirements of the
American National Standard for Information Sciences—Permanence of Paper
for Printed Library Materials: ANSI Z39.48-1992.

Typeset in Sabon

Composition by R. Lynn Rivenbark
Macon, Georgia

Printed by R. R. Donnelley and Sons
Harrisonburg, Virginia

To our siblings

Laurie Jordan, Bob Lindsay
and
Ann, Billy, and Kate O'Hanlon

Foreword

Should the United States deploy a national missile defense? This is one of the most important policy questions facing President George W. Bush. His decisions on missile defense will have potentially enormous consequences for America's security and international affairs.

The United States has never had a nationwide defense against missile attack. That raises questions about whether the United States will someday, out of fear of reprisal against its homeland, be deterred from projecting power abroad or at least from considering certain military options. Meanwhile, since the Pentagon's last major policy plan, the 1997 quadrennial defense review, the potential ballistic missile threat to the American homeland has increased as missile delivery system technology has proliferated, as noted in the Rumsfeld Commission report.

Yet deploying missile defenses would require modifying or even withdrawing from the Anti-Ballistic Missile Treaty. In light of the end of the cold war, the treaty's blanket prohibition on nationwide defenses arguably has been overtaken by events. Nonetheless, Moscow still values the treaty highly, as do many of America's key allies—this guarantees that efforts to deploy missile defenses will be extremely challenging diplomatically. In addition, there are obvious technical hurdles that must be surmounted to make national missile defenses work, not to mention the budgetary issues that will be fought out in Congress. Reduced to their essentials, they boil down to the familiar question: how much insurance is enough—a matter on which honorable men and women will surely differ.

James M. Lindsay and Michael E. O'Hanlon wrestle with these problems. Noting that missile defense proponents and opponents both make valid points, they nonetheless argue that each side is deaf to the other's concerns. This book searches for a proposal for national and allied missile defense that incorporates the most important and persuasive concerns of each view.

The authors are deeply grateful for the support and assistance they received from their colleagues in researching and writing this book. Richard Haass encouraged the project from the start and did much to create a lively, collegial, and constructive environment at Brookings, which greatly aided the authors as they wrote the book. The authors are also deeply indebted to Ivo Daalder, Tom Donnelly, Bates Gill, James Goldgeier, Philip Gordon, Richard Haass, and David Mosher for reading the entire manuscript and providing detailed and invaluable comments. Harold Feiveson, Steve Fetter, Richard Garwin, George Lewis, Frank von Hippel, and David Wright answered the authors' queries on a variety of technical issues.

Jason Forrester, Gregory Michaelidis, and Micah Zenko were superb research assistants who worked tirelessly and in good cheer to track down a dizzying array of facts and figures. Todd DeLelle made the process of verifying the manuscript a pleasure. Theresa Walker edited the manuscript, Carlotta Ribar proofread it, and Julia Petrakis prepared the index.

The authors thank the German Marshall Fund of the United States and the John M. Olin Foundation for their financial support of this effort.

The views expressed here are solely those of the authors and should not be ascribed to the persons whose assistance is acknowledged above or to the trustees, officers, or other staff members of the Brookings Institution.

MICHAEL H. ARMACOST
President

March 2001
Washington, D.C.

Contents

Abbreviations

ABL	airborne laser
ABM Treaty	Anti-Ballistic Missile Treaty of 1972
BMDO	Ballistic Missile Defense Organization
C1	Capability 1
C2	Capability 2
C3	Capability 3
CIA	Central Intelligence Agency
CTBT	Comprehensive Test Ban Treaty
DoD	Department of Defense
DoE	Department of Energy
ESDP	European Security and Defense Policy
GPALS	Global Protection against Limited Strikes
IAEA	International Atomic Energy Agency
ICBM	intercontinental ballistic missile
INF	Intermediate-Range Nuclear Forces Treaty
IRBM	intermediate-range ballistic missile
MAD	mutual assured destruction
MRBM	medium-range ballistic missile
MIRV	multiple independently targetable reentry vehicle
MTCR	Missile Technology Control Regime
NATO	North Atlantic Treaty Organization
NIE	National Intelligence Estimate

NMD	national missile defense
NPT	Nonproliferation Treaty
NTW	Navy theater-wide defense
PAC	Patriot Advanced Capability
RV	reentry vehicle
SBIRS	space-based infrared system
SLBM	submarine-launched ballistic missile
SDI	Strategic Defense Initiative
SRBM	short-range ballistic missile
START	Strategic Arms Reduction Treaty
THAAD	theater high-altitude area defense
TMD	theater missile defense
WMD	weapons of mass destruction

CHAPTER ONE

Defending America

S HOULD THE UNITED STATES build a national missile defense (NMD) to protect the American people, and possibly key allies as well, against attack by long-range ballistic missiles? President Bill Clinton's September 2000 announcement that he was deferring the decision on whether to deploy an NMD system puts this question squarely on the Bush administration's agenda. The United States currently has no nationwide defense against missile attack. Should President Bush fulfill his campaign pledge to "build effective missile defenses, based on the best available options, at the earliest possible date," the decision will have potentially seismic consequences for both American national security and international affairs.[1] Most countries, including many of America's closest allies, warn that missile defense will trigger an arms race and jeopardize three decades of arms control efforts.

Within the United States, reactions to national missile defense have broken down along well-worn lines. Opponents, most of whom are Democrats, complain that the benefits of national missile defense are uncertain and the costs steep. They argue that effective missile defenses are difficult to build—not the least because America's adversaries have every incentive to find ways to defeat them—and that the investment of billions would produce only a high-tech sieve. At the same time, deploying an NMD system would strain relations with Russia, China, and

1

Europe and threaten three decades of arms control. Even those who believe that formal superpower nuclear arms control has become anachronistic should worry. A hasty, ambitious NMD deployment could worsen U.S. security by impeding cooperative programs to secure Russia's nuclear weapons and materials, and by reducing the odds that Moscow and Beijing will tighten their controls over the proliferation of weapons of mass destruction. The result may well be a world with more intercontinental ballistic missiles (ICBMs) and weapons of mass destruction that would leave America less secure, not more secure.

Supporters of national missile defense, most of whom are Republicans, insist not only that the United States should build defenses but that it must. They argue that revolutionary developments in radar, laser, and data processing technology are transforming missile defense from the stuff of science fiction into a here and now reality. These technological breakthroughs come as nuclear and ballistic missile technology is spreading to states that are virulently hostile to American power and values. According to this view, a national security policy that deliberately leaves the American people vulnerable to attack when technology makes it possible to protect them is immoral and unacceptable. Not only does it fly in the face of common sense to leave the nation undefended, but it could hamstring America's role in the world. If hostile countries such as Iraq felt they could threaten the United States, and thereby deter it from defending its allies and global interests, these countries might feel less constrained about threatening or attacking their neighbors. Moreover, vulnerability to long-range ballistic missile attacks could cause America's friends and allies to doubt its willingness to stand by its security commitments, thereby weakening support for the United States around the world.

Both sides in the NMD debate make valid points. But rather than generating a serious discussion of how each side's legitimate concerns can be forged into a sensible policy for the country, the current debate has degenerated into a dialogue of the deaf. Each side repeats its claims with evangelical fervor, often exaggerating the harm or promise of missile defense. National missile defense, however, should not be an ideological issue to champion passionately or oppose resolutely. The issues are complicated, not clear cut. What is needed is not partisan or ideological cheerleading but a sober analysis of the role national missile defense can play in American national security. That is what this book seeks to provide.

Déjà Vu All Over Again?

Whether to defend the United States against ballistic missile attacks is not new to American politics. The current debate over national missile defense marks the third round in a decades-long debate over the merits of defense in the nuclear age.

Although initial research programs had begun a decade earlier, the first major missile defense debate began in 1967 when the Johnson adminis-tration proposed building the Sentinel system, which would have placed nuclear-tipped interceptor missiles at fifteen sites around the country, including ten near major metropolitan areas.[2] People living near the planned sites rebelled, however, because they feared that putting the mis-siles in their backyard would greatly increase their chances of becoming the target of an attack. The Nixon administration recognized that Sentinel was politically unsustainable and changed course. It abandoned the idea of defending American cities and proposed instead to use the same interceptor technology to defend a portion of America's land-based ICBMs. The new program, named Safeguard, proved politically contro-versial as well, and it barely survived congressional opposition led by a coalition of Democrats and liberal Republicans. In October 1975 the lone Safeguard site opened in Grand Forks, North Dakota. Less than two months later, however, anti-Safeguard forces prevailed on Capitol Hill, and Congress voted to close the base, effectively writing off an investment of more than $20 billion (in 2001 dollars).[3]

With the passing of Safeguard, missile defense disappeared as a politi-cal issue until Ronald Reagan resurrected it in his famed 1983 "Star Wars" speech.[4] The result was a new, high-profile program, the Strategic Defense Initiative (SDI), that sought to defend the United States with ground-based and space-based weapons. Like Sentinel and Safeguard, SDI polarized Congress, though this time largely along party lines. Pro-ponents (mostly Republicans) argued that defending America was a moral imperative; critics (mostly Democrats) argued that it was wasteful and dangerous. Unlike Safeguard, however, SDI never left the research and development stage. The Bush administration reduced the program's political profile and focused it on long-term research. The Clinton admin-istration initially went even further. At the behest of many in the military, it redirected spending away from national defenses and toward theater missile defenses (TMD) designed to protect U.S. troops and allies against attacks by shorter-range missiles like the infamous Scud that played such a prominent role in the 1991 Persian Gulf War (figure 1-1). In contrast to NMD programs, TMD programs have enjoyed widespread political support during the past decade because the threat of attack on U.S. troops from shorter-range missiles has been judged considerable and because TMD systems are usually not seen as threatening the deterrents of other major nuclear powers.

The Sentinel, Safeguard, and SDI programs all foundered on two obstacles. The first was technological—none of the three programs offered the prospect of an effective defense. The Johnson administration acknowledged from the start that Sentinel could not defend the United States against a Soviet attack—the system was justified as a "thin" defense against a possible Chinese attack. (China did not deploy long-range missiles capable of reaching U.S. soil until 1980.) Even in that limited role it raised major worries because it sought to destroy incoming warheads in their terminal phase by detonating nuclear warheads in the atmosphere over the United States. The Safeguard system's interceptor missile flunked nearly half of its flight tests. Even if the interceptor missile had worked flawlessly, the Soviet Union could easily have overwhelmed the lone Safeguard site (which is why the Ford administration acquiesced in the congressional decision to shut it down). The SDI proponents insisted that the United States was on the verge of mastering exotic technologies such as x-ray lasers. By the end of the Bush administration, however, the Pentagon had concluded that such weapons were decades away from being ready.

The second, and in many ways more important, obstacle to missile defense was strategic. Critics argued that even if highly effective defenses could be built, they would—at least in the context of the U.S.-Soviet rivalry—produce a more dangerous world, not a less dangerous one. One problem is that they would have likely fueled a superpower arms race. Moscow would build more offensive weapons in order to be certain it could overwhelm any U.S. defense, and Washington would respond similarly to any Soviet defense. Worse yet, defenses might have made war more likely. Both countries would fear that the other side could attack first and then use its defenses to blunt a retaliatory attack. This would have created an incentive to strike first, before the adversary could attack. Moreover, the incentive to "use them or lose them" would be strongest at the worst possible time—during a crisis. Finally, given the state of technology, defenses would probably not have worked in any case—especially in light of the enormous strategic arsenals each side wielded against the other.

The conviction that national missile defenses fuel arms races and make crises more dangerous led the United States and the Soviet Union to sign the Anti-Ballistic Missile (ABM) Treaty in 1972. The treaty flatly banned all forms of national missile defense that could provide territorial defense for the United States or Soviet Union against long-range missile attack. It did not, however, ban defenses against strategic or long-range missiles outright. Instead, it permitted both countries to operate two small missile defense systems (like Safeguard), one around its national capital and the other around an ICBM site, each equipped with no more than one hundred interceptors designed for local defense. (In 1974 the United States and the Soviet Union agreed to cut the number of permitted sites and interceptors in half; Russia continues to maintain its site around Moscow.) The treaty permitted a certain amount of radar capability for each defense site; it also permitted early-warning radars along each country's periphery and facing outward (and in certain overseas locations) as well as satellites for similar purposes. But to create firebreaks against any rapid or clandestine expansion of these limited defenses, the treaty barred other types of sensors, the development and testing of sea- and space-based defenses, as well as other mobile national missile defense systems. It also banned exports of long-range missile defense technologies. Both countries retained the right, however, to develop and build theater defenses, conduct basic research on virtually all missile defense technology, and develop and test fixed land-based ABM technologies as long as any deployments met the treaty's strict guidelines.

In sum, the core motivation behind the ABM Treaty was that neither country should develop a *strategically significant* defense, that is, one that could render the adversary vulnerable to a disarming first strike, or spark an arms race. However, the letter of the treaty bans all national missile defenses—that is, any system, however limited in scale, that could defend all of a country's territory against long-range missile attack.

In signing the ABM Treaty, Washington and Moscow formally embraced the idea that, at least in the case of their superpower rivalry, mutual vulnerability helped prevent nuclear war and dampen a wasteful arms race. (The two sides were not so enamored with vulnerability that they agreed to restrict air defenses or antisubmarine warfare capabilities.) The wisdom of this decision has been debated ever since; indeed, it was hotly debated during the 1980s, when the cold war continued. Missile

Figure 1-1. *U.S. Spending on Missile Defense*
Billions of constant 2001 dollars

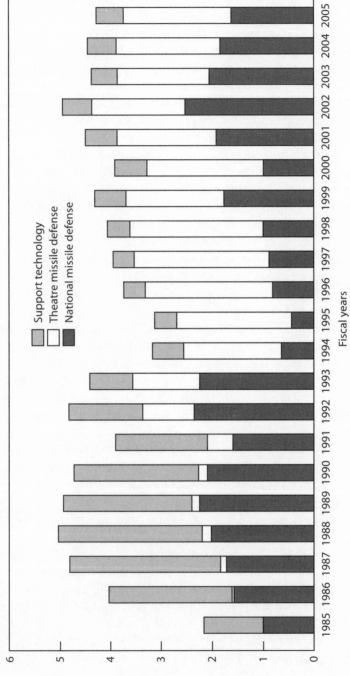

Legend:
- Support technology
- Theatre missile defense
- National missile defense

Fiscal years: 1985 1986 1987 1988 1989 1990 1991 1992 1993 1994 1995 1996 1997 1998 1999 2000 2001 2002 2003 2004 2005

Source: Walter Slocombe, undersecretary of defense (policy), "U.S. Limited National Missile Defense Program," presented at Harvard-CSIS Ballistic Missile Defense Conference, Cambridge, Mass., May 2000, p. 27.

Note: Spending for fiscal years 2001–05 is projected.

defense critics acknowledge that the logic of mutual assured destruction (MAD) is counterintuitive, but they insist it forms the cornerstone of strategic stability. Many NMD proponents, however, reject the idea that a MAD world has an overriding virtue. They argue that any policy that leaves the United States vulnerable to a nuclear attack, whether accidental or intentional, is immoral.[5] What is often overlooked amid this sparring is another, more nuanced, possibility: a limited defense against small powers may have virtue even if there is no alternative to a MAD world between the great powers.

Is the Third Time a Charm?

Has anything changed since the Sentinel, Safeguard and SDI debates to warrant rethinking the idea of national missile defense? Proponents say yes. They make three points. First, U.S.-Russian relations have improved greatly with the end of the cold war, easing fears that defensive deployments will inevitably spark an offensive arms race. The warmer strategic climate also has lowered the bar for judging any missile defense worthwhile. A missile defense that would have been pointless during the cold war given the size of the Soviet threat may make sense today (table 1-1). Second, the United States faces a greater threat of attack as missile technology spreads to more countries. Many of these new ballistic missile powers are deeply hostile to American values and interests. Third, technology has improved, making it possible to build effective defenses against the smaller threats that the new ballistic missile powers pose.

There is more truth to each of these claims than critics are willing to acknowledge. The changes are not as dramatic, however, as missile defense proponents would have it.

Better Relations with Russia (Though Don't Forget about China)

With the end of the cold war, the United States and Russia are no longer enemies and have begun to take important steps to reduce the threat they pose to each other. They no longer deploy huge land armies against each other. They have negotiated the Strategic Arms Reduction agreements (START I and START II), which if implemented will bring the number of strategic nuclear warheads on each side down to 3,000–3,500. They are committed to using the START III negotiations to cut their arsenals to no more than 2,000–2,500 strategic warheads apiece. Under the

Table 1-1. *Evolution of U.S. National Missile Defense Programs*

Item	Mission	Threat size	Space-based laser	Space-based interceptors	Ground-based interceptors
Strategic Defense Initiative (1980s)	Counter massive Soviet ballistic missile strike	1,000s	10s	4,000	1,500
GPALS (early 1990s)	Defeat accidental or unauthorized ballistic missile launch	200	No	1,000	750
Limited national missile defense (2000)	Defend against very small rogue state threat	A few to a few 10s	No	No	100 to 250

Source: Walter Slocombe, undersecretary of defense (policy), "U.S. Limited National Missile Defense Program," presented at Harvard-CSIS Ballistic Missile Defense Conference, Cambridge, Mass., May 2000.

Department of Defense (DoD) Nunn-Lugar cooperative threat reduction initiative and related Department of Energy (DOE) programs, American scientists visit Russian nuclear weapons labs and vice versa, U.S. technology helps protect Russian weapons and nuclear materials from theft and diversion, and American dollars pay for the partial dismantlement of an aging Russian nuclear arsenal.[6]

The fundamental transformation in U.S.-Russian relations clearly creates the opportunity for new discussions on missile defense, as Moscow itself acknowledges. In 1997, then-Russian president Boris Yeltsin agreed to consider Bill Clinton's request to negotiate changes to the ABM Treaty to permit the deployment of a limited national missile defense. In 2000, the new Russian president, Vladimir Putin, acknowledged that missile defenses have a role to play in the post–cold war world and proposed that Russia and NATO work jointly to develop them.

But claims about a new strategic climate are easily pushed too far. Although Russia and the United States have better relations, they are not allies. Substantial suspicion still marks the relationship—witness the tensions over NATO's 1999 war against Serbia and Russia's ongoing war against Chechen rebels. The distrust is especially strong in Moscow. It understandably fears defenses that theoretically could some day render its nuclear deterrent obsolete and further diminish its already sinking international status. So Washington should not be surprised that Moscow does not enthusiastically embrace its missile defense proposals.

The focus on how much warmer U.S.-Russian relations are than U.S.-Soviet relations also overlooks another key player in the missile defense debate: China. Unlike Russia, China is not a declining power but a rising one; and again, unlike Russia, China has specific territorial issues (notably Taiwan) over which it could conceivably wage a war with the United States. How does the missile defense debate look in Beijing, then?

China is not a signatory to the ABM Treaty, but missile defense clearly affects its interests. With only about twenty ICBMs in its arsenal, China has never had a robust second-strike capability against the United States. Deployment of even a "limited" NMD system could, depending on the specific architecture chosen, make the value of its nuclear deterrent even more questionable. Missile defense looks especially threatening to Beijing coming as it does on the heels of a decade of seemingly closer U.S. support for Taiwan—a rogue, breakaway province in China's eyes—as well as a 1997 White House decision to add Chinese political and military installations back into U.S. strategic nuclear targeting plans after a twenty-year absence.[7] No one should be surprised, then, that Beijing looks skeptically on President George W. Bush's claim that "America's development of defenses is a search for security, not a search for advantage."[8]

It is tempting to dismiss Russia's and China's complaints as their problem. But that view is too simplistic, even from the perspective of enhancing U.S. security. At a minimum, deploying defenses over Russia's objections could jeopardize President Bush's hopes to make deep cuts in offensive nuclear weapons. Until the day that Russia sees the United States as entirely unthreatening—an outcome to be hoped for but not one on the immediate horizon—it will continue to link its offensive deployments to U.S. decisions on missile defense. Fiscal constraints will hamper its ability to do so, but Moscow will still retain some low-cost options for deploying a sizable nuclear arsenal—such as retaining the multiple-warhead ICBMs it is supposed to destroy under START II. Chances are, then, that the more robust the U.S. defense, the larger the Russian nuclear arsenal. The same goes for China.

Some may say, so what? After all, with the cold war over, superpower arms balances no longer have the importance they once did. And if China builds up its offensive strategic forces to counter a U.S. defense, at least it will have fewer resources to spend on other military instruments—such as the amphibious forces that would be needed to seize Taiwan.

But the fallout from a push for missile defenses would probably redound to America's disadvantage. Both Russia and China would probably improve their existing countermeasure technologies—particularly against so-called midcourse defenses that attempt to destroy enemy warheads in space—a step that any country with the resources to test missiles repeatedly can probably take with considerable success. If Moscow and Beijing feel threatened by a U.S. missile defense, they might also respond by deploying their nuclear forces on states of hair-trigger alert. (Russia already does so, but future arms control efforts could change that.) This would substantially increase the risk of accidental war, hardly the desired outcome of missile defense.

Russia might also curtail its cooperation with the United States to secure its nuclear arsenal. Cooperative programs have consolidated and secured most of Russia's nuclear weapons to date, but challenges remain. Surplus nuclear materials that are not inside actual nuclear warheads remain widely dispersed and vulnerable to theft. In addition, large numbers of Russian weapons scientists, many of whom are now working on temporary contracts that reduce their incentives to emigrate to radical states seeking their expertise, do not yet have self-sustaining civilian jobs within Russia.

Finally, Russia and China might stop cooperating on issues that matter to Washington, particularly nuclear proliferation. Indeed, pursuing national missile defense over Russian and Chinese objections might encourage them to sell technology for developing weapons of mass destruction, building missiles, and defeating defenses to countries such as North Korea, Iran, and Iraq, creating a situation in which the cure aggravates the disease. And China might reduce its efforts to moderate North Korea's behavior, and raise the temperature in its dealings with Taiwan, to complicate U.S. foreign policy and make Washington pay a price for ignoring China's strategic interests.

To be sure, at this point these worries are hypothetical. No one knows for certain how Russia or China would react to a U.S. NMD deployment that trampled on its interests. However, the vociferousness of Moscow's and Beijing's objections to NMD suggests that their responses would not be benign. So do the normal competitive security dynamics between countries that view each other as rivals. The U.S. National Intelligence Council shares our concerns, concluding, among other things, that Moscow and Beijing may sell countermeasures to other countries if the United States deploys an NMD system.[9] And domestic political pressures may also push Russia and China to react. For example, many Russians view the Nunn-Lugar cooperative threat reduction program as a sophisticated and well-camouflaged U.S. espionage effort. This sentiment has been fueled by a growing irritation with the United States, first because of NATO expansion and then because of the Kosovo war and frequent Western criticisms of the Chechnya conflict. Coupled with an NMD deployment, this irritation could greatly complicate U.S.-Russian relations, possibly undermining cooperation on the Nunn-Lugar or nonproliferation fronts.[10]

None of this is to gainsay then-governor Bush's claim during the 2000 presidential campaign that "it is possible to build a missile defense, *and* defuse confrontation with Russia."[11] Both can be done. But it will not be easy. And defenses are not all created equal. Some types will likely intensify confrontation between Moscow and Washington, as well as Beijing and Washington.

The Spreading Threat

Missile defense proponents argue that the United States faces a growing ballistic missile threat. Missile defense critics respond by arguing that the long-range ballistic missile threat facing the United States has decreased during the past decade. By some measures the critics are right. During the 1980s, the Soviet Union possessed 2,318 long-range missiles. Today Russia has roughly 1,100, a decline of more than 50 percent. That number will fall further if Washington and Moscow make good on their START III pledge. Meanwhile, no other potential adversaries besides China have built ICBMs, and Beijing's arsenal remains small. And countries such as Argentina, Brazil, Egypt, and South Africa that sought to develop long-range missile technology in the 1980s abandoned their programs in the 1990s.[12]

These measures, however, ignore the more important trend for the future of American national security: the number of states hostile to the United States and possessing long-range missile technology is likely to grow during the coming decades. The U.S. intelligence community believes that by 2015 the United States will face ICBM threats not just from Russia and China but also from "North Korea, probably from Iran, and possibly from Iraq."[13] Even more troubling, the intelligence community warns that any of these countries may be able to flight test a functioning "ICBM with a reentry vehicle (RV) with little or no warning."[14] So the United States may not have the luxury of waiting for evidence of a clear and present danger before taking steps to counter the missile threat.

The threat that spreading ballistic missile technology poses, while real, should be kept in perspective. North Korea, Iran, and Iraq may succeed in building ICBMs, but they will not recreate the Soviet missile arsenal. All three countries operate under substantial financial and technological constraints, and according to the U.S. intelligence community, will be able to produce only "a few to tens [of missiles], constrained to smaller payloads, and less reliable than their Russian and Chinese counterparts."[15] Their accuracies may also be poor, and their warheads may or may not survive the descent to earth given the difficulty of building heat-resistant reentry vehicles. All three countries will be even harder pressed to build more than a few nuclear warheads. North Korea has the most advanced nuclear program of the three, and the U.S. intelligence community estimates that it has enough nuclear material for two warheads at most.[16] Any such warheads may not be small enough to place atop a missile. Of course, North Korea, Iran, or Iraq could use chemical and biological warheads instead, but doing so would, most probably, diminish significantly the lethality of any attack (while still risking nuclear retaliation). Consider the situation with a biological agent like anthrax. Not only is it difficult to deliver anthrax effectively by high-speed warhead, but if a missile were fired at the United States, Americans would know they had been attacked, possibly giving them valuable time to take cover and in any case providing an opportunity to seek prompt medical treatment against infection.

The threat facing the United States also is not immediate. Although the U.S. intelligence community contends that North Korea, Iran, and Iraq "could" deploy long-range missiles, considerable disagreement exists over whether they will anytime soon.[17] Moreover, recent political trends give reason to be optimistic that ballistic missile technology may not spread as rapidly as feared. North Korea agreed to freeze its missile flight-test program in 1999, in June 2000 the leaders of the two Koreas held a historic summit meeting in Pyongyang, and in October 2000 Secretary of State Madeleine Albright became the first senior U.S. official to visit the hermit kingdom. Iranian voters elected a more moderate Parliament in February 2000, and relations between Teheran and Washington may be slowly warming. Positive political trends do not extend to Iraq, however. Sanctions remain in place on Baghdad, slowing Saddam Hussein's pursuit of missiles and weapons of mass destruction, but international support for maintaining the embargo has frayed.[18] If the sanctions regime ends, or if countries further ignore it, all signs indicate that Iraq will move rapidly to rebuild its arsenal.

That some political trends are now working against missile proliferation and sanctions remain in place against Iraq weaken claims that the United States must launch a crash course to build missile defenses. Washington probably has time to do missile defense right and not just fast. Put differently, the risks of rushing outweigh the risks of being a bit more patient. By the same token, however, encouraging political trends are no reason to shelve the idea of missile defense or to adopt a casual and relaxed attitude toward missile-defense research. Political trends can reverse themselves overnight; North Korea may resume flight testing at a moment's notice, reformers may not gain control of Iran's military, and Iraq may succeed in acquiring a long-range missile capability. Indeed, continued vigorous U.S. missile defense efforts will keep the pressure on the international community to take nonproliferation more seriously; both China and Russia have pushed Pyongyang to moderate its behavior in a bid to show the world that the U.S. fear of North Korea is exaggerated. And in the long run, with the advent of a networked world and easy access to information, it may prove impossible to stem the proliferation of missile technology.

Better Technology

For decades, effective defenses against long-range ballistic missiles were derided as fantasy. Now many NMD critics agree that some kinds of defenses are becoming feasible. But considerable disagreement exists over which missile defense architectures make sense and how effective they are likely to be.

The missile defense architecture that has attracted the most attention is the Clinton administration's proposal to build a midcourse interceptor system using "hit-to-kill" technology. Under this plan, the United States would eventually be able to launch interceptor missiles from bases in Alaska and North Dakota. Upon reaching space, these defensive rockets would launch "exo-atmospheric kill vehicles" that would try to destroy the attacker's warheads by ramming into them. In October 1999 the Pentagon demonstrated the basic feasibility of "hitting a bullet with a bullet" in a controlled test in which a kill vehicle destroyed a warhead 140 miles above the Pacific Ocean. Equipment malfunctions disrupted the next two tests, however, and the interceptors failed to hit their targets.

These flight-test problems highlight the difficulties that plague the development of any major weapons system, especially one as complex as missile defense. Programs seldom proceed as smoothly, rapidly, or inexpensively as their strongest supporters contend. And while the Pentagon may eventually solve the engineering problems that have beset the NMD system that the Clinton administration proposed building, it remains questionable how well any midcourse interceptor can be made to work under operational conditions. Critics contend that because midcourse interceptors operate in the weightless vacuum of space, where there is no air resistance to help separate heavier warheads from lighter decoys, they are inherently vulnerable to simple countermeasures.[19] Pentagon officials acknowledge that early versions of its midcourse interceptor would be vulnerable to "sophisticated countermeasures" but insist that its capabilities will be upgraded over time.[20] It will be years before the tests needed to settle the issue can be conducted, but basic physics suggests that the Pentagon faces serious and innate disadvantages in trying to make a midcourse NMD system work against anything but a crude attack.

The vulnerability of the Clinton administration's proposed system to countermeasures has prompted considerable interest in boost-phase technology.[21] These defenses would shoot down missiles shortly after launch, before they reached space, and most important, before they could deploy warheads or decoys. In theory, boost-phase intercepts should be easier than midcourse intercepts. When a warhead reaches space, it is small, cold, and fast, making it difficult to locate and hit. By contrast, during boost phase an ICBM is moving relatively slowly and its rocket plume makes it easy to locate. The operative words, however, are "in theory." Serious work on boost-phase defense is only just beginning, and perhaps its leading proponent, physicist Richard Garwin, acknowledges that making it work will be "technologically challenging."[22] No one knows yet how long it would take to build an operational system or how effective it would be under real world conditions.

Even when the Pentagon solves these technological challenges, boost-phase defenses based on land or sea or in the air—the variants that have drawn the most political support thus far—are inherently limited: because missiles remain in their boost phases for only a few minutes, these defenses can work only if the defensive weapon is based within a few hundred miles of the launch site of the offensive missile. In many instances, therefore, boost-phase defenses would need to be based on foreign territory. This raises serious questions about such a defense's reliability in wartime. Moreover, earth-based boost-phase defenses cannot be used to protect the United States against Chinese or Russian missile attack— deliberate, accidental, unauthorized, or erroneous—because both countries are too large. That fact is seen as a virtue by some (including us), because it should ease the effort of gaining Russian or Chinese support for the system, but it is seen as a weakness by others. The geographical limitations inherent in earth-based boost-phase defenses lead many missile defense proponents to champion space-based boost-phase defense. But deploying boost-phase interceptors in space, and keeping them in good operational condition there, would be a monumental technological and logistical challenge that makes the idea a rather distant prospect.

Technological optimists may turn out to be right, and missile defense technology may move ahead rapidly. Even then, however, Americans will remain vulnerable to chemical, biological, and nuclear attack. Neither the Clinton administration's proposed midcourse system nor a system using boost-phase interceptors is designed to shoot down cruise missiles or short-range missiles launched from ships, which are easier for any attacker to build than long-range ballistic missiles because the basic components are more readily available and the engineering challenges are less severe. Hostile states (or terrorists) may also resort to nonconventional means of attack.[23] This is especially true for weak states that cannot conduct rigorous missile flight tests because of financial or political constraints. And in the case of biological weapons, a nonconventional attack probably would be more deadly than a ballistic missile because Americans might not learn of the attack until it was too late to take cover or seek early medical treatment.

The recognition that America will remain vulnerable to attack even with national missile defense does not mean that defense is pointless. The fact that the United States cannot defend itself perfectly against every threat is no reason to give up the effort. Taking steps to defend the country against long-range missile threats is especially worthwhile because missile threats differ fundamentally from "suitcase bombs"—which are much bigger and less easily concealed than that phrase suggests, especially in the key case of nuclear weapons. Missiles deliver warheads very quickly—making them especially dangerous during a crisis or in a war. They are also inherently more useful than suitcase bombs as instruments of coercive diplomacy because the attacker does not have to issue a threat; the fact that a potential assailant possesses missiles may be sufficient to deter. Finally, it is not true that Americans are defenseless against suitcase bombs or terrorist attacks. The United States spends billions of dollars every year on intelligence and law enforcement activities that attempt to track terrorists, monitor borders, and foil bomb plots. As for cruise missiles, several TMD programs have the capability to address this emerging threat.

But even if a limited NMD system is feasible and desirable, one does not have to be a Luddite to be skeptical about claims that robust national missile defenses capable of defeating large-scale attacks are within reach—or wise, even if possible. The Pentagon has made important strides in recent years, but it has only established that it might be able to build a limited national missile defense. Much work remains to be done to build an operational system. That will take time, and the ultimate effectiveness of any defense remains to be seen. What is clearly not in the cards any time soon is a technological magic bullet that erases the threat of nuclear annihilation. For that reason, talk of moving toward a "defense dominant" world or substituting mutual assured security for mutual assured destruction is wildly premature. Ronald Reagan's dream of rendering nuclear weapons "impotent and obsolete" remains just that.

Why Not Prevention, Preemption, and Deterrence?

The strategic climate may have changed, the threat may be potentially more widespread, and technology may be better, but does national missile defense fill a niche not met by traditional policy tools? Critics say no. They argue that the United States should deal with ballistic missile threats as it has for forty years, through a combination of prevention, preemption, and deterrence. The problem, however, is that all these policy tools have shortcomings.

Consider prevention. The United States has long controlled the export of high-technology goods, and it has pressed other advanced industrialized countries, including Russia and China, to follow suit. It has imposed sanctions on states judged to be proliferators. It has pioneered arms control agreements such as the Nonproliferation Treaty (NPT) and the Comprehensive Test Ban Treaty (CTBT), though the Senate has refused to consent to the latter. It has created the Missile Technology Control Regime (MTCR), a supplier cartel composed of more than three dozen countries that seeks to deny missile technology to missile-seeking states. And it has used military force (against Iraq) and implicitly threatened to use force (against North Korea) to launch preventive attacks designed to disrupt other countries' proliferation efforts before they could produce operational weapons. Despite these efforts, nuclear and missile technology continues to spread, though at rates that vary from weapon to weapon and decade to decade.

If proliferation does occur, the United States could resort to a preemptive attack if it received reliable information that a country was preparing to launch a ballistic missile attack.[24] But preemption is easier to urge than to carry out. For a preemptive attack to succeed, the United States would need to know where enemy missiles were located. Although ICBMs are larger than Scuds, the abject failure of the U.S.-led coalition to find Iraqi Scuds during the Gulf War underscores the difficulty of this strategy. If a country such as North Korea or Iraq put ICBM silos inside large buildings or even under tents, the United States might not know where they were. Worse yet, a preemptive attack may trigger what it sought to avoid: an attack on the United States or one of its allies. Should U.S. forces lose the element of surprise or should they fail to destroy all the adversary's missiles, the opposing country would be able to launch its own attack.

The difficulties inherent in preventing proliferation and preempting attackers explain why the United States has also relied on deterrence in dealing with missile threats. This reliance will continue even if more states acquire long-range missiles. Despite claims to the contrary, no good reason exists to believe that the leaders of countries such as North Korea, Iran, or Iraq are inherently undeterrable. To the contrary, the behavior of all three countries suggests that they respond to incentives and punishments in a rational manner. For example, Pyongyang has refrained for nearly a half century from attacking its more powerful neighbor to the south. (It also showed it could respond to incentives and punishments by suspending its nuclear program after Washington, Seoul, Tokyo, and other capitals offered compensation, and the United States threatened to use military force.) Iraq refrained from using weapons of mass destruction against U.S.-led coalition forces in the Gulf War, quite possibly because it was warned that any such attack would be met with a devastating response.

The problem with deterrence is that, while generally reliable, it can fail. No one seriously contends that North Korea or Iraq will attack out of the blue or even under most conceivable circumstances. Missiles come stamped with a return address, which is one reason deterrence works. But in a few situations a missile attack might become thinkable. Perhaps the likeliest scenario is a regime on the verge of collapse. The Soviet Union's peaceful demise does not mean that other dictatorial regimes will go quietly as well. A government in its death throes might care little about the calculus of deterrence, either because it has nothing to lose by lashing out or because it loses control over its arsenal. Indeed, should a regime in Pyongyang or Baghdad find itself losing a civil war, it could conceivably attempt to blackmail Washington into coming to its rescue. Alternatively, in a more traditional interstate war, a foreign leader may rationally threaten missile attack if U.S.-led forces try to overthrow his regime.

This scenario points to a broader problem: weak nations want long-range missiles not only because they can serve as operational weapons of war, and help assure regime survival in such a war, but also because their very presence makes them useful for coercive diplomacy. Missile defense proponents rightly ask whether the United States would have been willing to liberate Kuwait in 1991 if Iraq had possessed a nuclear missile capable of hitting American soil. Even if the answer had been yes for the Bush administration, it might not be for a future president in a similar situation—or for a future Congress. (After all, Congress just barely approved Operation Desert Storm.) Perceptions of American vulnerability could have equally important consequences for U.S. alliance relations. Friends and allies could come to doubt whether the United States would make good on its security guarantees, thereby undermining America's interests around the world.

National missile defense, then, could help the United States remain a global superpower, reducing the odds that it would be dissuaded from projecting decisive power in a future crisis or conflict out of fear that its own territory might then be attacked by weapons of mass destruction. As a practical matter, the United States would not be able to act with impunity just because it had a shield for its homeland against missile attack. It would not be sure that shield would work perfectly; it would have to worry that other, clandestine means of attack could be undertaken against U.S. territory (even if such attacks are hardly guaranteed to succeed, as argued above); it would have to worry that its friends and allies, particularly those in immediate proximity to the enemy, could be attacked with weapons of mass destruction as well. There is no doubt that, as a general principle, the United States needs to be especially careful about fighting countries with weapons of mass destruction, and NMD would not change that fact. However, taking account of all constraints and dangers, once Washington and its allies had settled on a policy choice, even an imperfect national missile defense might save tens or even hundreds of thousands of American or allied lives in a given conflict.

National missile defense could also affect the perceptions and incentives of U.S. enemies. Whether the system was perfect or not, potential adversaries might assume that it would help steel the resolve of the United States in a crisis or conflict, and make it more likely to intervene militarily to oppose acts of aggression. If that were the case, NMD would already have aided American national security policy—quite possibly by deterring conflict (or even deterring a potential enemy's desire to develop long-range missiles in the first place).

Missile defense, then, has a role to play in U.S. national security policy because the unthinkable could happen and that prospect will shape the behavior of the United States, its friends, and its foes. If defenses can be made to work, they can provide the United States with a measure of insurance against an unlikely but potentially catastrophic event, preserve America's freedom of maneuver abroad, and reassure others of America's security guarantee. And, it is important to note, in the case of small missile attacks, a defense does not need to be perfect to be useful. Assuming that the attacker targeted several cities rather than concentrating its attack on just one, a system that could strike down one in two incoming warheads could still save hundreds of thousands of Americans from nuclear annihilation. And even a porous missile defense could enhance deterrence by forcing an attacker with limited capability to contemplate the possibility that any attack would be futile and fatal.

But even if the Pentagon succeeds in building highly effective defenses—and that remains a big if—defense will not provide a substitute for other tools in dealing with proliferation. Just as buying personal life insurance is no reason to start smoking, eat poorly, or behave foolishly, the United States will need to continue policies of prevention, preemption, and deterrence. All four tools should be part of an integrated strategy for dealing with ballistic missile threats.

Sensible Defense Means Limited Defense

If missile defense can provide insurance in the event other policy tools fail, how much defense should the United States seek given what we know about the strategic climate, threat, and technology? Should America limit its efforts to defend against small attacks, as the Clinton administration proposed with its NMD system? Should it seek to defend itself "against any missile launch," as President Bush proposed at one point during the 2000 presidential campaign?[25] Or should it seek to develop something in between? These questions go to the heart of the debate over missile defense.

Many missile defense enthusiasts argue that the United States should build ambitious defenses. While most recognize that an impermeable peace shield remains decades off, they favor building defenses that could defeat any attack up to and including a large-scale unauthorized Russian launch. Such a system has immediate appeal. Who would not want to be protected against an accidental missile launch if it could be done at an acceptable cost? If Russia's command and control system fails, it might fail big, possibly leading to the launch of many dozens of missiles. That would mean the end of American society as we know it.

Proposals for ambitious defenses, however, suffer from two fatal flaws. First, we are decades away from developing missile defenses capable of blunting a large and technologically sophisticated attack. A defense against a large-scale accidental launch—unlike one against a small attack—needs to operate close to perfection to be worthwhile. Faced with

200 incoming warheads, even a system with an 80 percent kill rate—which would be a daunting technological achievement—would still allow 40 warheads to reach American soil.

Second, ambitious defenses come with strategic and diplomatic costs that are unacceptably high. Any system capable of defeating a large-scale unauthorized launch could also give the United States a first-strike capability against Russia. Moscow would be faced with a choice between basing its nation's security on assurances of American goodwill or finding a way to defeat the U.S. system. Given the current state of U.S.-Russian relations, there is little doubt that it would choose the latter. That would mean keeping missiles on high states of alert (to avoid a surprise attack), maintaining large stockpiles of nuclear weapons (to increase the chances of overwhelming the defense), and developing better countermeasure technologies (to penetrate the defense). The first is relatively easy to do, and the second two steps can be taken, despite Moscow's budgetary woes, if Russia disregards START II's ban on land-based missiles with multiple warheads and puts some of its excellent rocket scientists back on the job of developing countermeasures. The United States would almost surely be safer with just a limited defense, combined with deep cuts in offensive nuclear arsenals, lower states of weapons alert, enhanced efforts in the Nunn-Lugar cooperative threat reduction program and related activities in Russia, and possibly accidental-destruct technologies that either side could use to destroy an unapproved attack by its own forces.

What about building a less ambitious defense that could defeat China's much smaller nuclear arsenal? This proposal also has considerable surface appeal. Chinese officials have on at least two occasions issued veiled threats to use nuclear weapons against the United States to keep it from coming to the aid of Taiwan in a possible future war.[26] Whether China really would threaten nuclear attack or not under such auspices, it is only natural that the United States would want to have some protection against the possibility, if it could be had at an acceptable cost. Having a defense against such a possible attack could also dissuade China from issuing threats in the first place—or from thinking that it had the upper hand over Washington in any crisis concerning Taiwan. That in turn could reduce the odds of dangerous conflict.

However, such a U.S. defense capability against China is almost certainly unattainable. The problem is not, as is often alleged, that the United States will end up in an arms race with China. The United States can afford an arms race far more easily than can Beijing. Some would even argue that such an arms race would be desirable for the simple fact that it could deprive China of resources needed to improve its conventional military capabilities to seize Taiwan. The problem instead is that there is no reason to believe that when the race ends, the United States will have a defense that can defeat a modernized Chinese arsenal. Midcourse interceptors are vulnerable to countermeasures—technologies the Chinese have developed and no doubt could improve; earth-based boost-phase systems cannot reach China's long-range missiles, except for those deployed near its eastern coast; and space-based defenses will not be ready for perhaps two decades. At best, any attempt to render China's nuclear deterrent obsolete will become an expensive version of tic-tac-toe; the United States is likely to end up where it started—vulnerable to Chinese attack. At worst, it will poison U.S.-Chinese relations and aggravate the missile threat the United States faces—not only from China, but other countries to which Beijing might transfer technology—while also consuming large sums of money that might do much more for U.S. armed forces, and U.S. national security, if spent in other ways. Nor is it clear that China would spend less on its conventional military forces during a nuclear buildup; it might simply elect to spend more on its military if persuaded it was engaged in a major competition with the United States.[27]

In the end, efforts to build anything other than limited defenses will prove a fool's errand. Technology may some day allow the United States to build ambitious defenses, and U.S. relations with China and Russia may some day improve to the point that neither will see such defenses as threatening. But neither is true today. Americans can insist that they mean no harm with national missile defense, but that will not stop China and Russia from taking steps to protect their interests. And because these steps would probably diminish U.S. security, any effort to develop robust national missile defenses would likely be counterproductive and dangerous.

A Modest Proposal

The fundamental purpose of any American NMD effort at this point should be to build a system that can defend the United States and its allies against attack by hostile emerging ballistic missile states, which in practical terms means small attacks of no more than a couple dozen missiles lacking sophisticated countermeasures. This is the extent of the clearly identifiable missile threat that North Korea and, possibly, Iran or Iraq could pose over the next ten to fifteen years. It is also the realistic extent of what defense technology will permit over that same period. Above all, the system should be designed to minimize the threat it poses to the Chinese and Russian nuclear deterrents, keeping only a capability against a small, accidental or unauthorized launch from their arsenals. And the United States should continue a vigorous missile defense research program, to keep open the possibility of deploying a more ambitious NMD system if the evolution of the threat warrants it and the advance of technology permits it.

Contrary to the claims of both the Clinton administration and the more zealous missile defense proponents, there is no need to rush to build an NMD system by mid-decade. Neither the evolution of the threat, the state of technological development, nor the status of missile defense diplomacy warrants haste. It is far more important that missile defense be done right, in technical and political terms, than done quickly. Moreover, taking the time to do national missile defense right would enable the United States to coordinate NMD deployment with the deployment of advanced TMD systems, now currently scheduled for no earlier than 2007. Until these TMD systems are ready, America's major allies, and the American troops and citizens they host, will be vulnerable to attack and the United States still vulnerable to blackmail, even if a U.S. NMD system is deployed.

But can the United States design a defense against missile attacks from North Korea, Iran, and Iraq that Beijing and Moscow could live with? There are solid grounds to believe that the answer is yes. The key is to develop a limited, two-tier defense system, with a total number of interceptors constrained by treaty—or, failing that, unilateral U.S. statement— not to exceed 200. Considerably fewer numbers of interceptors would probably need to be deployed in the near to medium-term future, so adopting a ceiling of 200 interceptors—the original limit in the 1972 ABM Treaty—should provide ample room for adequate deployments.

The first layer of defense should consist of a modest number of boost-phase interceptor missiles, based either at sea or on land near the threatening countries. The exact number of interceptor missiles and their placement would depend on which states acquired the ability to threaten the United States. A boost-phase capability has the advantage of reassuring European capitals, which fear that any defense that protects the United States alone would make them tempting targets for longer-range attack. (U.S. friends and allies in the Middle East and East Asia do not have the same concerns; they face a more immediate short- and medium-range missile threat that is more easily addressed by U.S. TMD systems.)

Boost-phase interceptors could hit almost any long-range missile that a country launched, regardless of its ultimate destination—provided the country was sufficiently small and geographically accessible. Fortunately for the United States, most likely new ballistic missile powers meet these criteria.

A scaled-down version of the midcourse interceptor architecture that the Clinton administration favored should also be built to back up the boost-phase layer. There are several reasons for a backup: earth-based boost-phase interceptors (or lasers) require the cooperation of other countries to deal with most threats; the time window for shooting down a missile in boost phase is quite short; and boost-phase interceptors only work if deployed near the country that ultimately poses a threat to the United States. The midcourse system should be small, consisting of no more than fifty interceptors and quite possibly only twenty-five or so for the foreseeable future, given the plausible magnitude of any possible threat. It should be based in Grand Forks, North Dakota, instead of Alaska as the Clinton administration proposed. Depending on the speed of the interceptors and their response time, deploying the defense in North Dakota may still permit coverage of all fifty states, with the possible exception of a few, sparsely populated islands at the westernmost end of the Aleutian and Hawaiian island chains. Those areas would still be covered by the boost-phase layer.[28] By contrast, relying on the Alaska site alone would leave most of the northeastern United States poorly protected against missiles fired from the Middle East. The North Dakota system would have limited effectiveness because of its vulnerability to countermeasures, but it could still provide some capability against relatively simple limited threats. Moreover, because the construction season is much longer in North Dakota than Alaska, there is less reason to rush a decision on beginning work there in 2001 or even 2002. The extra time would allow more opportunity for all-important diplomacy in the interim, without postponing the date by which the NMD system could be operational.

Would China and Russia accept such a limited, two-tier defense? China would be the harder sell. Boost-phase interceptors would have no capability against its long-range missiles, except any located near its eastern coast, because they could not be placed close enough to most Chinese launch sites. That China is developing a mobile ICBM force should prevent the United States from obtaining even a modest boost-phase capability against Chinese long-range missiles. The hit-to-kill interceptor would be more problematic for Beijing. Although the Pentagon would probably fire multiple interceptors at every possible target to maximize the chances of a kill and though the system would be vulnerable to sophisticated countermeasures, Chinese military planners might nonetheless conclude that in theory it threatened their nuclear deterrent.

However, this problem should be solvable. Beijing could ensure its ability to retaliate by modestly increasing the size of its long-range missile force and using countermeasures. It probably plans the former step already, even in the absence of a U.S. missile defense. No one can applaud having more Chinese missiles aimed at the United States, but even a three- or five-fold increase in the size of the Chinese ICBM force would not fundamentally alter the strategic balance between the two countries. Moreover, as long as China does not place its missiles on hair-trigger alert, a larger Chinese missile force would not imply a higher risk of accidental launch.

Moscow's response to a limited, two-tier missile defense should be more positive. Earth-based boost-phase interceptors pose no threat to Russian ICBMs, and even under the most pessimistic Russian budgetary projections, Moscow will retain more than enough survivable ICBMs to overwhelm the North Dakota defense we propose even in a second strike. President Putin has endorsed boost-phase defenses, and the commander of Russia's Strategic Rocket Forces has suggested it might be possible to live with a U.S. missile defense if the number of U.S. offensive missiles is cut.[29] Moreover, basing twenty-five to fifty interceptors in North Dakota is not only consistent with the ABM Treaty's core principle of banning strategically significant defenses, the treaty already gives the United States the right to deploy one hundred interceptor missiles in Grand Forks (even if not for the purposes of national missile defense). It is true that President Putin has consistently voiced strong skepticism about permitting national missile defense, but in a November 2000 speech and on other occasions he has also expressed a willingness to keep talking to the United States about possible modifications to the ABM Treaty. This may be just the type of proposal that would tap into his limited, but apparently real, willingness to consider treaty modifications provided that they not threaten strategic stability or the Russian deterrent.[30]

The United States should seek Moscow's agreement to modify the ABM Treaty—or to negotiate a successor agreement—to permit the deployment of this limited, two-tier defense (box 1-1). This means lifting the treaty's general ban against a nationwide defense as well as its specific bans on defenses based at sea or on foreign soil.

Box 1-1. Is the ABM Treaty Still in Effect?

When the United States and the Soviet Union signed the Anti-Ballistic Missile (ABM) Treaty in 1972, Russia was but one of fifteen Soviet republics. Many Soviet nuclear weapons and some other nuclear-related facilities such as early-warning radars were located on non-Russian soil. As such, when the Soviet Union dissolved in 1991, one of the two signatories to the ABM Treaty was replaced by fifteen countries with varying degrees of responsibility for what had been Soviet nuclear forces. So is the ABM Treaty still in effect? And if so, what former Soviet countries does it obligate?

The Clinton administration maintained that the ABM Treaty remains binding on the United States, a view that was widely shared, including by Governor George W. Bush during the 2000 presidential campaign. But some Americans, most (though not all) of them conservative Republicans, argue that the ABM Treaty is no longer in force because the Soviet Union left no obvious heir. For example, former CIA director R. James Woolsey argues:

> According to longstanding principles of international law, when one country has a bilateral treaty with another and is then "succeeded" by a different state (as Russia has succeeded to the rights and duties of the Soviet Union under a number of treaties), the bilateral treaty remains in effect only if both states so affirm—the new state and its predecessor's treaty partner. The only exception to what international lawyers call this "clean slate" rule is "dispositive" treaties—such as those that dispose of territory. In only these cases is the succession automatic. . . . But the administration does not assert that the 1972 U.S.-Soviet ABM Treaty is "dispositive."[1]

So far as it goes, this argument is correct. But it begs three other issues, the first two primarily legal and the third political. First, who in the U.S. system of government is constitutionally authorized to designate a successor state? Second, ten years after the Soviet Union's demise, has the United States already designated Russia as its successor? Third, is it realistic for the United States to expect to make one decision on the ABM Treaty and a different one on other U.S.-Soviet treaties?

In our judgment, the answers to all three questions affirm that the ABM Treaty remains binding. First, although the Constitution says nothing about whether presidents can designate a successor state on their own authority, and the case law on the matter is not settled, the Supreme Court's rulings in similar cases suggest that they can. In *Goldwater* v. *Carter* (1979) the Court rejected the argument that Jimmy Carter could not unilaterally terminate a mutual defense treaty with Taiwan because treaties require the Senate's advice and consent. If presidents are free to terminate treaties, they are presumably also free to decide which successor states inherit a treaty's obligations.

The power of presidents to designate successor states is important, because the Bush administration stated in 1992 that the ABM Treaty remained in force, with Russia as the natural successor to the Soviet Union under its terms. The administration even went so far as to propose amending the treaty to permit construction of missile defenses in formal talks with Russian officials. The Clinton administration also took the view that the treaty remains in force and that Russia is bound by its provisions. (The Clinton administration contended that the treaty's obligations extended to Belarus, Kazakhstan, and Ukraine—though not to all of the states that emerged from the Soviet Union—because all three had significant ABM assets. The administration negotiated a 1997 agreement formally designating all four countries successor states to the Soviet Union for the purposes of the ABM Treaty. Clinton never made good on his pledge to submit the succession agreement to the Senate for approval, and the obligations of Belarus, Kazakhstan, and Ukraine remain unsettled.)

Things do not change even if one believes that the Constitution requires some form of congressional approval. As law professor Michael Glennon points out, Congress acknowledged the continued standing of the ABM Treaty in 1996. At that point, the Republican-controlled Senate put restrictions on the president's ability to modify the ABM Treaty, something that logically and legally implied that legislators recognized the continued existence and relevance of the treaty.[2] And as Justice Robert Jackson wrote in the famed *Steel Seizure Case*, "When the president acts pursuant to an express or implied authorization of Congress his authority is at its maximum."[3]

These legal arguments form the core of the matter. But the broader political issue should not be trivialized. It would be bizarre, and transparently self-serving, for the United States to insist that the ABM Treaty no longer exists when the nation recognized it for a decade after the Soviet Union dissolved. Furthermore, it would run directly contrary to the position the United States has taken on who inherited the Soviet Union's obligations under other treaties. The United States agreed that Russia would inherit the Soviet seat on the UN Security Council, and it expects Russia to pay Soviet debts and abide by agreements on conventional forces in Europe, nuclear nonproliferation, offensive nuclear arms control, and many other matters. If the United States suddenly declares the ABM Treaty null and void, could it really expect Moscow to go along? Or would Russia also become highly selective about which treaties and obligations it would assume—and which it would not?

Washington could still calculate that the benefits of declaring the ABM Treaty void outweighed the likely consequences of Russian retaliation. But in this event, it would face the same types of calculations that it would face when considering outright withdrawal from the ABM Treaty. Deciding now to ignore the ABM Treaty would be tantamount to withdrawing from it. In our view, if the United States wants to abandon the treaty it would be better served by invoking its withdrawal provision than by fabricating a weak legal argument that few in the world would take seriously.

1. R. James Woolsey, "What ABM Treaty?" *Washington Post*, August 15, 2000, p. 23. See also Douglas J. Feith and George Miron, "Memorandum of Law: Did the ABM Treaty of 1972 Remain in Force after the USSR Ceased to Exist in December 1991 and Did It Become a Treaty between the United States and the Russian Federation?" Washington, Center for Security Policy, February 24, 1999.

2. Michael J. Glennon, "Yes, There Is an ABM Treaty," *Washington Post*, September 4, 2000, p. A25.

3. *Youngstown Sheet and Tube Co. v. Sawyer* (The Steel Seizure Case), 343 U.S. 579, 637 (1952).

The reason for pursuing negotiations with Moscow is not that the ABM Treaty is sacred but that a formal agreement on defenses would serve U.S. interests. It would reassure Moscow about American intentions. That would greatly increase the odds of agreeing on deep cuts in offensive nuclear weapons as well as other measures designed to reduce nuclear risk, substantially reduce the diplomatic costs of an NMD deployment, improve the prospects for a strong Nunn-Lugar cooperative threat reduction program, and reduce the chances that Russia would seek to undermine the U.S. defense system, for example, by selling countermeasure technologies to countries such as Iran, Iraq, and North Korea. Most U.S. allies are unlikely to object strongly to a U.S. missile defense if Moscow decides to accept it. A modified ABM Treaty may need to be further revised a decade or two from now should the evolution of the ballistic missile threat warrant it. But the United States should cross that bridge only when (and if) it comes to it.

Moscow may prove intransigent on missile defense and leave the United States with no choice but to withdraw from the ABM Treaty. But in doing so, Washington should still seek to allay Russian concerns. At a minimum, it should pursue a tacit arms control policy that keeps Moscow informed of its plans and unilaterally accept intrusive verification procedures on the size and nature of its NMD program. Because China can also make the costs of an NMD deployment exceed the benefits, Washington should pursue a similar policy of transparency toward Beijing.

No one should be under any illusion, however, that tacit arms control will be easy to establish. Not only is treaty withdrawal an inauspicious foundation on which to build a new relationship with Moscow, domestic political support for tacit arms control could prove elusive. Critics will ask why the United States is sharing sensitive information with Russia and China when both countries target American cities. The net result might be no arms control at all. Both Washington and Moscow should keep this in mind as they discuss the future of the ABM Treaty. It would be much more preferable to modify the treaty than to abandon it.

CHAPTER TWO

Missile Defense:
Concepts and Systems

THE BASIC IDEAS BEHIND how missile defense systems operate are not particularly complex. But it is important to have a clear mental picture of how ballistic missiles, and technologies designed to counter them, function. This chapter provides that background information, with a number of graphics, illustrating the main concepts.

Basic Elements of Ballistic Missiles

Ballistic missiles are rockets designed to accelerate to fast enough speeds so that they can fly relatively long distances before falling back to earth. They are first accelerated by the combustion of some type of fuel, after which they simply follow an unpowered—or ballistic—trajectory. They consist, most basically, of rocket engines, fuel chambers, guidance systems, and warheads, though the specifics vary a great deal depending on the range and sophistication of the missile.

Missile Parts and Types

For shorter-range missiles, the entire weapons system is generally simple. The missile usually consists of a single stage rocket, which fires until its fuel is exhausted or shut off by a flight-control computer and then ceases functioning for the duration of the flight. The missile body and warhead often never separate from each other, flying a full trajectory as a large, single object.

For longer-range missiles or rockets, the system consists of two or three stages, or separate booster rockets, each with its own fuel and rocket engines. The rationale for this staging is to improve boosting efficiency and thereby maximize the speed of the reentry vehicle or vehicles. Putting all the fuel for a long-range rocket in one stage would make for a very heavy fuel chamber and mean that the rocket would have to carry along a great deal of structural weight throughout the entire phase of boosted flight. That would lower the ultimate speed of the warhead or warheads, reducing their range. With staging, by contrast, much of the structural weight is discarded as fuel is consumed. That makes it possible to accelerate the payload to speeds sufficient to put it on an intercontinental trajectory. Long-range warheads must reach speeds of about 4.5 miles a second (roughly 7 kilometers a second), or almost two-thirds of the speed any object would need to escape the earth's gravitational field entirely (roughly 7 miles, or 11 kilometers, a second). To reach such speeds with existing rocket fuels, efficiency in design—including rocket staging—is essential.

On long-range rockets, warheads are designed so that they can be released from the missile body during flight. Generally, warheads and any decoys are released after boosting but while the rocket is still going up—that is, in the ascent phase of flight.[1] Releasing warheads from the missile is clearly necessary if multiple warheads with multiple aim points are to be used. It is also desirable since large missile bodies are subject to extreme forces on atmospheric reentry that could throw them, and any warheads still attached to them, badly off course.

In fact, warheads do not fly free and exposed. They are instead encased within reentry vehicles. These objects provide heat shields and aerodynamic stability for the eventual return into earth's atmosphere. They protect the warheads from melting or otherwise being damaged by air upon reentry and also maximize the accuracy with which they approach their targets.

Missiles may be powered by solid fuel or liquid fuel. If liquid fuels are used, it is usually considered desirable that they be storable and not require cooling or other special treatment that would involve extensive preparation before launch. Advanced intercontinental ballistic missiles (ICBMs) can use either type of fuel; Russian SS-18s use liquid fuel, for example, whereas modern U.S. missiles use solid fuel.[2]

Missile guidance must be exquisitely accurate. Warhead trajectories are determined by the boost phase, meaning that their course is set hundreds or thousands of miles before they reach their targets. To land within a few hundred feet of a target—or even a couple miles—requires considerable care in how long the rocket motors are fired and in what direction the rocket is directed to take by their firing. Generally, rockets use inertial guidance systems to measure the acceleration provided by the boosters at each and every stage of their burning. Computers then integrate those measurements to plot out a trajectory for the warheads; a feedback loop then corrects any inaccuracies in how the rockets have been firing, so that when they are shut off, the warheads' ballistic flight will take them halfway around the world and land them perhaps within a couple football fields of their designated aim point.

Bombs, Bomblets, and MIRVs

Although streaking shards of metal can cause terror, damage, and casualties, it is of course the warhead placed atop a missile that is most feared and most capable of causing serious harm to an enemy.

The standard, simple missile carries a single warhead. It is generally large as warheads go, but not enormous—typically weighing about as much as bombs dropped from aircraft (several hundred pounds up to perhaps a ton in weight).

Both shorter-range and longer-range rockets can also carry large numbers of bomblets instead of warheads. These can carry conventional, chemical, or biological agents in smaller packages, or submunitions, distributing their aggregate effects over a larger area than a single warhead could. They could also carry radiological payloads—basically radioactive waste, designed not to explode but to contaminate, injure, and kill directly.

But one cannot build a nuclear bomblet. Most modern nuclear weapons weigh hundreds of pounds, and crude devices such as the Hiroshima and Nagasaki bombs weigh tons. They weigh so much because they produce critical masses of fissile material not through efficiency of design but rather brute force—meaning large amounts of enriched uranium or plutonium, as well as correspondingly large amounts of conventional explosive to compress that fissile material.

Both warheads and bomblets can be designed to explode on impact, or when reaching a certain altitude, or after a certain time of flight. Bombs designed to explode at a certain altitude or after a certain time may—or may not—explode if they accidentally strike the ground. Much depends on the details of their design; as a rule, modern U.S. warheads would not explode under such circumstances, but simpler weapons could. This fact is relevant to certain types of missile defenses that could destroy a missile but not the warheads it carried.

Long-range missiles can also have multiple independently targetable reentry vehicles, or MIRVs. Britain, France, Russia, and the United States have developed and deployed this technology. It works in the following manner. All warheads are initially within a "bus," or vehicle-sized object that separates from the rocket's third stage at the end of powered flight. The bus has mini-booster rockets of its own, which it can use to modify its own position and speed before releasing a reentry vehicle (RV) containing a warhead (and any decoys or chaff to accompany it). It can then reposition itself before releasing another RV. Based on their minor differences in position and velocity, the warheads can then travel slightly different trajectories. Magnified by the effects of fifteen to twenty minutes of high-speed, long-distance flight, these minor changes in trajectory can translate into impact points distributed throughout a "footprint" perhaps 100 miles by 300 miles in size.[3]

A missile bus may also carry decoys. These are objects designed to resemble warheads, thereby confusing the defense's sensors and preventing them from identifying the true warhead or slowing the defense's response time. In the vacuum of space, even extremely light decoys move at the same speed as heavy warheads, making it particularly straightforward to fool simple sensors during exoatmospheric flight. More advanced sensors that can gauge the size, shape, rotational motion, temperature, or radar reflectivity of an object may be able to distinguish warheads from decoys—unless the decoys become more sophisticated or unless the warheads are camouflaged to make them resemble decoys.

The Trajectory of a Ballistic Missile

Ballistic flight is unpowered flight within the earth's gravitational field. In other words, it corresponds to what is essentially the free fall of a fast-moving object. Once a rocket stops burning, the only forces acting on it—or any warheads or decoys released from it—are because of gravity or air resistance. That makes flight trajectories predictable and essentially parabolic with respect to the earth's surface. But the other details of the trajectories vary greatly and depend on the speed of the rocket when its boosters stop firing, as well as the angle at which the rocket is pointed.

Boost Phase

As figure 2-1 shows, the first, or boost, phase of a ballistic-missile trajectory is a powered flight typically lasting one to five minutes. This boost phase generally lasts about a fifth of a missile's total flight time.

For shorter-range missiles, the boost phase occurs entirely within the earth's atmosphere; for long-range missiles, it generally extends beyond the atmosphere into space. Either way, during boost phase, the missile gains an upward and an outward or horizontal component to its velocity. For an ICBM, the missile will usually be about 200 to 500 miles downrange of its launch point and have reached an altitude of about 125 to 400 miles at the end of its boost phase.[4]

Midcourse Flight: Ascent, Apogee, and Descent Phases

Once boost phase is complete, the remainder of the upward flight is often termed the ascent phase. Upward flight ends at the trajectory's apogee, or highest point above the earth. The missile then begins to accelerate back to earth in its descent phase.

For existing ICBMs, the ascent phase occurs entirely outside the atmosphere. It would be possible for a sophisticated country to build a fast-burn missile that would complete its boost phase within the atmosphere, but that has not yet been accomplished.[5] (The atmosphere is generally considered to end at roughly sixty miles or one hundred kilometers above the earth's surface, even though in fact there is no true cutoff but instead an exponential decline, and some air molecules are found even above one hundred miles.)

Since a long-range missile's apogee and descent phase also occur outside the atmosphere, midcourse flight is also described as the exoatmospheric phase of flight. For ICBMs, most of the missile's total flight time is spent in this exoatmospheric phase.

During exoatmospheric flight, the horizontal element of the velocity of the missile and any warheads or decoys remains constant. The vertical component of velocity is reduced by gravity, eventually slowing to zero and then reversing as the missile and any objects it has released return to earth. The result is, as noted, essentially a parabolic trajectory, as the missile continues in a generally upward motion until gravity turns its trajectory first flat and then downward.

Figure 2-1. *Trajectories of Ballistic Missiles (for Standard, Minimum-Energy Flight)*

Altitude, in kilometers

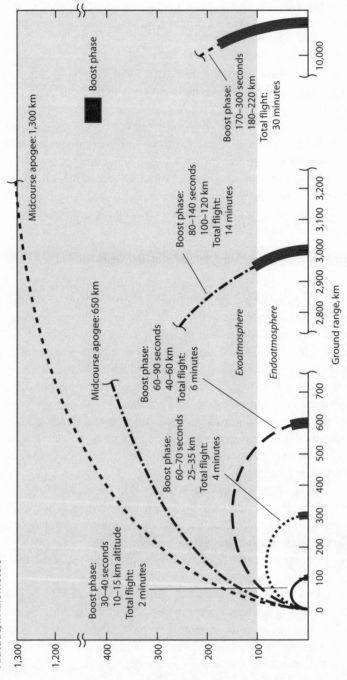

Source: Ballistic Missile Defense Organization, *1993 Report to Congress on the Theater Missile Defense Initiative (TMDI)*, Union of Concerned Scientists.

The Terminal Phase—Atmospheric Reentry

Finally, the missile and any objects it releases, including warheads, bomblets, and decoys, reenter the atmosphere—assuming that they reached a high enough altitude to have left it in the first place. Typically, missiles with ranges of 300 miles (about 500 kilometers) or more leave the atmosphere; those with shorter ranges do not.

Missile bodies, warheads, and decoys slow because of air resistance in a manner that depends on their weight, size, and shape. As a result of this air resistance, descending objects heat up; they are also subject to strong forces that may damage them structurally if they are not well built.[6]

Minimum-Energy, Lofted, and Depressed Trajectories

As figure 2-2 shows, missiles may also be flown on several different types of trajectories. A missile that flies a minimum-energy trajectory will travel the maximum distance given the speed at which its rocket burns out. But missiles may also fly on what are known as lofted or depressed trajectories for certain purposes. These names are fairly self-explanatory. Lofted trajectories are those on which the rocket's flight attains a higher altitude than a minimum-energy trajectory for the same horizontal range. Depressed trajectories, by contrast, stay closer to the earth's surface than is normal for long-range flight.

Missiles and warheads on lofted or depressed trajectories require extra energy, and extra speed, to cover a given distance. But there are advantages to such flight profiles. Depressed trajectories can help missiles and reentry vehicles avoid radar detection. By staying close to earth they are shielded from the view of distant radars due to the planet's curvature. For shorter-range rockets, they can also keep a ballistic missile within the earth's atmosphere at all times—rendering them invulnerable to those types of missile defenses that must work outside the atmosphere.

Lofted trajectories also have their uses for an attacker. A missile or reentry vehicle on such a flight profile would come back to earth at a greater speed than one traveling a standard trajectory. That means the objects would reach earth more quickly in its final descent, and with greater speed and energy. It also means that they would be within the earth's atmosphere only a relatively short time during the terminal phase of flight, giving certain kinds of missile defenses less time to try to shoot them down.

Figure 2-2. *Trajectory Phases*

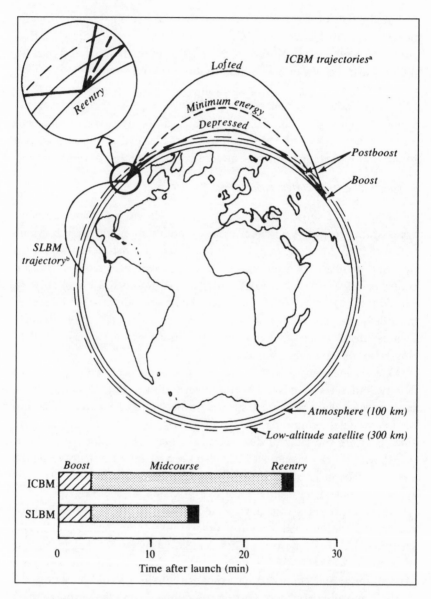

Source: Ashton B. Carter and David N. Schwartz, eds., *Ballistic Missile Defense* (Brookings, 1984), p. 51.
a. Range of intercontinental ballistic missiles is 10,000 km in this example.
b. Range of submarine-launched ballistic missiles is 5,000 km in this example.

Missile Types

Missiles are sometimes given the rather arbitrary designations of short range, medium or intermediate range, and long or intercontinental range (the last also being known in the cold war superpower context as strategic). The corresponding acroynms are SRBM, IRBM, and ICBM. In the standard U.S. lexicon, theater missile defenses generally cope with SRBMs and IRBMs, and national missile defenses try to destroy ICBMs (though they may also at times go after IRBMs). Table 2-1 shows the basic flight characteristics of IRBMs and ICBMs.

Most Scuds are SRBMs. Iranian Shahabs, North Korean NoDongs, and Indian Agni missiles are IRBMs. Superpower strategic systems such as the Minuteman, MX, SS-18, and SS-25 are ICBMs.

Most short-range missiles have ranges of up to about 300 miles (500 kilometers), meaning that all or virtually all of their trajectories are within the atmosphere. However, the category of SRBMs also generally includes missiles with ranges up to roughly 600 miles or 1,000 kilometers. Medium-range and intermediate-range missiles can travel 600 miles to 3,500 miles (1,000 to 5,500 kilometers, roughly speaking). ICBMs have ranges up to 6,000 miles (roughly 10,000 kilometers) or even more.

Submarine-launched ballistic missiles, or SLBMs, are generally of intercontinental range (that is, they are generally ICBMs). But they are sometimes only capable of shorter flight—and sometimes are flown on shorter flights, regardless of their maximum ranges, if the launching submarine is reasonably close to its targets when missiles are fired.

These various range distinctions can become confusing because some authors define them in different ways. But the idea of three distinct categories is useful, since there are three different classes of missiles in terms of sophistication, cost, and prevalence around the world.

Basic Types of Missile Defenses

Missile defenses can be categorized by the range of the offensive missile they are designed to defeat. Actual defenses do not always fall neatly into one category or the other, but most do. This is the approach the Pentagon generally takes and is the approach that we use. The main categories of interest are theater missile defense (TMD) and national missile defense (NMD).

Table 2-1. *Flight Characteristics of Ballistic Missiles*

Range	Initial angle of trajectory relative to earth's surface[a]	Missile speed at rocket burnout	Time of flight (approximate)
Short-range ballistic missiles (SRBMs)			
600 miles	43°	1.8 miles/second	7 minutes
(1,000 km)		(2.9 km/ second)	
Intermediate-range ballistic missiles (IRBMs)			
1,000 miles	41°	2.4 miles/second	10 minutes
(1,600 km)		(3.0 km/second)	
2,000 miles	38°	3.2 miles/second	16 minutes
(3,200 km)		(5.1 km/second)	
Intercontinental ballistic missiles (ICBMs)			
5,000 miles			
(8,000 km)	27°	4.3 miles/second	27 minutes
		(6.9 km/second)	
6,000 miles	23°	4.5 miles/second	31 minutes
(10,000 km)		(7.2 km/second)	

Source: Albert D. Wheelon, "Free Flight of a Ballistic Missile," *ARS Journal* (December 1959), pp. 916, 917, 919.
a. Information shown is for minimum-energy trajectories—that is, trajectories that provide maximum range for a given rocket burnout speed. Conversions to kilometers are rounded off to two significant figures.

Theater Missile Defense versus National Missile Defense

The distinction between TMD and NMD is not perfect, but for a country like the United States located far away from possible threats, and given most current defense technologies, the distinction works fairly well. Technologically, TMD defends against shorter-range missiles—SRBMs and IRBMs—and NMD defends against long-range threats or ICBMs as well as most SLBMs and many IRBMs. Conceptually, for the United States, that means TMD systems would protect American troops deployed abroad, as well as the territories of friendly countries near potential conflict zones, whereas NMD systems would protect U.S. territory (or allies a long distance from likely threats). NMD is sometimes also de-scribed as strategic missile defense.

These latter distinctions between TMD and NMD obviously fail for U.S. allies located near potential combat zones. For them, TMD systems are what would provide national defense. For the United States, TMD could have national defense implications as well, if offensive missiles were fired from a ship near U.S. territory, or from the northern half of Latin America. It could also have NMD relevance if the TMD systems also had the capability to intercept longer-range systems. In general, TMD inter-ceptors are not sufficiently fast or maneuverable to hit high-speed war-heads; moreover, if they had only been tested against slow-moving threats, their owner would probably not have confidence that they would work against faster objects even if that was theoretically possible. There may be exceptions to these broad generalizations, however.

To avoid confusion, we use the term NMD only to mean defense against long-range missile threats—ICBMs, SLBMs, and some longer-range IRBMs. We apply it to all technologies that could provide such protection, ranging from the Clinton administration's proposed system (which, lacking a proper name of its own, is also confusingly called NMD as if that were its actual designation rather than simply its mission) to boost-phase con-cepts to more advanced, futuristic approaches. We also note any situations where TMD systems would be likely to have NMD capabilities.

In fact, the United States and Russia have attempted in recent years to clarify the distinction between TMD and NMD. As defined in a 1997 U.S.-Russian accord known as the demarcation agreement, TMD systems are considered those capable of working against missiles with ranges not exceeding 3,500 kilometers (roughly 2,100 miles). In addition, that agree-ment defines TMD systems as those whose interceptor missiles do not exceed 3 kilometers per second in speed, and those that are tested only against offensive missiles with speeds below 5 kilometers per second.[7] The reason speed is so important is that faster intercepts require greater maneuverability in order to ensure that the interceptor collides with the streaking warhead in the short time available for terminal homing. Systems designed for slower flight are unlikely to have the necessary high acceleration and maneuverability. Missile defense systems with faster interceptors that are tested against longer-range, faster threats are defined as NMD. Missile defenses exceeding some but not all of the ceilings for TMD are in a legally ambiguous state.

Alas, even the technical distinction between TMD and NMD can break down for certain types of systems. That is especially the case for boost-phase defenses that would intercept an enemy rocket in its first phase of flight, while its engines were still firing. Defenses that were capable of hitting a medium-range missile in its powered flight might well be intrinsically capable of hitting a long-range rocket in that phase of flight as well, since there is much less difference among SRBMs, IRBMs, and ICBMs in their initial phases of flight than in subsequent phases. It is also possible that other weapons designed and tested for TMD may be capable of being upgraded to work as NMD, perhaps by linking them to advanced sensor networks, if their interceptors were given sufficient maneuverability to hit fast-moving objects as well.

Eventually, these facts may make it impractical to limit NMD without also limiting at least certain types of TMD. But for the near-to-medium-term future the distinction between the two types of defenses can probably be maintained for most purposes. Moreover, very capable TMD systems can be designed without exceeding most or all of the above speed and range restrictions from the TMD/NMD demarcation agreement. In particular, the Navy theater-wide system should have tremendously wide coverage, and it is doubtful that greater coverage would be needed for theaters of special concern to the United States such as East Asia and the Persian Gulf.

Boost-Phase, Midcourse, and Terminal Defenses

One can further subcategorize defenses by considering where in an offensive missile's trajectory the defense would try to destroy a threat and what technologies the defense would use to find, track, and destroy a threat. The main categories based on the offensive threat's trajectory are as follows:

—Terminal defenses that would work as warheads reentered the earth's atmosphere (if they had left it) but in any case in the final minutes of an offensive missile's flight;

—Midcourse defenses that would work while enemy warheads were outside the atmosphere (with some defense systems focusing on the ascent phase, relatively early in the exoatmospheric flight, and others on the descent phase); and

—Boost-phase defenses that would work in the first few minutes of the offensive missile's flight.

Finally, the different technologies used in missile defense range from land- and sea-based interceptor missiles to air-based or space-based interceptor missiles to various types of lasers. Within each of these main areas of technology, there are also other variations, depending on how any interceptor would physically destroy a threat and how it would be guided toward that threat.[8]

The following discussion uses the above taxonomy. At the broad level, defenses are broken down into TMD and NMD categories—that is, systems that would intercept SRBMs and most IRBMs, on the one hand, and those designed primarily against ICBMs on the other.

Types of Theater Missile Defenses

Most theater missile defenses today operate in either the midcourse or terminal phases. Some operate in both, so the following discussion considers those categories together. But they can be subcategorized by how they destroy a target. In addition, there is at least one boost-phase concept being considered for TMD.

Terminal and Midcourse Defenses

These defenses are of two main types, depending on how they destroy a warhead.

TRADITIONAL EXPLOSIVES. Most theater missile defenses that have been built or developed to date work in a fairly straightforward and similar fashion, and a way not so different from the way a radar-guided surface-to-air missile works against an airplane. First a defense battery is "told" of a missile launch, usually by communication from an early-warning satellite that senses the heat or infrared signal from the offensive missile's booster rockets. The defense battery's radar then begins to scan the sky looking for the incoming threat. Once it locates and begins to track the threat, and the incoming object is at the proper distance, an interceptor missile is launched. Its trajectory is chosen to put it in the right place to meet the incoming threat; a computer linked to the radar makes the necessary computation.

From that point on, the defense battery radar does double duty, tracking the incoming threat and the outgoing defensive interceptor missile. The interceptor missile may have a radar receiver that allows it to pick up radar echoes from the target. (Placing a radar receiver on the interceptor missile allows for more precise tracking; it is referred to as semiactive homing.) At the proper moment, a ground control station sends a radio signal to the interceptor, causing it to detonate a conventional-explosive warhead. The explosion then creates shrapnel that, if sufficiently close to the incoming warhead, should destroy that warhead. This is the basic way the existing Patriot missile defense system, known as the Patriot PAC-2, functions.[9]

HIT-TO-KILL INTERCEPTORS. More advanced theater missiles, such as the next generation of the Patriot (or PAC-3), the Army's theater high-altitude area defense (THAAD), and the Navy's area defense and theater-wide programs, use more advanced interceptors. Patriot PAC-3 may be deployed in 2001; Navy area defense by 2003; and THAAD and Navy theater-wide (NTW) by 2007 or so. Equipped with many miniature boosters, they are intended to maneuver so well that they can collide directly with incoming threats, obviating the need for (and weight of) explosives. They generally also will use either their own radar (as with Patriot PAC-3) or advanced infrared sensors (both Navy systems and THAAD) for the final homing, having first been steered to the general vicinity of a target by radar. These approaches are known as hit-to-kill technology.

Hit-to-kill technologies generally operate when an enemy missile or warhead is in its descent phase or terminal phase of flight. However, the NTW system is designed to work anywhere outside the atmosphere, be it in the ascent or descent phase. Theoretically, it may even be able to work against missiles still in boost phase. However, it can only work outside the atmosphere, and many shorter-range missiles do not have boost phases that continue beyond the atmosphere. In addition, it is not clear that the NTW missile has sufficient maneuverability to hit a target that is still accelerating.

Boost-Phase Defenses

Boost-phase defense may provide TMD as well, less so against SRBMs (given their very short boost phases) than against IRBMs. Such boost-phase defenses could be either interceptor rockets or lasers.

For example, a laser based on an airplane may ultimately be used to shoot a high-energy beam at a burning rocket, rupturing its metal skin and causing it to explode. A current program exists to develop such a laser, known as the ABL (for airborne laser); the Pentagon hopes to have it operational by 2010. Eventually, and with much work, such lasers could eventually also be based in space. Alternatively, small interceptor rockets could be based on airplanes or in a low orbit in space a few hundred kilometers above the earth's surface. Larger interceptors on land or at sea could also perform this mission, as we discuss in a moment.

Types of National Missile Defense

As is true of TMD, NMD systems can work at various places along an incoming warhead's trajectory.

Terminal Defenses

Terminal defenses are useful for defending small or high-value targets. They are poorly suited to national missile defense for a large country like the United States, however. Since they only work against incoming threats during the last minute or so of flight, and their interceptor missiles can realistically fly no more than fifty to one hundred miles in that time, they must be based near the city or small region they are designed to protect. More than one hundred defense batteries—and perhaps even two or three times that number—would be needed to defend an area the size of the United States in this way.

It may, however, eventually be possible to combine the advantages of terminal defense with those of midcourse defense. An interceptor missile could theoretically leave the atmosphere, fly hundreds or thousands of kilometers to where an incoming threat was headed, then reenter the atmosphere to conduct an intercept. It would need a local radar to guide the final approach to its target, but would not need to be based near the region it was defending.[10]

Midcourse Defenses

Midcourse missile defenses generally have fifteen to twenty minutes to work against ICBMs, which is one of their appeals. During that time, interceptor missiles could travel thousands of miles, meaning that in theory it is practical to defend an entire land mass such as the United States with a single base or two of missiles.

The interceptors could be fired as soon as an enemy launch was noticed by an infrared-detection satellite. More likely, they would be launched after radar picked up the missile following a few minutes of flight. The United States presently has radars for such purposes on its own continental coasts, in Alaska, in England, and in Greenland. These types of radars have long wavelengths that are optimal for long-range detection. A different type of radar, generally using shorter wavelengths and thus having less range but more accuracy, would then track the threatening objects. It would guide interceptors toward targets until the interceptors were close enough to pick up the threats with their own sensors. In the final approach, such sensors would provide much more accurate readings of the location of the threats than distant radars could.[11]

Several interceptors might be launched more or less simultaneously at a single threat, to account for the possibility of random failures. Alternatively, if time were sufficient, a first interceptor could be launched, and then a second or third would be launched if previous efforts had failed. This latter technique is called "shoot-look-shoot" defense.

In fact, it could take four or five interceptors to reliably shoot down a single warhead, not only for midcourse NMD but for most types of missile defense using interceptor rockets. That is the reason why the Clinton administration advertised its proposed one-hundred-interceptor system as capable of destroying only a couple dozen warheads.[12] Several problems could cause a given interceptor to miss. Rocket boosters can fail; for example, during the cold war, superpower ICBMs were generally considered to have no more than 80 to 85 percent reliability.[13] Or the so-called kill vehicle could miss its target, because of random error, a manufacturing defect, or some other cause. Even if the overall interceptor reliability were as high as 80 percent, very high reliability is needed against a nuclear weapon. To obtain 99 percent confidence of a successful intercept, in this example, three interceptors would be needed per warhead. Even more might be required if several interceptors could fail for the same reason (that is, if their probabilities of failure were not simply random, and independent from each other, but linked and systemic). Since there is not a great deal of time in which to intercept warheads, moreover, it might be impractical to attempt one intercept before firing a second and third and perhaps a fourth and fifth interceptor just in case they were needed. In other words, "shoot-look-shoot" defensive tactics may not be possible, necessitating a launch of several interceptors at once against a given warhead.

Boost-Phase Defenses

Boost-phase defenses that worked against theater-range missiles (SRBMs and IRBMs) would generally also work against longer-range missiles (notably, ICBMs). In fact, since the latter begin at the same speed as short-range rockets and burn longer and higher into the atmosphere and beyond, they are generally easier to intercept in this initial phase of missile flight than are shorter-range missiles.

A major difficulty with boost-phase defenses is that they must be based near the enemy missile launch point. That could be on land, at sea, or in the air—but it would need to be near the enemy missile launch points in any case. Since boost phase lasts only three to five minutes, or less for shorter-range missiles, an interceptor does not have much time and cannot cover much distance. As a result, it must begin its flight near its target. This problem is not serious if the potential missile threat comes only from small countries that border U.S. allies or international waterways. But it makes boost-phase defense generally impractical against missiles launched from countries with large land masses, like Russia or China.

The exception to this rule would arise if a boost-phase defense were based in a low orbit in space. Even then, however, a space-based interceptor would need to be in the right place at the time a missile was launched, since it would not have much time to complete the intercept before the offensive booster stopped burning. So the defender would need to put interceptors in many different orbits, spacing them so that some would be in the correct position at all times against plausible threats (the interceptors would be in constant motion relative to the earth's surface). A simple calculation shows that only one out of several dozen interceptors might be, by chance, in the right place at the right time to intercept a given ICBM. So even to have the capacity to intercept five to ten enemy missiles, several hundred interceptors could be needed.[14]

Even lasers, which produce beams traveling at the speed of light, would need to be located near missile launch points. Otherwise, their beams would be too weakened by the atmosphere, or by the inevitable spreading of a light beam that occurs over distance (known as diffraction) even in the vacuum of space. The beams could also simply be blocked by the earth's curvature.

Boost-phase defenses, as well as other types of TMD and NMD, would generally be alerted about the launch of an enemy missile by infrared-detection satellites high above the earth. The satellites would see the strong heat signature of the rocket. Although such signals have occasionally been confused with forest fires and other hot emissions from earth over the years, the combination of experience, more sensitive satellites, and better computers makes such confusion less likely all the time. U.S. early-warning satellites are "parked" in geosynchronous orbit about 22,000 miles (or roughly 36,000 kilometers) above the earth's surface. At that height, an object orbiting the earth completes a full revolution once every twenty-four hours—the same speed at which the earth's surface rotates. As a result, the satellite remains above the same region of the planet continuously.

Decoys and Other Countermeasures

Clearly, intercepting a missile or warhead moving at up to several miles per second is a daunting task. To date, the United States is capable of carrying out this task only for lower-speed warheads that are no more than a couple dozen miles away from a defense battery. Its capability is improving with time, however, and will continue to do so—the test failures that occurred in 2000 notwithstanding.

Eventually, a nation that could put a man on the moon in the 1960s can probably figure out how to hit a bullet with a bullet, or with a laser beam. But that may not be good enough. The moon was not trying to get out of the way or confuse us as to its true location. By contrast, even relatively unsophisticated enemies would do everything in their power to make a defense's job as hard as possible—and they would probably have some fairly simple ways to do so.

One approach would be to fire more missiles than the defense has interceptors, simply saturating the defense and ensuring that some offensive weapons could not be intercepted. If the attacker had MIRV technology, saturating a midcourse or terminal defense would be even easier and require even fewer missiles.

Decoys against Midcourse Defenses

Against defenses that can only work outside the atmosphere, in the vacuum of space, an attacker could choose to fly its shorter-range missiles on trajectories that would never leave the atmosphere. Some defenses only work in outer space (or in the very high parts of the atmosphere) because they depend on sensitive infrared detectors to home in on a target—and such detectors can be blinded by the heat generated by air resistance, particularly if an interceptor missile is traveling at high speed. Keeping trajectories within the atmosphere would require an attacker to shorten the range of many of its missiles. But for many scenarios that would not be a steep price for an attacker to pay. Rather than flying its missiles on depressed trajectories, an attacker might also move its missiles as close as possible to their target (for example, Chinese missiles aimed at Taiwan could be placed near the Taiwan Strait before launch, as indeed they have been by Beijing). In that case, their natural trajectories would be lower and their durations of flight would be reduced—preventing some defenses from having enough time to intercept them.

Against any defense that must work in the vacuum of outer space, the attacker has its greatest range of options.[15] In this exoatmospheric or midcourse region, a warhead would generally have separated from its missile—or could be designed to do so almost immediately after boosting was complete. (As noted, an advanced country could design even its long-range missiles to complete their boosting while within the atmosphere, though a less sophisticated country might not be able to.)[16]

Outside the atmosphere, air resistance will not separate out the generally lighter decoys from the heavier warheads (as it would do for the Patriot and other TMD systems that operate within the atmosphere).[17] In outer space, even extremely light decoys would fly the same trajectory as true warheads, so speed could not be used to distinguish the real from the fake. To mimic the infrared heat signature of a warhead, thereby fooling sensors that measure temperature, decoys could be equipped with small heat generators, perhaps weighing only a pound. To fool radars or imaging infrared sensors, warheads and decoys alike could be placed inside radar-reflective balloons that would make it impossible to see their interiors.[18] Decoys could also be spun by small motors so that the balloons surrounding them rotated at the same speed as real warheads, in case the defense's radar was sensitive enough to pick up such motion.

There is some chance that lighter decoys could be distinguished from heavier warheads based on how they moved away from the bus. If pushed away by something like springs, lighter decoys would tend to move faster than heavy warheads, assuming springs of similar force. But detecting such differences in motion would require extremely precise sensors. The attacker might also compensate by releasing chaff just prior to releasing decoys and warheads—to prevent radars from seeing what happens during the release—or by designing a more sophisticated release mechanism that makes decoys and warheads indistinguishable even at the moment of separation from the bus. It is for these reasons that the decoy problem is acute, and possibly not solvable for the foreseeable future, in the case of midcourse defenses.

Decoys like those mentioned above are not trivial to make, however—
and might work only if repeatedly flight tested. Balloons need to be
inflated in outer space. Some type of mechanism needs to physically separate each decoy from its host vehicle as well—easy to do for Russia (or
the United States, Britain, or France), the countries that have mastered
MIRV technology, but a bit harder for one that has not. (Most states of
concern to the United States are highly unlikely to have MIRV technology
anytime soon; even China does not have MIRVs today.) The associated
technology is fairly simple, but making it work in the laboratory is not
the same as making it work at high speed in outer space, after a high-
acceleration trajectory through the earth's atmosphere.

Decoys against Terminal Defenses

Making decoys work *within* the atmosphere is what is truly hard,
however. It can be done, but it requires decoys that can overcome the
effects of air resistance so as not to slow down more quickly than real
warheads would.

Decoys that could mimic warheads within the atmosphere therefore
might need small booster rockets. Alternatively, they could be made small
and dense, so that they would fly the same trajectories as heavier but
larger warheads (since the rate of slowing from air resistance increases
with an object's size as well as its weight), though in that case their radar
signatures might give them away.

Countermeasures against Boost-Phase Defenses

Against boost-phase defenses, countermeasures are also possible,
though they are relatively difficult to make. As noted, boost phases could
theoretically be shortened to minimize the time a defense would have to
home in on the hot rocket booster. Against interceptors that would track
a rocket's plume, contaminants could be put in the rocket fuel to make
its plume asymmetric and potentially lead interceptors that home in on
the midpoint of the plume astray (unless the interceptors also had an
additional sensor). Against lasers, a rocket could be rotated, or given a
shiny external surface that would reflect most incoming light. Finally,
rockets could also be launched from remote locations and launched on
cloudy days when infrared detection satellites might not detect their heat
signatures immediately—reducing the time when boost-phase defenses
could work.

In short, the missile defense job involves not only very advanced technologies but a complex interaction between offense and defense. Moreover, the tools available to each side are different, and in many cases advantageous to an attacker, meaning that even a less sophisticated attacker may be able to compete successfully with a technologically advanced defender. The broad message, picked up again in chapter 4, is that one must ask about the likely offensive countermeasures that could be deployed against each and every different type of defense. Missile defense is not pure science; it is an interactive, competitive, action-reaction process.

CHAPTER THREE

The Threat

DOES THE UNITED STATES confront a threat that justifies building a national missile defense? Although claims are frequently made that ballistic missiles are rapidly proliferating around the world, the current and likely future missile threat to the U.S. homeland comes from only five countries: Russia, China, North Korea, Iran, and Iraq. The first two already have long-range missiles and nuclear weapons; the others might acquire both during the next fifteen years. The nuclear powers India and Pakistan might also join the intercontinental ballistic missile (ICBM) club in the coming decade, though few see their missile programs as a threat to the United States (as opposed to each other).

The spread of long-range missiles and weapons of mass destruction warrants concern not because any of these countries is likely to attack the United States. They are not—both because they have no immediate incentives to do so and because of the threat of devastating retaliation. Rather, the problem is that a missile attack *could* happen, with consequences for the United States that would dwarf the horrors of the Oklahoma City bombing and potentially claim as many victims as the Civil War—if not more. And that prospect has the power to constrain how the United States conducts itself abroad and to undermine the confidence U.S. friends and allies have in American security guarantees. Missile attack is not the only such threat to the United States, but it is among the most serious.

A Growing Ballistic Missile Threat?

The fear that ballistic missile technology is rapidly spreading across the globe fuels the American push for missile defense. National missile defense (NMD) proponents note that thirty-eight countries now possess ballistic missiles and more are likely to acquire them in the coming decade. The image of the United States amid a sea of hostile countries armed with missiles is alarming. But it is not one that describes the world we live in or are likely to live in during the next decade.

Why? Because most countries have neither the ability nor the interest to attack U.S. territory. As table 3-1 shows, of the thirty-eight countries believed to possess ballistic missiles, twenty-seven own only missiles with ranges of about 600 miles or less. Many of these countries, such as Hungary, Poland, and the Czech Republic, are U.S. allies and friends. Most own aging Scud missiles that they bought or inherited from the Soviet Union. A few, like South Korea and Turkey, own American-made missiles. Most show no interest in shouldering the financial and political costs of developing the capability to build their own ballistic missiles. Most important, none of them has developed nuclear weapons, and most show no interest in doing so. A few—Kazakhstan, Belarus, Ukraine, South Africa—have even given up their nuclear weapons.

The pool of countries capable of attacking U.S. territory—as opposed to U.S. allies and bases overseas—or that might become capable of doing so during the next decade is small. Only four countries currently possess the ability to strike the United States from their own territory: Russia, China, Great Britain, and France. No one seriously worries about a British or French threat, a fact that highlights the important distinction between capabilities and intentions. The main fear with Moscow is an accident and not a deliberate attack. U.S.-Chinese relations have been rocky in recent years, and it is possible that the two countries could come to direct blows over Taiwan, but neither a U.S.-Chinese cold war nor an all-out strategic competition is preordained. Six other countries possess medium- or intermediate-range missiles. Two of these are potential U.S. adversaries (Iran and North Korea); two are close security partners (Israel and Saudi Arabia); and two are friendly countries (India and Pakistan). Other countries with latent missile potential in the form of space-launch programs, such as Brazil and Japan, are U.S. friends or allies.

What may be most striking about table 3-1 is who does not show up as possessing intermediate- or long-range ballistic missiles. In the mid-

Table 3.1. *Countries Possessing Ballistic Missiles*

Countries possessing only short-range missiles (<600 miles)

Afghanistan	Egypt	Slovakia
Algeria	Georgia	Syria
Argentina	Greece	Taiwan
Armenia	Hungary	Turkey
Azerbaijan	Iraq	Turkmenistan
Belarus	Kazakhstan	United Arab Emirates
Bulgaria	Libya	Ukraine
Congo	Poland	Vietnam
Czech Republic	South Korea	Yemen

*Countries possessing short- and intermediate-range missiles
(between 600 and 3,500 miles)*

India	Israel	Pakistan
Iran	North Korea	Saudi Arabia

Countries possessing short-, intermediate-, and long-range missiles (>3,500 miles)

China	Russia	United States
France	United Kingdom	

Source: Todd Sechser, "Countries Possessing Ballistic Missiles," Carnegie Nonproliferation Project, Washington, undated, pp. 3–5.

Note: Six hundred miles is roughly equal to 1,000 kilometers, and 3,500 miles is approximately 5,500 kilometers.

1980s, Argentina, Brazil, Egypt, and South Africa all had programs to develop long-range missiles. All have now ended these efforts.[1] This missile "de-proliferation" is no less important because it has gone largely unnoticed in the American national security debate. Nor was it an accident. The United States and its allies devoted considerable diplomatic effort to persuading these countries to abandon their missile programs. This underscores the fact that regardless of the outcome of the NMD debate in the United States, diplomacy should remain a key part of the U.S. strategy to encourage deproliferation.

Russia

The scale of the potential threat that Russian long-range missiles pose to the United States dwarfs that of any other country. Like U.S. missiles, Russian missiles can be fired on a moment's notice. Russian missiles are also highly accurate, and can be used to target both American cities and well-protected military installations such as missile silos.

Table 3-2. *Russian Strategic Nuclear Missile Forces, 2000*

Type	Name	Launchers[a]	Year deployed	Warheads × yield (kiloton)	Total warheads
ICBMs					
SS-18	Satan	180	1979	10 × 550/750 (MIRV)	1,800
SS-19	Stiletto	150	1979	6 × 750 (MIRV)	900
SS24 M1/M2	Scalpel	36/10	1987	10 × 550 (MIRV)	460
SS-25	Sickle	360	1985	1 × 550	360
SS-27	Sickle	20	1998	1 × 550	20
Total		756			3,540
SLBMs					
SS-N-18 M1	Stingray	176	1978	3 × 500 (MIRV)	528
SS-N-20	Sturgeon	60	1983	10 × 200 (MIRV)	600
SS-N-23	Skiff	112	1986	4 × 100 (MIRV)	448
Total		348			1,576
Grand totals		1,104			5,116

Source: "Russian Nuclear Forces, 2000," *Bulletin of the Atomic Scientists,* vol. 56 (July–August 2000), pp. 70–71.

a. Russia also possesses 69 long-range bombers equipped with approximately 790 warheads.

As table 3-2 shows, as of mid-2000, Russia possessed 756 land-based ICBMs equipped with 3,540 warheads, as well as 348 submarine-launched ballistic missiles (SLBMs) equipped with 1,576 warheads.[2] These numbers will likely fall further during the next decade. Under the terms of the second Strategic Arms Reduction Talks (START II), which have yet to go into effect, Moscow and Washington have agreed to deploy no more than 3,000 to 3,500 strategic nuclear warheads apiece. Under this overall ceiling, they have also agreed to eliminate land-based multiple warhead missiles and to deploy no more than 1,750 warheads on SLBMs. And Moscow has agreed to destroy its largest and most destructive land-based ICBM, the SS-18.

U.S. and Russian officials are also engaged in discussions on a START III treaty. In March 1997, Presidents Bill Clinton and Boris Yeltsin agreed at the Helsinki summit that the two countries should cut their strategic nuclear warheads to between 2,000 and 2,500 apiece. The formal start of the START III talks was delayed for three years because the Russian Duma refused to consent to START II. After the Duma relented in March 2000 (though with conditions that have prevented the treaty from going into effect), Russian officials proposed going down to between 1,000 and 1,500 warheads. The Clinton administration stuck by the original Helsinki numbers, on the grounds that the United States needs at least 2,000 warheads to maintain its nuclear deterrent. The Bush administration may be more open to so-called deep cuts, however; during the campaign President Bush emphasized that "the Cold War logic that led to the creation of massive stockpiles on both sides is now outdated. Our mutual security need no longer depend on a nuclear balance of terror."[3]

The size of the Russian strategic nuclear arsenal may fall even without progress at formal arms control talks. Russian Defense Minister Igor Sergeyev admitted in 1998 that by 2010 Russia will be unable to afford more than 1,500 strategic nuclear warheads.[4] Some experts believe that budgetary pressures may force Moscow to go to 500 or fewer warheads.[5] (Estimates of Russia's annual military spending range between $20 and $50 billion, far less than the roughly $300 billion the United States spends annually.)[6] But while a steep drop in the number of Russian strategic warheads is likely, it is not inevitable. Much depends on whether Moscow adheres to START II, which it has threatened to abandon if the United States builds an NMD system.[7] U.S. intelligence officials and civilian observers agree that without START II—the only thing preventing Russia from keeping its multiple warhead missiles—Moscow could maintain a force of 3,000 to 4,000 strategic warheads (not to mention its many thousands of short-range nuclear weapons) for at least the next decade.[8]

However much Russia's nuclear arsenal shrinks, its missiles will remain equipped with countermeasures. Russian interest in developing countermeasure technology dates back to the earliest work on missile defenses in the 1960s, and it escalated in the mid-1980s as the United States began work on the Strategic Defense Initiative. According to the 1999 National Intelligence Estimate (NIE), which summarized the official view of the U.S. intelligence community, Russia has "developed numerous countermeasures."[9] These countermeasures reportedly include decoys that simulate warheads, "chaff" that confuses enemy radars, and maneuverable warheads that can evade interceptors.[10] Reportedly, the SS-18 ICBM may hold about thirty decoys in addition to its ten nuclear warheads, for example.[11] And Russia's leading missile designer said in 1999 that the Topol-M rocket, the newest addition to the Russian arsenal, had "from the very beginning design capabilities enabling it to effectively penetrate a potential ABM system of any state."[12]

Russia's countermeasure technology presents a problem for any U.S. missile defense that relies on midcourse interceptors, regardless of whether an attack were deliberate, accidental, unauthorized, or erroneous.[13] And while the prospects for a deliberate Russian first strike are exceedingly slim, the possibility of an accidental, unauthorized, or erroneous launch, while low, may be growing. Nearly 60 percent of Russia's ballistic missiles have exceeded their operational life span, and its modernization programs are hampered by a lack of funds.[14] Making a bad situation worse, those aging missiles remain on hair-trigger alert, with the coordinates of U.S. targets in their computers, ready to launch at a moment's notice.

Russia's early warning systems may be even worse off. In January 1995, Norwegian scientists launched a rocket to study the northern lights. Russian ground radar mistook it for a nuclear attack on Moscow. President Yeltsin was alerted, and the Russian nuclear codes activated before the mistake was discovered.[15] Today, most of the satellites that told Russian officials that the initial ground report was false no longer work or have reached the end of their operational lives. As a result, "Currently, Russia is totally blind to a Trident [submarine missile] attack from the Atlantic and Pacific, and, for all practical purposes, it is equally blind to a Minuteman or MX [missile] attack from the continental United States."[16]

Despite these problems, the U.S. intelligence community believes "that an unauthorized or accidental launch of a Russian strategic missile is highly unlikely so long as current technical and procedural safeguards are in place."[17] Whether that assessment is accurate can be debated. We are not fully reassured, given the witches' brew of aging weapons on hair-trigger alert, aging warning systems, and underpaid troops now found in Russia's military.

How large would an accidental or unauthorized Russian launch be? No one knows for sure.[18] Everything depends on why the launch occurred. If it stemmed from an equipment malfunction or human error, it might involve just one missile and one or several warheads. If it stemmed from the unauthorized, rogue actions of a single Russian ICBM launch-control center, ten missiles each with a single warhead (assuming START II's ban on multiple warhead missiles is implemented) could be fired. By contrast, an unauthorized launch by a single submarine could send between 48 warheads (if it were one of Russia's new generation of submarines) and 200 warheads (if it were one of its older generation of submarines that are now being retired).

What if Russia deliberately attacked in response to an erroneous report of a U.S. first strike? In such a situation, it might fire a thousand warheads or more at the United States. Dozens, perhaps hundreds, of warheads could also hit America's NATO allies and other countries deemed to threaten Moscow.[19] Moreover, deep cuts in the Russian arsenal will not solve the problem that an erroneous Russian launch could mean dozens or even hundreds of warheads headed toward American soil. Moscow is likely to retain several hundred ICBMs if it proceeds with de-MIRVing, and its SLBMs will remain MIRVed.

China

China's strategic nuclear arsenal of twenty single-warhead ICBMs is only a fraction the size of Russia's and far less sophisticated.[20] China's one ballistic missile submarine seldom leaves port and has missiles with a range of about 1,000 miles (table 3-3). These liquid-fueled rockets are based on 1960s designs and are relatively inaccurate. As a result, they are most likely targeted against American cities rather than U.S. missile fields. Beijing is believed to have opted for this minimal deterrent posture rather than the far larger counterforce arsenals that the United States and Russia developed because of cost considerations and because China believes the threat to destroy major population centers is sufficient to deter Washington and Moscow from attacking its territory.[21]

China is now modernizing and expanding its strategic forces.[22] It is developing two ICBMs. Both are road mobile—a response to the vulnerability of stationary ICBMs to a U.S. or Russian attack—though only one is believed to have a range sufficient to hit targets anywhere in the United States. China is also developing an SLBM that could hit targets in at least some parts of the United States from Chinese territorial waters. None of these new missiles is expected to be deployed for several years.

Many NMD critics point to China's modernization program as evidence that it intends to contest U.S. preeminence, not only near Taiwan but strategically and globally as well. The so-called Cox report that a special House of Representatives panel issued in 1999 accused the Chinese government of systematically stealing U.S. nuclear weapons secrets. The

Table 3-3. *Chinese Nuclear Missile Forces, 2000*

Type	NATO designation	Number	Year deployed	Range (miles)	Warheads × yield	Number of warheads
ICBMs						
DF-5A	CSS-4	20	1981	8,050	1 × 4–5 Mt	20
DF-31	CSS-?	0	2000?	4,950	MIRV × ?	?
New ICBM	CSS-?	0	2010?	7,450	MIRV × ?	?
Total		20				20
IRBMs						
DF-3A	CSS-2	40	1971	1,750	1 × 3.3 Mt	40
DF-4	CSS-3	20	1980	3,400	1 × 3.3 Mt	20
DF-21A	CSS-5	48	1985	1,100	1 × 200–300 kt	48
Total		108				108
SLBMs						
Julang-1	CSS-N-3	12	1986	1,050	1 × 200–300 kt	12
Julang-2	CSS-NX-4	0	2010?	4,950	1 × 200–300 kt	?
Total		12				12
Grand total		140				140

Source: "Chinese Nuclear Forces, 2000," *Bulletin of the Atomic Scientists,* vol. 56 (November–December 2000), p. 78.

report has deservedly attracted criticism for its worst-case reading of the available evidence, but its broader point that China has sought to get access to U.S. military technology holds true.[23] That said, however, China's decision to modernize its relatively primitive nuclear forces should not be alarming in and of itself. After all, the United States is still modernizing its SLBM forces even as it cuts its stockpile of nuclear weapons.[24]

The more relevant question is whether China will substantially expand the number of ICBMs and ICBM warheads it possesses. Experts disagree on the answer, though they do agree that China is not likely to approach even sharply reduced U.S. or Russian arsenals. U.S. intelligence analysts believe that "by 2015, China will likely have tens of missiles targeted against the United States, having added a few tens of more survivable land-based and sea-based mobile missiles with smaller nuclear warheads."[25] For their part, Chinese officials repeatedly state that they will tie the size and speed of their modernization efforts to what the United States decides to do on missile defense.[26]

Like Russia, China has extensive experience with countermeasures.[27] That is largely because one potential target of Chinese missiles is Moscow, which is protected by the world's only operational (though not necessarily effective) defense against long-range missiles. China's new generation of long-range missiles almost certainly will be equipped with countermeasures. When China conducted the first flight test of its new road-mobile ICBM in August 1999, it included decoys.[28]

China might well launch all of its ICBMs in an attack against the United States. (Beijing could calculate that any missile not fired in the first salvo would be targeted in an American retaliatory attack.) The number of missiles that would be fired in an accidental launch is unclear, though the chances of it occurring are even lower than that of an accidental Russian launch.[29] Unlike Russia, China maintains its ICBMs without fuel or warheads, a posture that makes it impossible for Beijing to strike quickly or to fire its missiles accidentally or erroneously under normal nonalert conditions.[30] Beijing maintains this low alert posture even though it makes its deterrent vulnerable to a first strike by highly accurate U.S. missiles. Analysts expect that China will deploy its next generation of missiles mated with their warheads as the United States and Russia both do. Even if China takes this step, it probably will not adopt a launch on warning posture (which might increase the chances of an attack triggered by a false alarm); it lacks the early warning radars needed to detect a missile strike.[31]

North Korea, Iran, and Iraq

The Clinton administration justified its proposed NMD system on the need to respond to the potential threat posed by three countries that the State Department once called "rogue states" but now refers to as "states of concern": North Korea, Iran, and Iraq. Assessments of this threat have changed greatly over the years. In the mid-1990s, the U.S. intelligence community downplayed it, stating flatly that "no country, other than the major declared nuclear powers, will develop or otherwise acquire a ballistic missile in the next 15 years that could threaten the contiguous 48 states and Canada."[32] In the late 1990s, the view that new ballistic missile powers posed a threat that was "broader, more mature and evolving more rapidly" than anticipated gained ascendancy.[33] By 2000, however, critics pointed to encouraging political trends and argued that fears of ballistic missile proliferation were overblown.

North Korea

North Korea has the most advanced missile and nuclear weapons programs of the three states of concern.[34] For a decade Pyongyang has produced and exported short-range missiles based on Soviet Scud designs. These missiles have ranges of 180 to 300 miles (300 to 500 kilometers). These weapons are suited for use against South Korea; they cannot reach Japan or any other American ally in East Asia. North Korea also appears to have deployed the No Dong, a single-stage liquid-fueled, intermediate-range missile that it first tested in the early 1990s and which is believed capable of traveling 800 miles (1,300 kilometers). The No Dong gives North Korea the ability to hit targets anywhere in Japan. North Korea is believed to have the ability to produce roughly one hundred Scuds a year at present. Estimates for the number of No Dongs produced to date range from roughly ten to one hundred.[35]

Despite North Korea's progress in building short- and medium-range missiles, the U.S. intelligence community initially downplayed North Korea's ability to build effective long-range missiles. The November 1995 NIE noted that North Korea was developing a missile that might be able "to strike portions of Alaska and the far western portion of the Hawaiian Island chain (more than 1,000 kilometers west of Honolulu)," but it regarded North Korea as "unlikely to obtain the technological capability to develop a longer range ICBM." Furthermore, it stated that the United States would be "likely to detect any indigenous long-range ballistic missile program many years before deployment."[36]

NMD supporters attacked this relatively benign assessment.[37] As a result of the controversy, Congress created the bipartisan Commission to Assess the Ballistic Missile Threat to the United States. Known more widely as the Rumsfeld Commission, after its chair, the current secretary of defense Donald Rumsfeld, it concluded in July 1998 that the intelligence community had underestimated the North Korean threat. The commission reached this conclusion not because it received new intelligence information but because it rightly worried about the security of all fifty U.S states, not just the continental forty-eight, and because it questioned the assumptions that had guided previous estimates. It argued that Pyongyang would not build missiles to the same high standards the United States employed and that it could do much of its work in secret.

The commission also used a different standard for assessing the threat. Rather than attempting to determine whether North Korea was *likely* to build long-range missiles, as previous estimates had, it focused instead on whether North Korea *could* build them.[38] The commission's answer was yes. In its view, North Korea "would be able to inflict major destruction on the U.S. within about five years of a decision to acquire such a capability" and "the U.S. might well have little or no warning before operational deployment."[39]

North Korea's surprise test of a long-range version of its Taepo Dong-1 missile in August 1998 made the commission's case. The test was not a complete success—the third stage booster apparently meant to launch a satellite into space failed to ignite. But it indicated that North Korea was developing the ability to build multistage missiles capable of traveling intercontinental distances. Faced with a far greater threat materializing much earlier than anticipated, the Clinton administration moved on the diplomatic front to persuade Pyongyang to halt its missile test flights, with former secretary of defense William Perry leading the effort. After the United States agreed in September 1999 to lift some of the economic sanctions it had imposed a half century earlier, North Korea announced it would halt its missile tests "while the talks [with the United States] are underway."[40] It later declared a moratorium on missile flight testing. North Korea did not, however, pledge to stop its missile program entirely. As a result, it is highly likely that North Korean scientists continue to work on developing the Taepo Dong-2 and other missiles in their laboratories.

How long it would take North Korea to build an operational ICBM if it resumed flight testing is unclear. Clinton administration officials repeatedly invoked the year 2005. Secretary of Defense William Cohen testified before Congress, however, that 2005 was targeted "by the Ballistic Missile Defense Organization as the soonest it would be ready to deploy" an NMD system.[41] The Rumsfeld Commission said only that countries could "acquire the means to strike the U.S. within about five years of a decision to acquire such a capability."[42] The 1999 NIE ventured no further than to speculate that North Korea would "develop ICBMs capable of threatening the United States during the next 15 years."[43] In other words, the best guess of the U.S. intelligence community is that North Korea might have an ICBM deployed before 2005—or possibly not until after 2010. It just does not know.

One difficulty in determining when the North Korean threat might become real is that its 1998 test flight showed only that it had made surprising (though incomplete) progress in building long-range missiles. North Korea has not yet demonstrated that it has mastered the harder tasks of building the guidance systems and reentry vehicles needed to turn a missile into an operational weapon.[44] Guidance systems are crucial to ensuring that missiles hit their target rather than fly wildly off course. They remain difficult to build for ICBMs even in the age of global positioning satellites because it is essential to know not only a rocket's precise position but its precise speed to set its course accurately. And with long-range missiles, the standards for accuracy are unforgiving. An ICBM that falls five miles east of Chicago—a trivial error over an intercontinental distance—would fall into Lake Michigan and be far less lethal. But building accurate guidance systems requires "precision machining, the ability to fabricate advanced materials, and access to computers used by the accelerometers, gyroscopes, and associated subcomponents."[45]

The technology needed to build reentry vehicles that can survive the stress of reentering the atmosphere is only slightly less complicated. It requires not only manufacturing a device that can withstand physical stress but also one that will not be too heavy (thereby limiting the size of the warhead) while still fitting on the missile without degrading accuracy. And while North Korea has developed reentry vehicles for its short-range and medium-range missiles, it is harder to develop them for long-range missiles because their greater speeds subject their reentry vehicles to stresses roughly ten times greater.[46]

With its test-flight program suspended, North Korea's ability to meet these challenges and its actual long-range missile capabilities remain a matter of speculation. The 1999 NIE concluded that if North Korea solved the third-stage booster problem—it made no specific mention of either the guidance or reentry issues—the Taepo Dong-1 would be theoretically capable of delivering "a light payload (sufficient for a biological or chemical weapon) to the United States, albeit with inaccuracies that would make hitting large urban targets improbable."[47] However, a nuclear warhead would be too heavy for the Taepo Dong-1.

The longer-range Taepo Dong-2 missile, which North Korea has not yet flight tested, appears to have substantially greater capability. "A two-stage Taepo Dong-2 could deliver a several-hundred kilogram payload to Alaska and Hawaii, and a lighter payload to the western half of the United States. A three-stage version of the Taepo Dong-2 could deliver a several-hundred kilogram payload anywhere in the United States."[48] Because even a three-stage Taepo Dong-2 would have significant payload limitations, North Korea probably could target only cities in the western United States with nuclear weapons. Early-generation nuclear weapons may weigh a ton or more; making them light enough to be delivered by a missile presents a substantial technological challenge.[49] North Korea might not be able to build a sufficiently light warhead unless it acquired an advanced design from another country.

North Korea would also need nuclear materials to build a bomb—and it is possible it already has modest quantities that would allow it to do so. Despite being a signatory to the Nonproliferation Treaty, Pyongyang maintained an active nuclear weapons program in the late 1980s and early 1990s and diverted material from Soviet-designed nuclear reactors, possibly producing weapons-grade plutonium. The discovery that North Korea had diverted nuclear material touched off a crisis that was finally resolved in 1994 with the signing of the Agreed Framework. Under its terms, North Korea agreed to close its one functioning nuclear reactor, stop construction of two others, seal a factory designed to turn material irradiated in the reactors into weapons-grade plutonium, and ultimately allow for removal of spent fuel rods to a third country. In exchange, the United States, Japan, and South Korea agreed to help it build two nuclear reactors that could not be easily used to produce weapons-grade plutonium.[50]

The United States suspended work on the reactors following the August 1998 Taepo Dong-1 test. Suspicions immediately arose that North Korea had resumed its effort to develop nuclear weapons. The U.S. Defense Intelligence Agency argued that Pyongyang had built as many as ten new installations for conducting a clandestine nuclear weapons program. Other U.S. intelligence agencies rejected this assessment, however. North Korea twice allowed U.S. officials to inspect one suspected site, and they found nothing suspicious. Another suspected site turned out to be an underground vault for storing the North Korean leadership's memorabilia.[51] But the Defense Intelligence Agency's fears do not appear entirely unreasonable. The International Atomic Energy Association (IAEA) expressed "concern" in September 2000 over North Korea's nuclear program and stated that it could not be certain that it was halted.[52] Even if Pyongyang has abided by the terms of the Agreed Framework, it may possess enough nuclear material, based on what it diverted before the agreement was reached, to build "at least one or possibly two weapons."[53]

Like its nuclear program, Pyongyang's chemical and biological capabilities are shrouded in secrecy. According to the Rumsfeld Commission,

North Korea "possesses biological weapons production and dispensing technology, including the capability to deploy chemical or biological warheads on missiles."[54] Ballistic missiles, however, are not ideal vehicles by which to distribute chemical or biological weapons. The effectiveness of such agents varies greatly with the conditions under which they are released.[55] For example, winds may disperse chemical and biological pathogens, substantially reducing the lethality of an attack.[56] Developing chemical or biological warheads that can be placed on an ICBM is also a challenging task because long-range ballistic missiles travel at extremely high velocities as they reenter the atmosphere, which potentially exposes chemical or biological agents to temperature fluctuations that could render them useless.

If North Korea develops long-range missiles, however armed, would they be equipped with countermeasures? Most experts say yes. The Union of Concerned Scientists (UCS) argues, "Any country that has both the technological capability and the motivation to build and potentially use long-range ballistic missiles would also have the technological capability and motivation to build and deploy countermeasures that would make those missiles useful in the presence of the planned U.S. NMD system."[57] The 1999 NIE largely concurs, noting that North Korea and other countries "*could* develop countermeasures . . . by the time they flight test their missiles."[58] But whether and how well North Korea could get its countermeasures to work, or be confident they would work—especially in the absence of rigorous flight testing—is unclear.[59] The UCS report notes that emerging ballistic missile powers "may not be in a position to evaluate the performance of their own countermeasures through flight testing (because they do not have the large radar and other sensors required to observe the behavior of countermeasures in tests)."[60]

North Korea might circumvent this problem by buying countermeasures from Russia or China. The 1999 NIE contends that Moscow and Beijing "are probably willing to sell the requisite technologies."[61] The unclassified NIE gives no evidence to support this claim, and it is debatable whether Moscow and Beijing would help another state build sophisticated long-range missile forces—especially if the United States refrained from abrogating the ABM Treaty, or at least respected its basic spirit and numerical constraints while deploying any NMD system in the years ahead. Selling countermeasures to North Korea and helping it deploy them on its missiles would be a deeply hostile act against the United States that would fuel domestic pressures for more robust defenses, precisely the outcome China and Russia hope to avoid. It would also probably lead Congress to impose serious economic penalties on Moscow and Beijing.

Moscow and Beijing, however, have contributed substantially to the shorter-range missile capabilities of countries such as Iran. Whether because of strategic design, a desire to earn hard currency, or simple neglect, they have often failed to prevent companies and institutes within their countries from aiding the ballistic missile programs of countries that cause the United States considerable concern. Because they have already assisted states like Iran in developing missile threats against U.S. allies and forward-deployed U.S. troops, there is ample reason to think they might continue this aid even if it contributed to direct threats to the U.S. homeland. (The odds would surely increase if a U.S. NMD deployment made them feel threatened or provoked.)

So a country such as North Korea might, or might not, be able to build long-range missiles equipped with functioning countermeasures. Even if evidence is inconclusive, the possibility is worrisome.

It is possible that the whole question may become moot. In 2000 North Korea suddenly abandoned its tradition of isolationism and began aggressively cultivating contacts with the outside world. In June 2000, it hosted a surprisingly cordial summit meeting with South Korean president Kim Dae Jung. The sight of the normally secretive North Korean president Kim Jong Il smiling and bantering with his South Korean counterpart raised hopes that North Korea had done an about face. Hopes grew further the following month when Russian president Vladimir Putin announced after a trip to Pyongyang that North Korea was willing to abandon its long-range ballistic missile development program if other countries agreed to help it launch satellites for scientific purposes. Then in October 2000, Secretary of State Madeleine Albright became the first senior U.S. official to visit North Korea.

Whether the promising political signals coming out of Pyongyang herald a fundamental change in North Korea's relations with the rest of the world remains to be seen, however. The first six months of the Korean rapprochement were more notable for their promise, and their positive atmospherics, than for any concrete and enduring accomplishments in improving security conditions in the region.[62] Although Russian officials insisted that they had had detailed talks with Pyongyang on its proposal to abandon its missile program, Kim Jong Il told visiting South Korean media executives that he had made the offer "laughingly."[63] Moreover,

North Korea's new policy of engaging the outside world, while highly desirable, poses a potential risk to the United States and its allies; Pyongyang may simply be looking for outside help in keeping its economy and political system intact while it continues to build long-range missiles. What is certain is that North Korea's long-range missile and nuclear infrastructure remains intact, and the country probably can resume both programs quickly. Thus, while offering carrots to Pyongyang in exchange for restraints on its missiles and weapons programs makes sense, excessive optimism over its new engagement strategy is not warranted.

Iran

Unlike North Korea, Iran has yet to test a missile potentially capable of intercontinental flight.[64] It has been developing medium-range missiles capable of hitting Israel, Saudi Arabia, and other targets in the Middle East. The current focus is on the Shahab 3, a one-stage missile with an 800-mile range and a one-ton payload capacity. Iran has tested it three times, the first in 1998 when it exploded during launch and twice again in 2000 when it apparently worked once and failed once.[65] Teheran is also working on the Shahab 4, which has a range of roughly 1,200 miles, and the Shahab 5, which has a range estimated between 1,800 and 3,300 miles.[66] To put those numbers in perspective, the closest major U.S. city to Iran is Boston, which is roughly 6,000 miles from Teheran (figure 3-1).

Iran used North Korean designs to build the Shahabs—which highlights how proliferators cooperate among themselves—but has improved them with the help of Russian and Chinese technology. Because Teheran has received help from Russia and China, the Rumsfeld Commission concluded that "the ballistic missile infrastructure in Iran is now more sophisticated than that of North Korea."[67] Given the quality of Iran's technological infrastructure and Teheran's commitment to acquiring medium-range missiles, the 1999 NIE states that "Iran *could* test an ICBM that could deliver a several-hundred kilogram payload to many parts of the United States in the latter half of the next decade, using Russian technology and assistance."[68] Intelligence estimates about the probability that Iran will acquire an ICBM in the next fifteen years vary widely, however. Some analysts contend the chances are "*likely* before 2010 and *very likely* before 2015"; others contend there is "*less than an even chance* by 2015."[69]

What would an Iranian ICBM be armed with? Teheran is not now believed to possess nuclear weapons. But it has probably had a nuclear

Figure 3-1. *Missile Flight Distances from Iran*

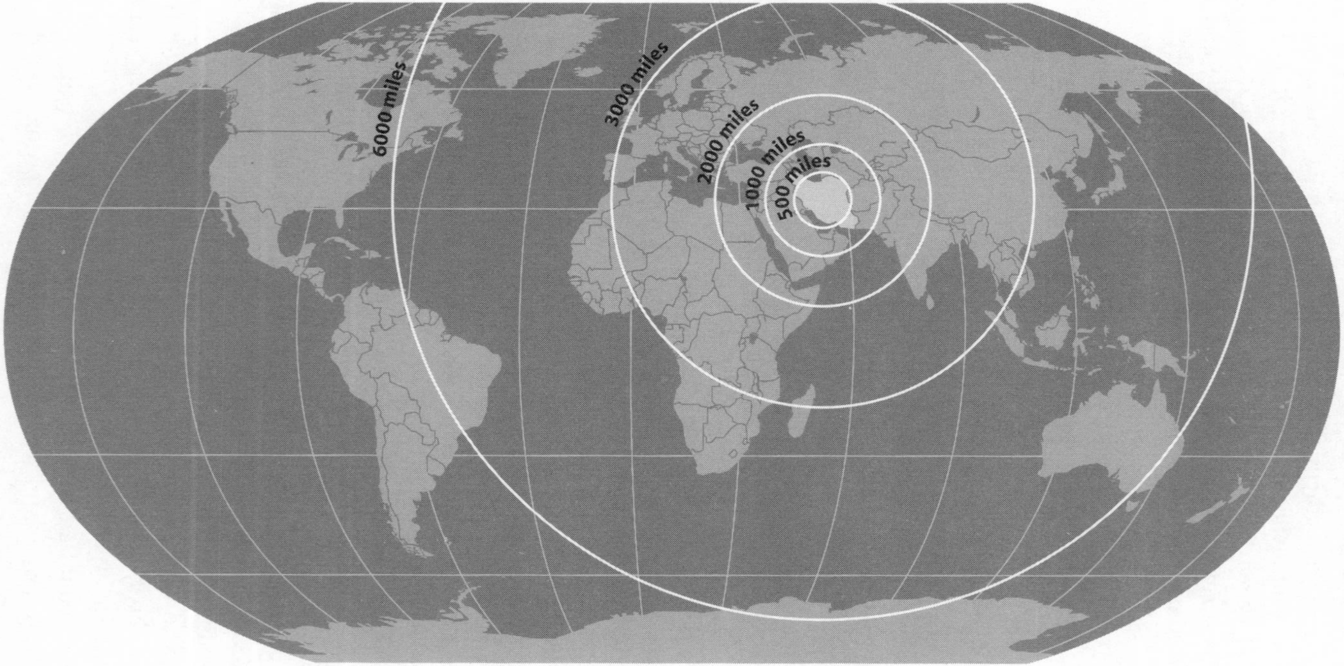

Note: As of year-end 2000, Iran was not believed to have any operational missiles with ranges greater than 500 miles.

weapons program for at least fifteen years, partly out of the apparent desire of Ayatollah Khomeini for an Iranian-Islamic bomb and partly in response to the very aggressive Iraqi nuclear effort. In its early years, the program may have benefited from a U.S.-supplied nuclear research reactor that had been acquired during the reign of the shah, and possibly used for weapons-related purposes even in that era.[70] U.S. intelligence analysts believe that Teheran "has set up an elaborate system of military and civilian organizations to support its effort" to acquire nuclear weapons.[71] Russia has played a key role in this effort by training Iranian scientists and helping Iran construct its first (legally permitted) nuclear reactor. China is also providing Iran with nuclear help.[72]

How long it will take Iran to build a nuclear weapon is unclear. Previous intelligence estimates have exaggerated Iran's progress; in the early and mid-1990s, U.S. intelligence reportedly predicted that Iran would achieve a nuclear capability by 2000.[73] Because the Iranian nuclear program is secret, the Rumsfeld Commission concluded that "The U.S. is unlikely to know whether Iran possesses nuclear weapons until after the fact."[74] Not surprisingly, Iran's main stumbling block is probably acquiring the fissile material needed to build a bomb. The reactor Russia is helping it build is ill-suited to producing weapons-grade plutonium.[75] Moreover, Russia has publicly conditioned its aid on Teheran's willingness to allow the IAEA's inspectors to examine its nuclear facilities. Thus far, Teheran has complied with this stipulation, and the inspectors have not turned up evidence that nuclear material is being diverted from civilian use. That has fueled speculation that Iran might be trying to obtain fissile material surreptitiously from other countries.

Similar uncertainty surrounds the status of Iran's chemical and biological weapons programs. Teheran retaliated against Iraqi chemical weapons attacks during the Iran-Iraq war with chemical weapons of its own. Most of these used hydrogen cyanide, a relatively ineffective chemical agent that is ill-suited for long-range ballistic missiles because it must be delivered in very large quantities to be lethal.[76] Iran may be developing more lethal nerve agents such as sarin gas and VX, but little is known about these programs. Even less is known about Iran's efforts to develop biological weapons. It reportedly has sought to hire scientists who worked on biological weapons for the Soviet Union.[77] The Central Intelligence Agency believes that Iran has sought to acquire the "ability to produce domestically the raw materials and equipment needed to support indigenous biological agent production."[78] Like North Korea, Teheran not only needs to develop or acquire the chemical or biological agent but also to fashion a warhead that can withstand the rigors of an ICBM or at least an IRBM trajectory. (Iran and Iraq used aircraft and artillery, not ballistic missiles, to deliver their chemical munitions during the Iran-Iraq war.)

The election of a reformist majority in Iran's parliamentary elections in February 2000 raised hopes that Iran might pursue a more moderate foreign policy. The Clinton administration quickly tried to encourage a new dialogue with Teheran by lifting some economic sanctions. There is no evidence that U.S. overtures are meeting with a response or that reformers' preferences are prevailing. Regardless, even if a U.S.-Iranian détente materializes, better relations between Washington and Teheran will not guarantee that Iran will forgo developing an ICBM. Iran's complicated government structure may enable hardliners to continue to control the country's military spending decisions. Moreover, moderates may share the hardliners' view that ballistic missiles and nuclear weapons are essential as symbols of national greatness and as deterrents to Western (particularly American), Israeli, or Iraqi coercion.[79]

Iraq

Iraq's ballistic missile program lags far behind those of North Korea and Iran. The stumbling block is not a lack of desire but the consequences of the Persian Gulf War. The United States and its allies destroyed much of Iraq's missile infrastructure during the war, and under the terms of the UN cease-fire resolution, Iraq agreed to forgo developing all weapons of mass destruction and all missiles with ranges greater than one hundred miles. UN inspectors subsequently discovered that Iraq had manufactured chemical and biological weapons and had made substantial progress toward building nuclear weapons. As many of the nuclear, chemical, and biological agents as could be found were subsequently destroyed, but there is no way to be sure other materials do not remain.

Iraq cooperated with UN inspections only grudgingly and repeatedly tried to conceal the true status of the banned programs.[80] For example, it was not until Saddam's ill-fated son-in-law temporarily defected and gave UN inspectors incontrovertible evidence of work on biological agents such as anthrax and botulism that Baghdad acknowledged it had a biological weapons program. In 1998 Iraq went a step further and barred inspectors from carrying out their duties. In retaliation, the United States and Great Britain in December 1998 launched Operation Desert Fox, which (among other things) sought to destroy Iraq's missile and weapons labs.

As U.S. and British officials predicted at the time, the 1998 bombing did not stop Iraq's ballistic missile program permanently. By 2000 Iraq had resumed test flights of a short-range missile as permitted under the UN restrictions, and it may have been pursuing other development efforts in secret.[81] Iraq is reportedly moving aggressively to acquire ballistic missile technology from Russia among other countries as well.[82] Iraq also refused to cooperate with the UN Security Council's 2000 decision to create a new inspection regime, saying it would not allow UN inspectors to enter the country until the UN first lifted economic sanctions.

Baghdad's history of misleading the United Nations about its weapons programs and its refusal to allow inspections strongly suggest it may be secretly continuing to develop missiles and weapons of mass destruction. How fast Iraq could reconstitute its ballistic missile program is a matter of conjecture. Before the Gulf War, the Iraqi missile program had been devoted to short-range missiles. Although allied bombings damaged or destroyed the physical infrastructure, Iraq retains a substantial knowledge base and may have hidden missile parts and production equipment from UN inspectors. The 1999 NIE concludes that "Iraq could test an ICBM capable of reaching the United States during the next 15 years."[83] The analysts were split, however, on the likelihood it would, with opinion ranging from "*unlikely* before 2015" to "likely before 2015."[84] Which prediction turns out to be correct depends on whether political change comes to Iraq, how much technology and equipment Baghdad hid from UN inspectors, whether an effective UN inspection regime resumes, and what level of foreign assistance Baghdad receives. As the 1999 NIE notes, "If Iraq could buy a Taepo Dong-2 from North Korea, it *could have a launch capability* within months of purchase."[85] Of course, that statement could apply to any country, but it is nonetheless a real worry.

Iraq's nuclear weapons program was, if anything, further along than its long-range ballistic missile program at the start of the Gulf War. Observers now estimate that in 1991 Iraq was a few months to four years away from building a nuclear device.[86] It had several programs for obtaining nuclear materials, ranging from the use of gas centrifuges and electromagnetic isotope separators for enriching uranium to chemical reprocessing plants for extracting plutonium from reactor fuel. Any bomb it built would probably not have been compatible with a missile; according to at least one Iraqi nuclear scientist, "Iraq faced many problems in trying to reduce and ruggedize its design to fit on top of a ballistic missile."[87] UN inspectors found a great deal of documentation on the Iraqi nuclear program, and blueprints of bomb designs developed by Iraqi scientists. They dismantled much of Iraq's nuclear infrastructure—some had been destroyed during the war, but much had not—and located a very small amount of fissile material that it had diverted for weapons production. How long it would take Iraq to reconstitute its nuclear program depends on its success in concealing key materials and technology, as well as any efforts it may make to acquire such technologies or fissile materials from abroad. It clearly retains technological know-how. As for chemical and biological weapons, Iraq has the medical, veterinary, and scientific facilities needed to reconstitute both programs very quickly—though it is doubtful that they were truly dismantled in the first place.

Unlike the case with both North Korea and Iran, political trends give no reason to be optimistic about future Iraqi behavior. By all accounts, Saddam Hussein remains firmly in power, and he gives no sign that Iraq's foreign policy will moderate. That could remain the case even under a successor, such as his son, Uday. Should the international effort to isolate Iraq end, it is likely that Baghdad will move aggressively to acquire weapons of mass destruction and the means to deliver them. And while only ICBMs would pose a direct threat to the territory of the United States, Baghdad is more likely first to develop IRBMs with which to threaten regional competitors and American allies.

The Iraqi experience reveals another lesson: it is very difficult to prevent, as opposed to slow or complicate, a country's acquisition of missiles and weapons of mass destruction. Neither Operation Desert Storm, nor Operation Desert Fox, nor for that matter the 1981 Israeli bombing of Iraq's Osirak reactor, could stop Iraq from building missiles, producing chemical and biological agents, and moving far down the path toward a nuclear weapons capability. Even the 1981 attack, which destroyed the Osirak reactor, had the long-term effect of driving Iraq's nuclear program underground and into smaller research facilities, not of ending it. To be sure, buying time was of critical importance, given who ruled Iraq during the past two decades. But without UN weapons inspectors—a type of capability that will rarely be deployable in other places—all of these missile and weapons of mass destruction programs would have continued in the 1990s, and in fact some have.

Intent

Why have North Korea, Iran, and Iraq sought to develop long-range missiles and weapons of mass destruction? This question gets to a core issue in the NMD debate. But intent is notoriously difficult to infer from behavior; judgments may reflect the observer's fears as much as they do the attacker's aims.

Status and regional rivalries clearly play a major role in the decision to acquire weapons of mass destruction. Possession of nuclear weapons can generate great national pride; witness the joyous public reactions in India and Pakistan in 1998 when both countries tested nuclear weapons. Chemical, biological, and nuclear weapons also can provide a military advantage or deterrent against threatening neighbors. North Korea is technically still at war with a far richer South Korea. Iran and Iraq fought a bloody eight-year war in the 1980s in which both sides used chemical weapons. The arms race dynamics are obvious. Iraq seeks to acquire weapons of mass destruction, and Iran feels compelled to follow suit, and vice versa.

But North Korea, Iran, and Iraq's apparent interest in ballistic missiles with ranges exceeding 2,000 miles cannot be explained in terms of regional rivalries. ICBMs have ranges too great to make them usable in any battlefield role, and the great expense it takes to build them makes them impractical as vehicles for delivering conventional warheads.[88] Their great value comes instead as political weapons that can be used to influence the behavior of distant powers. The United States is the obvious target partly because of its geographical position—North Korea, Iran, or Iraq does not need an ICBM to hit Russia or China and neither Iran nor Iraq needs an ICBM to hit Europe. It is also a target because of its superpower status—it has intervened directly in the affairs of all three countries and fought wars against two of them.

How then do these countries hope to influence U.S. behavior? At a minimum, they want to deter a U.S. attack. Long-range missiles armed with nuclear, chemical, or biological warheads constitute useful "don't-mess-with-me" weapons. Adversaries know that the willingness of the United States to march on Baghdad or Pyongyang and overthrow their regimes, should they launch another war of aggression in the future, will drop if they can threaten to kill tens or hundreds of thousands of Americans. They may even hope that the United States would be less inclined to defend the territory of its allies in the face of such potential threats. The latter type of logic also probably guides China's policy of not trying to match the United States missile for missile.

That China's nuclear deterrent caused little concern for more than two decades reminds us that the United States can tolerate (though not like) other countries having small arsenals when it is clear that the other side only wants to deter an attack. Unfortunately, the same arsenal that Saddam Hussein can use to persuade the United States not to overthrow him can also be used in an attempt to hold the United States at bay while Iraq attacks a neighbor. Moreover, that arsenal becomes a major obstacle should the United States decide in the future that its interests can be served only by overthrowing the Hussein government.

Of course, deterrence cuts both ways. Any country that threatens the United States with weapons of mass destruction risks devastating retaliation. Now some argue, as Samuel R. "Sandy" Berger, President Clinton's national security adviser, put it, that North Korea, Iran, and Iraq "may not be as susceptible to deterrence as the Soviet Union was."[89] Proponents offer no evidence for this claim, content to rely instead on popular prejudices about irrational Iranians, Iraqis, and North Koreans. However, North Korea has abided by a cease-fire with the vastly more powerful South Korea for half a century. Iran returned the American hostages twenty years ago and has avoided direct conflict with the United States even during its most revolutionary moments. Iraq has skillfully tried to split the UN Security Council on the question of sanctions; in addition, though it has caused crises since 1991, it has tended to back down rather than give the international community cause to launch anything but minor attacks against it. (That Saddam Hussein mistakenly believed that the multinational coalition would fracture during the Gulf War, and that he is fundamentally evil, does not make him irrational or insane.) Moreover, under even the most ambitious proposals to cut the U.S. nuclear arsenal, the United States will retain the ability to destroy what all three governments clearly value—their ability to stay in power.

The real problem, as chapter 1 pointed out, is not that the leaders of new ballistic missile powers are irrational but that even with rational leaders deterrence may fail. To begin with, there is what might be called the Samson scenario. Just as the tormented Samson brought down the pillars of the Philistine temple, killing his captors and himself, a North Korean or Iraqi leader on the verge of being overthrown and perhaps killed might attack the United States simply out of spite, especially if he believed that American officials had engineered his overthrow. In such a situation, no U.S. response could cause him greater harm than what he already faced. (A hyperrational leader might even conclude, probably wrongly, that the United States would not respond with nuclear weapons because once deterrence failed there would be no point in retaliating.) Similarly, if a government were crumbling, political control of weapons of mass destruction could be lost, and an extremist military commander with a deep-seated hatred of the United States might launch an attack nihilistically. If he had a martyr complex, he might not care about retribution.

Political stability, however, does not eliminate the threat that new ballistic missile powers pose to the United States. Deterrence of states with small, vulnerable missile forces may be harder to sustain than deterrence of states with large, invulnerable ones even if leaders on both sides act rationally. When the United States and the Soviet Union faced each other during the cold war, neither side had an incentive to strike first, even in a crisis, because the other had a second-strike capability. Such crisis stability may not characterize efforts to deter a small power like North Korea, Iran, or Iraq. Their missile forces are not only vulnerable to an American first strike, they are also vulnerable to preemption by conventional means. Any ICBMs they build are likely to be immobile and possibly readily identified. Such vulnerability creates powerful incentives for both sides to strike first. That impulse can be kept in check during ordinary times. During a crisis, though, the U.S. incentive to preempt and the adversary's temptation to "use-it-or-lose it" may lead to an escalation neither side wants.

There are also circumstances in which a leader might judge it perfectly rational to launch a missile. Imagine a modern-day version of the Gulf War in which Iraq—it could easily be Iran or North Korea—had two missiles armed with weapons of mass destruction. Confronted with his potential overthrow, Saddam could use one of his long-range missiles to attack a relatively low-value target in the United States (or perhaps one of its allies) and thereby demonstrate his ability and will. By holding another missile in reserve, he could hope to hold Washington hostage and force it to stop its march on Baghdad. Such a plan would reflect a brutal, evil, and totally self-consistent logic, but nothing says that leaders have to play by Marquis of Queensbury rules. And while such leaders are uncommon, they are not unknown.

Finally, crises do not have to erupt, and threats of attack do not have to be made, for the spread of long-range missiles to harm U.S. interests. The prospect of attack may be sufficient to deter the United States from resisting foreign aggression. Even if the United States is not deterred, its allies and friends might fear that it will be. And if they believe that the United States will not come to their aid, as it did with Kuwait in 1991, they may decide that discretion is the greater part of valor. As a result, regional bullies might gain what they want without firing a shot. Given

America's extensive political and economic interests in the Middle East and East Asia, a collapse of confidence in American reliability could seriously harm U.S. global interests.

Other Emerging Ballistic Missile Powers

North Korea, Iran, and Iraq draw the most attention in the debate over the spread of ballistic missile technology. They are not, however, the only countries capable of building ICBMs during the next decade or even the most advanced technologically. Israel has a missile in development with an estimated range of 1,200 miles; India and Pakistan have missiles in development with estimated ranges of roughly 2,000 miles.[90] And while neither Brazil nor Japan is currently seeking to develop medium or long-range ballistic missiles, both have active space-launch programs that could be converted quickly into ICBM development programs. Moreover, India, Israel, and Pakistan possess nuclear weapons; Japan and (to a lesser extent) Brazil have the technological and financial infrastructure needed to make them.

The ability of India, Israel, Pakistan, Brazil, and Japan to build weapons that could threaten the United States has not been a cause for alarm; the 1999 NIE on the ballistic missile threat mentioned none of them. The reason is obvious: none is hostile to the United States. Israel, Japan, and Brazil historically have had close ties with Washington; the United States and Pakistan have generally cooperated in the security realm; and U.S. relations with India have warmed appreciably during the past decade. The prospect of the U.S. military confronting any of these five countries during the next decade ranges from nonexistent for Japan, Israel, and Brazil to slight for India and Pakistan. The one potential exception might be if a fundamentally anti-Western, anti-American government came to power in Islamabad.

The biggest threat the United States faces from friendly or neutral countries gaining nuclear and ballistic missile technology is that they may sell technology or even complete weapons to one another or to countries (say Libya or Syria) that have no ballistic missile program of their own. Countries such as Israel and Japan are unlikely to encourage such proliferation; the likelihood that they will become the targets of the new ballistic missile powers far outweighs the economic benefits of selling sensitive technology abroad. Other countries may not be so restrained.

The potential for emerging ballistic missile powers to share technology highlights the importance of reinvigorating U.S. and international efforts to halt or slow proliferation. Thus, any missile defense deployment must be made with an eye toward these nonproliferation efforts; otherwise it could do more harm than good to overall U.S. national security.

Combating proliferation is not solely a U.S. responsibility. America's allies also have important responsibilities. China and Russia have much to do as well; both have supplied technology and expertise to potential proliferators. But a U.S. NMD deployment, particularly a hasty and large-scale one, could influence their actions—just as any further proliferation on their part could increase the scale of a future American missile defense system. All sides need to realize that their interests, even if not identical, are interrelated.

Alternative Threats

Much of the discussion of national missile defense understandably focuses on long-range missiles. But these are not the only means of delivering weapons of mass destruction. That makes the task of protecting the United States all the more difficult. But it hardly means, as some allege, that national missile defense is pointless. Other means of attack are not trivially easy to undertake, and the United States has means of trying to thwart them as well.

Perhaps the most important alternative means of delivering a weapon of mass destruction against the United States is the so-called suitcase bomb. A country or terrorist group might try to attack the United States by planting bombs in a ship's cargo bay, driving them across the border in a truck, or smuggling them into the country. Ships, trucks, and suitcases have several advantages over missiles in delivering weapons of mass destruction: they are less expensive, more technically reliable, more accurate, and they can hide responsibility and bypass a missile defense. They are also the most effective way of dispersing biological agents, which are most lethal when they are allowed to incubate in an unsuspecting population that has seen no evidence that it has been attacked.[91] And the temptation to use nonconventional means to deliver weapons of mass destruction is large because of "the huge amount of commercial traffic that enters this country every day: 550 ships and boats, 2,500 aircraft, and 45,000 shipping containers."[92] According to the CIA, "In the coming years, U.S. territory is probably more likely to be attacked with weapons of mass destruction from non-missile delivery means (most likely from non-state entities) than by missiles."[93]

For all the attention that this statement has garnered, and all the concern over suitcase bombs, the CIA did not state that the United States is more likely to be attacked by a nuclear bomb packed inside a suitcase than one atop a missile. The CIA said nothing about the kind of weapon of mass destruction it expects to be used in the unconventional attack it postulates. In practice, chemical and biological weapons are more likely to be used than nuclear weapons. Chemical weapons are the easiest type of weapon of mass destruction to produce; both chemical and biological materials are far easier to move about than are nuclear weapons. Indeed, Japan has already experienced such an attack—in 1995 the Japanese cult Aum Shinrikyo unleashed sarin gas in the Tokyo subway.

For nuclear weapons, the notion of a suitcase bomb is highly misleading. While chemical and especially biological weapons could be concealed in small packages, the same cannot be said for fission or fusion bombs. The history of nuclear weapons development suggests that any early-generation nuclear weapon will be heavy and bulky. It would probably weigh a half ton or more and be at least as large as a dishwasher, if not a refrigerator. Although such a weapon might be smuggled across a border, it would not be easy to move or hide, and it certainly could not be hidden in a suitcase. Rather than be described as a suitcase bomb, it would be better thought of as a truck bomb. Indeed, it may even be too heavy for many light aircraft to carry.

Furthermore, the requirements for building a nuclear bomb or even a sophisticated biological agent exceed the organizational, technical, and financial capacities of most terrorist groups.[94] For instance, Aum Shinrikyo failed in its attempt to manufacture biological weapons despite making a sustained effort to master the intricacies of germ warfare.[95] A terrorist group might acquire a biological or nuclear weapon from a country. That is one of the best arguments for making sure that any U.S. missile defense not antagonize Russia so much as to impede further collaboration to secure that country's nuclear weapons and materials. But many countries would worry that any weapons they provided a terrorist group could be turned back on them. Or they might worry that the United States would figure out who gave the terrorist group the weapons and retaliate against the original source. The specter of a terrorist group smuggling a WMD device, particularly a nuclear weapon, into the United States cannot be dismissed, but neither is it likely.

Governments capable of building weapons of mass destruction would face dilemmas of their own. They must mount a complex covert operation to deliver the weapon without getting caught by U.S. intelligence, customs, and immigration agencies or the U.S. Coast Guard.[96] They would need spies to determine how to enter the United States undetected and agents who could be trusted to deliver the weapon to the intended target and to detonate it. But "most dictators do not come to power by giving powerful weapons to a few subordinates who are then allowed to leave the country. . . . So, while a homemade missile depends on unreliable technology, smuggling a bomb depends on unreliable human beings."[97] Indeed, the problem could be even more serious than that. Not only would a hostile autocrat need trustworthy subordinates, need to keep word of the plot from U.S. intelligence, and need to find a means of evading the various agencies protecting and controlling U.S. borders. He might also need a cooperative third party such as a shipping company or foreign government to help transport the weapon across the oceans. In other words, several steps would all have to go right for the plan to work. Even if each of the above four separate steps had a high probability of being carried out—say, for the sake of illustration, 80 percent—the overall plan would have less than a 50-50 chance of success.

This type of operation would also require time and advance preparations. It would most likely require a ship to transport the weapon from Eurasia, its most likely point of origin, into the Western Hemisphere. Even if an airplane could be used to fly the weapon into a nearby country, it would then have to be smuggled onto U.S. territory using smaller vehicles or craft. If a country wished to use such a weapon of mass destruction as leverage during a conflict against the United States—the most likely way in which the U.S. homeland would be threatened by WMD, in our judgment—it would probably have to smuggle the weapon into the United States in advance. Waiting until the war was under way to do so might be too late. Moreover, U.S. surveillance of borders, ports, and airports would become more vigilant under wartime conditions, reducing the odds that a hostile foreign country could smuggle a truck-bomb-sized warhead into the country. In short, delivering a nuclear weapon directly onto the territory of the United States—or the territory of a major U.S. ally for that matter—would be difficult for any party, be it a terrorist group or a foreign government. They might succeed; they might also fail.

Besides using long-range missiles, countries looking to attack the United States could resort to so-called forward-based threats. They could fire shorter-range ballistic or cruise missiles at the United States from ships or planes off the U.S. coast. Not only are these systems less technologically challenging to build than an ICBM—the basic components are readily available—they would defeat many types of missile defenses. The Clinton administration's proposed NMD system can work only against missiles that leave the atmosphere, which neither cruise missile nor short-range missiles do. As planned, it would not work against missiles coming from the South, since it would neither see them coming nor have the capacity to guide interceptors to them. And earth-based boost-phases work only if they are located near the launch point. Forward-based threats mean not only more possible points of attack but also more potential attackers. Anyone with a short-range ballistic missile becomes a potential threat.

This concern is real. But it needs to be balanced with a recognition that forward-based delivery options have significant limitations. Countries just developing nuclear weapons capability would find that their "initial indigenous nuclear weapons designs are likely to be too large and heavy for a modest-sized ballistic missile."[98] This may be true for ICBMs as well—but that is a challenge the Scud-class missiles might not be able to surmount either. And launching weapons of mass destruction from a forward-deployed ship shares some of the same difficulties of delivering a nuclear weapon by truck or similarly large vehicle (though not all of them).

Moreover, contrary to what NMD critics say, the United States is not defenseless before all unconventional threats. The U.S. Navy, Coast Guard, Customs Service, FBI, and other law enforcement agencies offer at least some protection against other means of delivery, whereas the United States is naked before the long-range missile threat.

Finally, missile warheads differ fundamentally from truck- or ship-delivered bombs because they can be delivered very quickly—making them especially dangerous during a crisis or in a war. They also are far more effective as coercive instruments. Missiles speak for themselves as threats; a country trying to deter the United States would not need to explicitly threaten to use them. By contrast, to use a truck bomb to coerce, a state would both have to threaten Washington explicitly (otherwise, it would not know it was being threatened) and credibly (otherwise it would not know the threat was real). That would be a tall order. It would also be an extremely dangerous strategy to pursue, given how firmly Washington might react against any state claiming to have predeployed weapons of mass destruction on U.S. territory.

Still, defenses against other types of threats than long-range ballistic missiles may require improvement too. The United States may eventually need to consider national defenses against shipborne ballistic missiles and cruise missiles, and it certainly needs to continue to improve its ability to monitor the flow of illicit materials into its borders. Those who emphasize the threats that truck bombs and short-range and cruise missiles pose are right to do so—even if, in our judgment, they are wrong to suggest that the existence of such threats makes national missile defense a pointless endeavor.

The Consequences of a Missile Attack

How many Americans would die from a missile attack? The exact answer depends on a wide variety of factors but three stand out: how many missiles were fired, what their warheads carried, and how accurately they approached their targets. A deliberate, accidental, unauthorized, or erroneous Russian launch that unleashed a massive salvo would likely produce the same kind of unimaginable devastation that a full-scale Soviet attack would have: more than 100 million Americans dead and American society in ruins. If the United States retaliated, the death toll would double, Russian society would lie in ashes, and the rest of humanity would confront massive nuclear fallout.

A small accidental Russian launch would not threaten the future of civilization, but its consequences would still be grim. How many people die would depend on the specifics of the attack. But consider one of the most frequently talked about scenarios: the accidental or unauthorized firing of all the missiles aboard a Russian Delta-IV submarine, which will be the mainstay of the Russian submarine force for the next decade. This would lead to the launch of sixteen missiles, each equipped with four warheads. If those missiles hit eight major urban areas—Atlanta, Boston, Chicago, New York, Pittsburgh, San Francisco, Seattle, and Washington, D.C.—upward of 7 million Americans would probably die instantly, or about 150,000 per warhead on average. Radiation exposure and lack of proper medical care would drive the death toll higher for several months, perhaps even doubling it.[99] If the accidental launch involved Russia's Typhoon-class submarines—which carry up to 200 warheads and which Moscow is now in the process of retiring—the death toll would be much higher. Conversely, an accidental Chinese launch that involved, say, a handful of missiles would have a substantially smaller death toll.

What about the kind of attack that countries such as North Korea, Iran, or Iraq might be capable of launching during the next decade? Again, the exact consequences would depend on many factors, not the least of which is the city or cities targeted. But assume for the sake of discussion that North Korea attacked and struck Los Angeles with a single missile. Early-generation North Korean ICBMs are likely to be relatively inaccurate—at least compared with American and Russian missiles. So the North Korean missile would be unlikely to hit the most densely populated part of Los Angeles—downtown at mid-day on a work day—and instead would fall in some part of the city with a moderate population density.

Table 3-4 estimates the number of people that would be killed or injured if the missile that reached Los Angeles was equipped with a conventional, chemical, biological, or nuclear warhead. As the table shows, a nuclear warhead is far more lethal than a chemical or conventional warhead. Biological agents could also be extremely lethal if properly delivered and dispersed and if also unanticipated. The death toll in a biological or nuclear attack from a single missile could easily exceed the total number of U.S. soldiers who died fighting the Korean War and would probably be comparable to the casualties in Hiroshima and Nagasaki. And to emphasize, these are rough estimates only. If the North Korean missile landed ten miles to the west of downtown Los Angeles it would fall into the sea and might not kill anyone. By the same token, however, a missile armed with a nuclear warhead that landed on downtown at mid-day could kill 250,000 people instantly and tens of thousands more in the days and weeks to follow.[100]

The prospect of wholesale slaughter is what gives long-range missiles their coercive power. North Korea, Iran, and Iraq may never match American power on any dimension, but if they develop ICBMs equipped with weapons of mass destruction, they could inflict terrific devastation on the United States. Knowing that, the United States might lose its

Table 3-4. *Casualties Produced by a Hypothetical Missile Attack on Los Angeles*

Type of warhead	Dead[a]	Injured[a]
Conventional (1 ton of high explosives)	5	13
Chemical (300 kilograms of sarin)	200–3,000	200–3,000
Biological (30 kilograms of anthrax spores)	20,000–80,000	...
Nuclear (20 kilotons)	40,000	40,000

Sources: Steve Fetter, "Ballistic Missiles and Weapons of Mass Destruction," *International Security,* vol. 16 (Summer 1991), p. 27; and correspondence from Steve Fetter, July 2000.

a. Numbers based on a medium-density city (3,000 people per sq/km) such as metropolitan Los Angeles.

resolve to defend its interests around the globe, and its allies might lose confidence in its security guarantees. Deterrence might forestall an attack on the United States or its allies, but deterrence can fail. That possibility makes arguments for building a national missile defense attractive. Before signing up to build an NMD system, though, it is essential to understand the different approaches to defending the United States and the costs and benefits that come with each one.

CHAPTER FOUR

Missile Defense Programs and Architectures

IF A NATIONAL MISSILE DEFENSE makes sense in theory, what kind of system is most likely to provide prudent protection at a reasonable budgetary cost? Should the system be based on land, at sea, in the air, or in space? How many interceptors or other defensive weapons should be deployed and at how many sites? And how many years would it take to develop and deploy a system? This chapter provides technical background to answer these questions. It does so by examining several basic types of NMD technologies and concepts. Chapter 5 presents the strategic and diplomatic dimensions of the problem.

Midcourse Defense:
The Clinton Administration Program

The debate in recent years over the wisdom of national missile defense has focused on one specific architecture: the midcourse defense the Clinton administration proposed to build, with an initial base in Alaska and a second eventually to be built in North Dakota. Although this system is not the only possible type of national missile defense, or even the only type of midcourse defense, it has been the primary focus of the Pentagon's NMD efforts. The United States has no other NMD system in the development or testing stage, though it is pursuing several types of theater missile defense (TMD) programs (box 4-1).

The Clinton Proposal

The Clinton administration committed itself in 1997 to developing a limited midcourse defense. The administration's proposal envisioned that NMD deployment would proceed in three phases. The first phase, which the Pentagon designated Capability 1 (C1), was to involve deploying twenty interceptors at a single site, either in North Dakota or Alaska, by 2003. The goal of this initial deployment was to be able to shoot down up to as many as five warheads equipped with either crude countermeasures or none at all. The administration then hoped to increase the number of deployed interceptors to one hundred by 2005. This theoretically would give the United States the capacity to intercept up to tens of warheads, again with either no countermeasures or only crude ones.

To make it possible for the interceptors to hit their targets, the C1 capability also called for building a new "x-band" radar (with relatively high frequency and thus relatively high accuracy), as well as upgrading various U.S. early-warning radars around the world, to detect incoming threats and guide interceptors to them. The proposed site for the x-band radar was Shemya Island, one of the westernmost of Alaska's Aleutian Islands (figure 4-1). Although Shemya Island is an ideal site for tracking missiles launched at the United States from Asia, it has two disadvantages. One is that extreme weather conditions make it possible to do heavy construction work on Shemya Island for only three months out of the year. As a result, construction of the x-band radar is estimated to take at least five years to complete. The other disadvantage is that Shemya Island is potentially difficult to defend against enemy attack, especially in light of the heavy volume of shipping traffic in the vicinity—though security would surely be enhanced in any crisis or wartime situation, mitigating the latter worry substantially.[1]

In the second, or C2 phase, the Clinton administration proposed making the NMD system capable of defending against an attack by warheads with more sophisticated countermeasures. In this phase, the number of deployed interceptor missiles would remain at one hundred, but the United States would build three more x-band radars, upgrade the interceptor missiles, and expand the communications infrastructure so that various sensors could share data. The C2 phase would also add the advanced space-based, infrared sensor, low altitude (SBIRS-low) surveillance satellite constellation to the ground-based radars used with the C1 capability.

Box 4-1. The State of Major Theater Missile Defense
Interceptor-Based Programs

Whatever President George W. Bush decides about NMD, he will almost surely deploy additional types of TMD systems to counter shorter-range ballistic missiles.

Since the Persian Gulf War, the United States has significantly improved its only existing missile defense system, the Patriot. Patriot's radar now has greater range and can track more objects simultaneously. Starting in 2001, the Pentagon is to deploy a further-improved version of the Patriot, known as the Patriot Advanced Capability 3 (PAC-3). That is later than initially expected—another reminder of the difficulty of developing even relatively simple missile defense systems—but the new Patriot shows every sign of doing its job well. It will have the ability to identify warheads so that it will not be fooled by an enemy's use of simple decoys or the breakup of a missile's body during atmospheric reentry (as early vintages of Patriot were in Desert Storm). It will also possess a new "hit-to-kill" interceptor missile that has been tested successfully several times. Whereas the existing Patriot system, known as PAC-2, can defend an area with a radius of roughly ten miles, the new PAC-3 will triple that coverage. The PAC-3 interceptor has its own self-contained radar for homing in on a target. It also features 180 small thrusters for fine steering in the final phases of intercept (earlier Patriots have fins for steering and blast-fragmentation warheads).[1]

The Pentagon is also developing a low-altitude theater defense based on Navy Aegis-class ships that uses a modified form of the Standard antiaircraft missile. Known simply as the Navy area defense system, it is designed to cover a zone somewhat larger than that of the Patriot PAC-3. Recent tests to validate the capabilities of the system's individual components—the missile and the ship radars—have been successful.[2] The Navy hopes to deploy this system by 2003 and to install it on at least forty ships.

The Patriot and Navy area defense system would work at relatively low altitudes, where air resistance would aid a defense by filtering out lighter—and thus slower—decoys. Sensors could easily determine which object was a real warhead, unless an enemy developed sophisticated countermeasures such as those of the British Chevaline system. But those types of countermeasures are far harder to design and produce than light decoys meant to operate only in space.[3]

The Pentagon's more ambitious TMD programs are not nearly as far along in research and development. The Army's theater high-altitude air defense (THAAD) has often been in the news because of its testing difficulties, but it is promising on the whole. Its problems were more often the result of shoddy workmanship than the viability of the hit-to-kill concept.[4] THAAD finally scored a direct hit during a June 1999 test and then again two months later. The intercepts, which used THAAD's infrared seeker to guide the missile's final approach, occurred at a much higher altitude and greater distance from base than Patriot is capable of—

they occurred at roughly sixty miles' altitude, generally considered the approximate dividing line between the earth's atmosphere and space.[5] But THAAD can also intercept within the higher-altitude regions of the atmosphere, meaning that it has some innate capability to filter out light decoys from real warheads.

The Navy theater-wide (NTW) program is not as far along in testing. Tests to date have focused on validating the performance of the missiles, with the first attempts to intercept mock enemy missiles scheduled to take place in 2001.[6] The NTW system is supposed to work against an enemy missile at any point in its exoatmospheric trajectory. That could pertain to boost phase, or more likely the postboost/ascent phase, as well as to midcourse and descent parts of the ballistic trajectory. In fact, if a single ship with NTW aboard were based to the east of the Korean demilitarized zone within a couple hundred kilometers of shore, its ascent-phase intercept capabilities could protect most of Japan—at least in theory.[7] In practice, however, to the extent it had to work outside the atmosphere, it would be vulnerable to simple decoys just as any exoatmospheric interceptor system would.

Whichever of these programs, THAAD or NTW, turns out to advance more rapidly is to be fielded in 2007, the other sometime thereafter—though THAAD enthusiasts, only recently on the ropes after six straight test failures, have been talking about speeding THAAD up in light of their pair of successes in 1999.

1. Bradley Graham, "Army Hit in New Mexico Test Said to Bode Well for Missile Defense," *Washington Post*, March 16, 1999, p. 7; James Glanz, "Missile Defense Rides Again," *Science*, April 16, 1999, p. 417; and David Hughes, "Patriot PAC-3 Upgrade Aimed at Multiple Threats," *Aviation Week and Space Technology*, February 24, 1997, pp. 59–61.

2. Robert Holzer, "U.S. Navy Missile Defense Effort Wins Support," *Defense News*, July 26, 1999, p. 3.

3. David A. Fulghum, "Advanced Threats Drive Arrow's Future," *Aviation Week and Space Technology*, October 12, 1998, p. 56.

4. Bradley Graham, "Low-Tech Flaws Stall High-Altitude Defense," *Washington Post*, July 27, 1998, p. 1.

5. The first intercept occurred at White Sands Missile Range, New Mexico, at an altitude of just under sixty miles, with both target and interceptor traveling at about 1.5 kilometers a second on impact. The second occurred a few miles higher, but at considerably higher interceptor speed (2.5 kilometers a second), and against a reentry vehicle descending from 300 kilometers' altitude. See "World News Roundup," *Aviation Week and Space Technology*, June 14, 1999, p. 56; and Robert Wall, "THAAD at Crossroads after Intercept," *Aviation Week and Space Technology*, August 9, 1999, pp. 29–31.

6. Anthony Sommer, "Defense Missile Test Will Be Held Off Kauai," *Honolulu Star-Bulletin*, July 11, 2000.

7. Captain Mike Moe, deputy director, Theater Air Warfare, "Navy Theater Ballistic Missile Defense," presentation at the Brookings Institution, June 2000.

Figure 4-1. *C1 National Missile Defense*

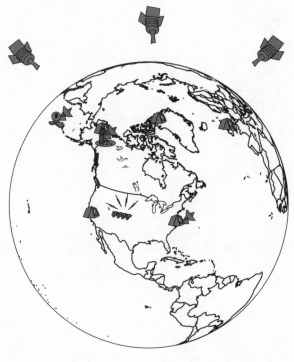

Ground-Based Interceptor		Battle Management/Command Control, and Communications
Upgraded Early Warning Radar		In-Flight Intercept Communications System
X-Band Radar		
Defense Support Program/ Space-Based Infrared System (High)		

Source: Andrew M. Sessler and others, *Countermeasures: A Technical Evaluation of the Operational Effectiveness of the Planned U.S. National Missile Defense System* (Union of Concerned Scientists/Massachusetts Institute of Technology Security Studies Program, April 2000), p. 22 (www.ucsua.org/arms/CM_toc.html [March 2001]).

Note: Locations shown are approximate. For more exact information, see table 4-1.

These added sensors would offer several advantages. First, as noted, x-band radars are very accurate, making it possible not only to obtain a good indication of the trajectory of a warhead early in its flight but also even to tell warheads from some types of decoys by comparing their size and shape and radar reflectivity. It may even be possible under some circumstances to watch a missile "bus" release warheads and decoys—a process that may allow the defense to distinguish between warheads and decoys based on their weight differences. Second, SBIRS-low can also obtain accurate tracking data early in a warhead's flight and help distinguish warheads from decoys based on their heat signature as well as on how they reflect visible light.[2] So the theory goes at least.

Besides being capable of handling more complex threats, the C2 capability would be more capable of handling threats from the Middle East (especially Iran), which the U.S. intelligence community estimated might materialize around 2010. The expectation was that the C2 capability would be deployed by that year. Figure 4-2 presents the basic elements of a C2 system.

Finally, the Clinton administration envisioned the possibility of a C3 phase that would involve more interceptors and the ability to shoot down warheads armed with sophisticated countermeasures. Table 4-1 shows how the various elements of the C3 capability stack up against the C1 and C2 systems. We discuss the C3 capability more fully later in the chapter.

The Evolution of the Clinton Proposal

The Clinton administration came to its support for national missile defense only after much prodding. During its first few years in office, it cut overall spending for missile defense but increased funding for TMD programs with the dollars that remained. Seeing Scud-class missiles in places like the Middle East as the real security worry, and unwilling to jeopardize offensive arms control or U.S.-Russian relations with an NMD program it saw as unnecessary, the administration cut spending on national missile defense from more than $2 billion annually to less than $1 billion (figure 1-1).

Political support for national missile defense grew when the Republicans took control of Congress in 1995; NMD deployment had been a plank of the House Republican candidates' Contract with America the previous fall. The Clinton administration responded to the growing political pressure by proposing an NMD system in 1997 and beginning an ambitious program to develop it. The effort intensified in 1998, after Iran and North Korea surprised the intelligence community with missile tests that showed rapid progress in their respective missile programs. In early 1999, the Clinton administration explicitly allocated money in its future years defense program to deploy the proposed NMD system. It added $6.6 billion to its defense plan for the years 2000 through 2005 for that

Figure 4-2. *C2 National Missile Defense*

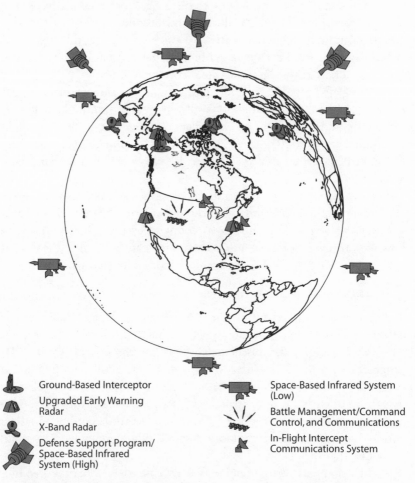

Ground-Based Interceptor

Upgraded Early Warning Radar

X-Band Radar

Defense Support Program/ Space-Based Infrared System (High)

Space-Based Infrared System (Low)

Battle Management/Command Control, and Communications

In-Flight Intercept Communications System

Source: Sessler and others, *Countermeasures*, p. 23.
Note: Locations shown are approximate. For more exact information, see table 4-1.

purpose (making a grand total of $10.5 billion for NMD over that period, including research and development costs).[3] Congress continued to add even more money to the missile defense development effort—and usefully so, based on statements from Pentagon officials responsible for the TMD and NMD programs.[4]

The Clinton administration also made several key decisions about its NMD program. In 1999 it decided to push the original deployment date back two years to 2005 and to aim to deploy one hundred interceptors by 2007. In 2000 the administration decided to base the system in Alaska, with North Dakota still a possible second site for eventual expansion of the system. The administration settled on an Alaska site because it offered the virtue of being able to defend the entire fifty states against an attack from North Korea or the Middle East. By contrast, a North Dakota site could not provide defense for the westernmost islands of the Aleutian and Hawaiian island chains. For that reason, the administration decided that a North Dakota site would be vulnerable to criticism, even if the combined population of the undefended islands amounted to only several thousand people.

The decision to pursue an Alaskan deployment rather than a North Dakota deployment came, however, at a cost. First, it required a rush to begin construction of the radar on Shemya, given the short construction season—thereby seriously complicating diplomatic efforts to convince Russia to modify the Anti-Ballistic Missile Treaty and U.S. allies to support NMD deployment. Second, although interceptor missiles based in Alaska could provide some defense to the entire country, they are poorly placed to defend the East Coast against missile attacks from the Middle East because of the distances involved and the mediocre radar coverage that the C1 capability would provide for that side of the globe. By contrast, while a North Dakota site would be less than optimal for defending western Alaska and Hawaii against an attack from North Korea, it would provide better coverage of the continental United States against a mix of North Korean and Middle Eastern threats. On balance, if one weighs the capabilities of the two sites by the sizes of the population bases they would defend well and poorly, North Dakota is the better choice, whereas if one insists on providing at least some coverage for every inch of American soil, Alaska is preferable. More comprehensive coverage of the entire country would come only with the deployment of the C2 and C3 capabilities.[5]

Besides its decisions about when to deploy the NMD system and where to locate its x-band radar, the Clinton administration also faced important decisions about the ABM Treaty. The C1 and C2 systems would fall within the treaty's guidelines allowing as many as one hundred long-range interceptors to be based at a single site. However, the treaty does not permit a territorial defense of any kind or size; the single missile defense site it allows is supposed to defend only the nation's capital or an intercontinental ballistic missile (ICBM) field. As a result, the administration committed itself to persuading Russia to modify the treaty or to withdrawing

Table 4-1. Proposed Clinton Administration Architecture for the C1, C2, and C3 National Missile Defense Systems

Item	C1 configuration	C2 configuration	C3 configuration
Number of interceptors deployed in Alaska	100	100	125
Number of interceptors deployed in North Dakota	0	0	125
Upgraded early-warning radars	Beale (Marysville, Calif.) Clear (Alaska) Cape Cod (Mass.) Fylingdales (England) Thule (Greenland)	Beale Clear Cape Cod Fylingdales Thule	Beale Clear Cape Cod Fylingdales Thule South Korea
x-band radars	Shemya (Alaska)	Shemya Clear Fylingdales Thule	Shemya Clear Fylingdales Thule Beale Cape Cod Grand Forks (N. Dak.) Hawaii South Korea
In-flight interceptor communications systems	Central Alaska Caribou (Maine) Shemya	Central Alaska Caribou Shemya Munising (Mich.)	Central Alaska Caribou Shemya Munising Hawaii
Early-warning satellites (SBIRS-high)	4[a]	5	5
Warhead-tracking satellites (SBIRS-low)	6[b]	24	24

Sources: Ballistic Missile Defense Organization, "C1/C2/C3 Architecture—Preliminary," briefing slide TRSR 99-082 25, Washington, March 3, 1999; Michael C. Sirak, "BMDO: NMD 'C3' Architecture Could Feature Up to Nine x-Band Radars," *Inside Missile Defense*, May 19, 1999, pp. 13–14; and Congressional Budget Office, *Budgetary and Technical Implications of the Administration's Plan for National Missile Defense*, April 2000, table 1, p. 9.

a. Existing defense support program satellites will also be used for national missile defense.

b. These satellites are planned engineering prototypes.

from it.[6] The target date for choosing between the two options was fall 2000 if the Alaska system were to be ready by 2005. The reason is that the ABM Treaty bans not only the deployment, but also the construction, of NMD systems. With the x-band radar on Shemya Island destined to take five years to build, construction would have to begin during the 2001 construction season. (Construction of the interceptor site would not have begun until 2003.) Because the ABM Treaty requires both parties to give six months' notice before withdrawing, that meant according to the administration that any withdrawal decision would have been needed the previous fall.

Speculation ran high during the first half of 2000 that President Bill Clinton might strike a deal with Russia to modify the ABM Treaty. President Vladimir Putin rejected that idea at the June 2000 Moscow summit, however, raising the specter that the United States might announce its withdrawal from the treaty. Speculation then turned to the possibility that Clinton might keep the NMD system on schedule for a 2005 deployment but avoid withdrawal by announcing that administration lawyers had decided that the excavation work planned for Shemya in 2001 would not violate the ABM Treaty's ban on "construction" of NMD elements. The pressure on the administration to keep NMD development on schedule faded in July, though, when a test of the interceptor rocket failed, the second test failure in six months. And in September 2000 Clinton decided that the 2005 deployment deadline was no longer realistic and announced that he was deferring any such decisions about NMD deployment and the ABM Treaty to his successor.[7]

Cost

What would it cost to construct the C1 system? As with most types of new technology that the Pentagon develops, it is difficult to say, since costs typically increase by 50 percent from a program's inception to its completion. Estimated acquisition costs for the Clinton NMD system are now $12.7 billion through 2005.[8] According to an April 2000 estimate by the Congressional Budget Office, they will reach a total of at least $20 billion (in constant 2001 dollars) including costs after 2005.[9] The Pentagon concluded later in 2000 that costs were likely to be greater, with its best estimate totaling about $25 billion for acquisition of the system.[10] Besides its acquisition cost, the C1 architecture would cost roughly $600 million a year to operate once deployed.[11]

The C2 capability would cost an additional $5 billion for radar and communications upgrades plus another $10 billion for the SBIRS-low satellite constellation.[12] That would make for a total acquisition cost of about $40 billion, plus $700 million a year thereafter in operating costs (for C1 and C2 elements in aggregate).

Even if costs increased further, they would hardly be enormous in comparison with Pentagon fighter, submarine, and destroyer programs expected to run into the several tens of billions each. Nonetheless, they would be significant for a Pentagon that already needs a real-dollar increase of up to $50 billion in its annual budget in the years ahead, primarily because of the need to replace aging equipment purchased in large amounts in the Reagan years, if current force structure and modernization programs are retained.[13] Even in an era of budget surpluses, such large defense spending increases may not prove practical; indeed, during the 2000 campaign President George W. Bush proposed adding only about $5 billion a year to the defense budget.[14] So while missile defenses may not be inordinately expensive in an absolute sense, they are not cheap either, and the Pentagon will likely face real opportunity costs in any decision to deploy them.

Are Development Schedules Realistic?

Was the Clinton administration's NMD development program sound in its pacing and schedule? Probably not. President Clinton partially recognized this when he decided against beginning construction of the Shemya Island radar and left that issue to his successor. That decision postponed the likely initial operational date for NMD until at least 2006. However, deployment even by 2006 is unlikely, and trying for that date is likely to continue creating more diplomatic and technological problems than programmatic benefits. Given the failure of the July 2000 intercept test, it may be more realistic to think of a 2007 or 2008 deployment, as the Pentagon's own Office of Operational Testing and Evaluation has suggested—assuming that this technology has a role to play in whatever NMD system the United States eventually does deploy.[15]

It does seem likely that someday, hit-to-kill technology against an incoming reentry vehicle flying a clear trajectory will work. The Pentagon conducted successful tests of the Patriot PAC-3, THAAD, and NMD systems in 1999. Those are notable accomplishments even if the NMD test was less than fully realistic, and somewhat lucky in that the kill vehicle mistakenly homed in on a decoy before finding and striking the real warhead during the final seconds of approach. A January 2000 NMD test failed when infrared sensors on the kill vehicle lost the target in the last few seconds before anticipated intercept. Water droplets in the kill vehicle's sensors froze, blocking the flow of coolant to the sensor and thus preventing it from reaching the low temperatures it needs to operate. A second failure occurred in July 2000, when the jury-rigged booster rocket being used to place the NMD kill vehicle on a high-speed trajectory failed to separate from the kill vehicle. That failure, the result of a rather sloppy mistake, largely wasted the $100 million spent on the test and meant that it provided little useful data while delaying the program by several months.[16]

Such problems are to be expected in high-technology development programs. They do not suggest that the technology is unworkable.[17] They add further evidence, however, to the contention that the testing program is imprudently rushed. A 1998 task force led by retired Gen. Larry Welch argued that missile defense research programs were being pushed too rapidly in what amounted to a "rush to failure."[18] The program was subsequently slowed modestly, as noted, with initial deployment delayed from 2003 to 2005, but much of the basic pace of the program remained unchanged. Notably, the Clinton administration decided to reach an initial decision on whether to deploy a national missile defense after completing only three of nineteen planned intercept tests of the candidate system. Joint Chiefs' Chairman Gen. Hugh Shelton, former director of the Ballistic Missile Defense Organization (BMDO) Lt. Gen. Lester Lyles, and current BMDO director Lt. Gen. Ronald Kadish, repeatedly acknowledged that the NMD development schedule was very ambitious.[19] In early 2000 the Pentagon's director of Operational Test and Evaluation predicted that the current missile defense development schedule would not hold.[20] And as noted, General Welch, whose panel vigilantly monitored NMD and TMD development programs, stated in the summer of 2000 that while deployment was not inconceivable by 2005, it was not likely either.[21] Those comments were all made before the July 2000 test failure, which only reinforced concerns about the NMD development schedule and slowed the process of gaining necessary information.

Leaving aside the fact that two of the first three tests were unsuccessful, the overall testing program is rather abridged and rushed. Although the MX was tested only 19 times in the research-and-development phase, all other major strategic missile programs were each tested at least 25 times, the Tomahawk cruise missile was tested 74 times, and the

Patriot—perhaps the most comparable, given its mission and its integration of missiles with an advanced radar—was tested 114 times.[22]

The actual booster of the planned NMD system will not be tested for the first time until at least 2001, and a production-quality version of that booster not before 2003. Those goals may slip; development of the production booster was delayed in 2000 by at least six months.[23] The fact that the actual booster had not been tested as of the end of 2000 is significant, because it will have greater acceleration than the surrogate rockets used in earlier tests—meaning that it will subject the kinetic kill vehicle to far greater stresses. It is possible that these stresses might damage the kill vehicle's multitude of sensors and small thrusters, thus necessitating some redesign.[24]

Overall, the Clinton administration clearly rushed development of its NMD system. The only real disagreement is over whether the haste reflected excessive optimism or imprudence. Whichever is the case, it is clear that even 2006 may be an optimistic target year for deployment.

The Decoy Question

As chapter 2 pointed out, midcourse defenses are inherently vulnerable to countermeasures, and the NMD system the Clinton administration proposed building is no exception (box 4-2). It may eventually have good enough sensors to recognize decoys that are larger, smaller, or cooler than real warheads, or that rotate and tumble in ways real warheads would not. Such capabilities might, for example, make it capable of identifying many of the decoys Russia is now believed to deploy with its SS-18 ICBMs.[25] But basic physics argues strongly that decoys closely resembling real warheads simply cannot be distinguished from actual threats by the U.S. sensor systems now in development.

Although the Pentagon claims that it will be able to deal even with advanced decoys, its argument is unpersuasive. For example, it claims that radars will be able to resolve the details of an object's shape and the polarization of its radar return.[26] But such radars are physically incapable of telling a radar-reflective balloon enclosing a spinning warhead from one containing a spinning decoy, since both objects would give the same radar returns. These types of decoys would also probably defeat other midcourse interceptors (such as the Navy theater-wide system deployed in its planned TMD mode or hypothetically on ships along U.S. coasts in a national missile defense mode).[27] Unless sensors could somehow deduce the relative masses of different objects as they left the missile bus that dispensed decoys and warheads—which would require extremely sensitive sensors in a best case, and which could be downright impossible in other cases (depending on the sophistication of the bus)—there would be no physical way to distinguish warheads from decoys.

Defenders of the Clinton administration's proposed NMD system often note that Britain had considerable difficulty in developing ballistic-missile countermeasures with its so-called Chevaline system. However, that system, designed to help warheads penetrate a Soviet endoatmospheric or terminal defense, was far more complex than what North Korea, Iran, Iraq, or any other country would need to defeat the planned U.S. system. Simple decoys work just fine in space; far more complex decoys are needed to mimic heavy warheads within the earth's atmosphere. Unfortunately for the United States, it is in space where its planned system would have to detect, discriminate, and destroy enemy missile warheads.

The news is not entirely bleak. It is not trivial to develop good decoy technology, including the means to dispense decoys in space. After all, the superpowers did not develop MIRV technology for releasing several independently targeted warheads from a single missile until they had had long-range ICBM missiles for a decade or so. (MIRV technology is more complex than decoy technology, since it must send warheads on more accurate trajectories than are necessary for decoys, but there are important parallels.) As such, it could take a country such as North Korea quite a while to perfect the needed countermeasures. An adversary is likely to require some realistic flight testing to have confidence that its decoys would work, and a state without the resources or diplomatic breathing room to test very much may not succeed in any limited period of time.[28] In its July 2000 NMD test, even a country with the technological sophistication and missile testing experience of the United States failed to get its countermeasure to work properly. The balloon decoy failed to inflate properly, making it straightforward for radar to distinguish it from the real warhead.[29] So all hope is not lost on the decoy front, even if the overall thrust of technology clearly favors even a relatively unsophisticated attacker—and even if, to quote BMDO's chief scientist, "Countermeasures threats are emerging sooner than originally expected."[30]

It is true that a country such as North Korea or Iraq might not need to develop decoys on its own, instead acquiring countermeasures technology from Russia or China. But such proliferation is hardly preordained, given that it would unmistakably be a hostile action against the United States. True, Beijing or Moscow might decide to provide such countermeasures

Box 4-2. Countermeasures

A common criticism leveled against midcourse NMD systems is that an attacker could defeat them by equipping its missiles with countermeasures. By some accounts these countermeasures are relatively inexpensive and easily available. So just how serious a problem are countermeasures for a midcourse defense?

The countermeasure debate has been dominated by an April 2000 report prepared by a study group organized by the Union of Concerned Scientists (UCS) and the Security Studies Program of the Massachusetts Institute of Technology.[1] The eleven study group members had impressive scientific credentials: eight had Ph.D.'s in physics and several had previously advised the government on ballistic missile technologies, including one who had served as a member of the Rumsfeld Commission that had warned of the spread of long-range ballistic missiles. The group based its report solely on information in the public record, the same information that would be available to any country trying to build its own intercontinental ballistic missiles (ICBMs).

The UCS report highlights three types of countermeasures. The first is to load dozens of submunitions, or smaller warheads, carrying chemical or biological agents atop a missile. UCS projects that a ballistic missile that can carry a one-ton payload 6,000 miles could easily carry eighty-five to ninety submunitions weighing twenty pounds each. The missile would dispense the submunitions shortly after it stopped burning and left the atmosphere, either by using spring-loaded tubes or by using a small thruster to spin the missile in a way that would make the submunitions spread out in a wide radius of impact points. The number of submunitions from just a few missiles would easily outnumber the interceptor missiles in the NMD system the Clinton administration proposed building. The submunitions that survived interception would descend through the atmosphere, with the chemical or biological agents protected from excessive heating by heat shields. The submunitions would then release the chemical or biological agents by ground contact fuses or by barometric fuses that would discharge at a set altitude.

The second type of countermeasure that the UCS report discusses involves placing a single, large warhead in a metal-covered balloon, while also releasing a large number of balloon decoys. UCS also claims that fifty or more such balloons could be deployed per ballistic missile, once again overwhelming the supply of NMD interceptors. Once the missile entered its midcourse phase, the balloons could be inflated using a small nitrogen gas bottle. Once inflated, the metal-coated balloon with a warhead suspended inside would be indistinguishable from other balloons to a defender's radar, infrared, and visible sensors, provided that the attacker took several fairly simple steps in building the balloons. An attacker could ensure that the empty and warhead-carrying balloons gave off the same thermal signature by altering the balloons' surface coating or by placing small heaters inside the empty balloons to heat them to temperatures similar to the balloon holding the warhead. An attacker could also ensure that the falling and spinning motions of the empty balloons and warhead would be indistinguishable by attaching the warhead to the inside of the balloon with string to prevent tumbling, deliberately distorting the motion of the empty balloons by placing small weights in them or taking other similar steps.

The third countermeasure the UCS report highlights involves covering a nuclear warhead with a thin metal shroud. Once the warhead reaches an altitude above the atmosphere, liquid nitrogen could be pumped into the small cavity between the inner and outer walls of the shroud. The cooled shroud would dramatically reduce the warhead's infrared signature, making it far harder, if not impossible, for the interceptor's sensor array—which depends on infrared sensors to do the final homing in the last tens of kilometers—to locate the target in enough time to make an intercept. UCS claims that even if the kill vehicle could be modified to use a visible sensor in the final stages of homing, the attacker could still defeat the defense by keeping the missile's trajectory in the earth's shadow. The shroud could be removed from the warhead by a spring-loaded device, which would be activated by a timer.

The UCS report contends that all three of the countermeasures it analyzed are not only possible, but probable, given the technological advancement a state would have to reach to be able to build an ICBM in the first place. Although U.S. officials acknowledge that any midcourse NMD system faces daunting challenges, they argue that the UCS underestimates how much progress the Pentagon has made in being able to discriminate between decoys and warheads. They contend, based on information that remains classified, that a combination of different sensor technologies will enable the midcourse system the United States is developing to "be effective against the envisioned rogue [missile] threat of 2005."[2] However, U.S. officials have not defined the precise countermeasures they expect the new ballistic powers to possess in 2005, making a comparison with UCS claims impossible.

Although most scientific commentary has been critical of the Pentagon's position, a few experts have come to its defense.[3] These experts do not dispute the UCS claim that countermeasures could be built to complicate the task of a midcourse system. Instead, they, like the Pentagon, argue that the UCS report underestimates the progress being made in discriminating between warheads and decoys. They also charge that the UCS report greatly exaggerates the ease with which countermeasures could be built and how reliable they would be. According to these experts, mastering the ability to produce a long-range missile does not guarantee the ability to build countermeasures that can be counted on to work. That would come only after rigorous flight testing, which countries such as North Korea, Iran, and Iraq might not be able to afford or might have to forgo because of international opposition. Even if these countries do conduct flight tests, they lack the radar and other sensors needed to assess how well their countermeasures are performing. As a result, the attacker might end up building countermeasures that do not work.

On balance, the laws of physics make it clear that any midcourse NMD system faces a stiff challenge in distinguishing between warheads and decoys. But a fledgling missile power may not quickly master decoys. The Pentagon's critics appear to have a considerable edge in the countermeasure debate, but the issue is not fully resolved.

1. Andrew M. Sessler and others, *Countermeasures: A Technical Evaluation of the Operational Effectiveness of the Planned U.S. National Missile Defense System* (Cambridge, Mass.: Union of Concerned Scientists, April 2000).

2. Vernon Loeb, "Antimissile System Is Called 'No Defense,'" *Washington Post*, April 12, 2000, p. A15.

3. K. Scott McMahon, Stanley Orman, and Richard Speier, "Countermeasure Doubletalk," *Defense News*, June 19, 2000, p. 19.

capabilities to an extremist regime if persuaded that the United States had adopted a hostile attitude against them and their core security interests with its NMD program. But such actions might be prevented by a U.S. approach to national missile defense that took Russian and Chinese concerns into account—as our proposed NMD architecture would do.

Nor have all the criticisms of the Pentagon's recent use of decoys in missile defense tests been fair. It is true that only simple decoys have been used and only in small numbers. But the early phases of any weapon's test program cannot be expected to recreate all the conditions under which the deployed system is ultimately intended to work. There is nothing inherently objectionable about beginning with simpler tests and then moving on.[31] That said, it is possible that some contractors have attempted to mislead the government and public about the existing capabilities of sensors to discriminate warheads from countermeasures— nothing short of fraud, if true.[32]

Another point in defense of the Pentagon: although countermeasures would be unnecessary for an attack using many bomblets filled with chemical or biological agents, as chapters 2 and 3 pointed out, such attacks would probably be less dangerous than those with nuclear warheads. Chemical weapons are intrinsically less lethal than nuclear or biological agents, and biological agents tend to be most effective when the targeted country does not realize it has been attacked for a period of time. Ballistic missiles are therefore less than ideal means of delivering such agents.[33]

All in all, a limited nationwide defense based on midcourse, or exoatmospheric, interceptors would have serious limitations. But it may still provide some capability against the type of threat a North Korea or Iran could develop in the next decade or so—assuming that China and Russia do not retaliate against a U.S. NMD deployment by transferring countermeasure technology to such states, which the U.S. intelligence community fears they might do.[34] It also offers the advantage of providing some type of defense capability against both Mideast and North Korean threats (including threats not now foreseen, such as from Libya or a Pakistan taken over by Islamic fundamentalists hostile to the United States). It offers the political reliability and physical security of being based on U.S. soil. Finally, it could also be useful against a small accidental or unauthorized Russian or Chinese launch. If those countries choose not to deploy sophisticated decoys on their missiles under normal conditions—as they might not, if the United States had managed to reassure them that its limited NMD was nonthreatening—a rogue commander firing such missiles without permission from Moscow or Beijing might not be able to penetrate the U.S. defenses. For these reasons, the Clinton administration's plan to build such a defense was not without merit—even if its exclusive reliance on this system, and its preference to rush to build it in Alaska, was probably mistaken.

Larger Midcourse Defenses

Although they would share the vulnerabilities to countermeasures of the Clinton administration's C1 or C2 plans, midcourse defenses with more interceptors could counter larger attacks that did not include such countermeasures. Those with more bases could have greater effectiveness against missiles launched from places such as the Middle East, North Africa, the North Atlantic and North Pacific Oceans, and Latin America. Two possibilities are of particular interest: the Clinton administration's own C3 proposal and a proposal to use the radars and missile launch capabilities already found on the Navy's Aegis-class ships. At the same time, the United States could try to reduce its vulnerability to countermeasures by building endo-exo interceptors that constitute a cross between a midcourse and a terminal defense.

The C3 Capability

As one possible approach to national missile defense, the Bush administration might pursue what the Clinton administration called the C3 capability. Under this approach, the United States would build missile defense bases in both North Dakota and Alaska, each equipped with up to one hundred and twenty-five interceptor missiles, as well as nine advanced missile-tracking radars on U.S. and allied territory. Those x-band radars would be in Alaska (the Shemya facility); Clear, Alaska; South Korea; Fylingdales, England; Thule, Greenland; Hawaii; Beale, California; Grand Forks, North Dakota; and Cape Cod (figure 4-3). Of course, there is nothing magical in the number of bases, interceptors, and radars in the C3 capability. The Bush administration or its successor could expand each of these elements of the proposal if it wanted to.

The Clinton administration envisioned deploying the C3 capability by 2011.[35] However, the proposal's status was less official than that of the C1 capability; the administration never formally committed to it by allocating the necessary funds in long-term defense plans, as it did for the C1 system. The logic of the Clinton administration's overall position implies

Figure 4-3. *C3 National Missile Defense*

Ground-Based Interceptor		Space-Based Infrared System (Low)	
Upgraded Early Warning Radar		Battle Management/Command Control, and Communications	
X-Band Radar		In-Flight Intercept Communications System	
Defense Support Program/ Space-Based Infrared System (High)			

Source: Sessler and others, *Countermeasures*, p. 24.

Note: Locations shown are approximate. For more exact information, see table 4-1.

a need for C3, however. The C1 and even the C2 systems would not perform particularly well against Mideast threats or warheads equipped with advanced countermeasures—both of which Clinton administration officials acknowledged to be real concerns—so a more advanced system would presumably be needed.

The C3 capability might cost $10 billion more than the C2 option, roughly speaking. All told, that would make for about $50 billion in acquisition costs for the Clinton administration's entire NMD system. Once fully deployed, annual operational costs would total roughly $1 billion annually for the C3 system (which by definition includes C1 and C2 elements).[36]

If concerned about the long-range sea-based ballistic missile threat, the United States might also add one or two defensive bases along each coast, for a total of up to one-half dozen sites. Even if it expanded the number of sites further in that way, it would not necessarily need to increase the aggregate number of associated interceptor missiles. However, it could need new radars facing toward the oceans rather than northward toward the pole. Moreover, TMD systems might also need to be deployed to defend against short-range missiles launched from the sea that would not leave the atmosphere and hence could not be intercepted by the NMD system the Clinton administration proposed building.

Navy Aegis Systems

The Pentagon is developing the Navy theater-wide (NTW) defense system as a TMD system, but some have proposed expanding it to have an NMD capability as well. Either way, it would use the Aegis radar deployed on about sixty Navy cruisers and destroyers as its engagement radar. In TMD mode, it would employ a modified form of the Standard Missile as its interceptor, with a hit-to-kill final stage atop it. A faster missile would probably be needed for NMD purposes. An NMD version of NTW would be a midcourse defense, meaning that it would have the same vulnerabilities to countermeasures as the Clinton administration's proposed NMD system. It might be even more vulnerable. The kill vehicle now envisioned for NTW does not have outstanding sensors or maneuverability—meaning that it would have a harder time coping with even the simplest decoys than the NMD system that the Clinton administration proposed building.

Of all TMD programs, NTW is the only one that raises any ABM Treaty compliance issues. The treaty permits theater missile defenses without restriction but does not clearly define the demarcation point between theater and national (or strategic) missile defenses. As chapter 2 discusses, the United States and Russia reached an accord in 1997 that defined as unambiguous TMD any system using interceptors that do not exceed speeds of 3 kilometers per second, and that are not tested against incoming warheads with speeds greater than 5 kilometers per second or ranges greater than 3,500 kilometers. The accord has not been submitted to the U.S. Senate for its advice and consent but nonetheless has a certain de facto status. The NTW program is to stay below the two latter thresholds, but its Block II interceptor will have a maximum speed greater than 3 kilometers per second, making its status ambiguous.[37] The current U.S. intent is to test anyway, without restriction, so disagreements over the demarcation agreement are unlikely to affect U.S. TMD capabilities. (The NTW missile that would exceed 3 kilometers per second has not yet even been developed, much less tested; meanwhile, the Block I missile does not exceed the 3 kilometers-a-second threshold.)[38] In fact, despite the claims of critics, the ABM Treaty has not impeded development of any missile defense systems to date, though it could do so eventually.

But the dilemma remains in the NMD context. The NTW interceptor's speed is sufficient to raise concerns that, if tied in with advanced sensors and tested in an NMD mode, it could theoretically have some NMD capability when based in U.S. ports. That fact helps explain why even a limited NMD system that includes advanced sensors could cause concern in Moscow and Beijing about the possibility of a much more robust U.S. NMD.[39]

Seeing the Navy theater-wide's NMD potential as a virtue, in 1999 a group convened by the Heritage Foundation proposed using Aegis-equipped cruisers to form a nationwide defense capability. It would, in their eyes, be a near-term way to provide fairly "thick" nationwide defense relatively inexpensively. (Heritage had been proposing similar ideas in less detail since roughly 1996.) The 1999 commission advocated buying about 650 interceptors to deploy on twenty-two cruisers (more than half of which would presumably be in U.S. ports or coastal waters at any time, given normal Navy ship rotation schedules), as well as possibly a barge in the Great Lakes or a site in North Dakota. These interceptors would be tested against long-range missile warheads to be sure they would work against such high-speed threats. Their radar systems could eventually be interlinked with other sensors such as large early-warning radars and satellites, including the SBIRS-low system. The Heritage group estimated the basic cost of the system at about $3 billion.[40]

The Pentagon disagreed with the Heritage cost analysis, later estimating that the system's total cost would fall between $16 billion and $19 billion. That estimate included the costs of advanced land-based radars, since the Pentagon determined that the Aegis radars would not be sufficient by themselves to provide early tracking and discrimination information. It also included the costs of several dedicated ships (since defenses could be badly needed in wartime—when most of the Navy's Aegis warships could be deployed), as well as upgraded missiles with enough range, maneuverability, and nuclear hardness to provide reliable nationwide defense.[41] (The Pentagon claimed that the planned Standard missiles could not do the NMD job adequately.)[42]

However, the Pentagon did concede that an NMD version of the NTW system might do a good job of complementing a ground-based system by covering coastal areas better than ground sites in Alaska or North Dakota could and simply by providing additional radars and interceptors.[43] And in fairness to the Heritage proposal, some of the Pentagon's cost estimates could be challenged. For example, given the likelihood that some ships would remain near U.S. coasts even in wartime, an Aegis defense might well provide some NMD capability without necessitating the purchase of more ships. (That said, there is little doubt that the Navy would lobby for more ships if assigned more missions.)

Some have argued that because NTW interceptors could theoretically shoot down missiles early in their flight, NTW could function as a boost-phase NMD system. Indeed, it could even be tested as a boost-phase defense in a way that was consistent with the demarcation agreement— simply by using medium-range missiles as the targets—but then used for national missile defense because if NTW worked against medium-range threats in the boost phase it would probably work against ICBMs too.[44] In practice, however, NTW's utility as a boost-phase defense would be limited. For example, NTW interceptors could not provide complete boost-phase defense against North Korea because they will be too slow to defend against launches from many inland and western parts of the country. For similar reasons, they would not be of much use against most launch points in Iraq or Iran. In addition, NTW interceptors may not have sufficient acceleration and maneuverability to hit even a nearby missile in boost phase, when an outgoing missile's flight would be powered and hence somewhat less predictable than an object in its midcourse trajectory. In the end, NTW interceptors used in NMD mode would be a midcourse system, not a boost-phase system, with all the attendant limitations and vulnerabilities to countermeasures.

It may be possible to develop new NTW interceptors fast enough to function as a boost-phase defense but still small enough to fit within standard vertical launch tubes on Aegis ships. But that remains to be established.[45] Given current rocket propulsion materials and methods, the only way to make fast missiles is to make big missiles with lots of fuel.

The Endo-Exo Interceptor: A Cross between Midcourse and Terminal Defense

In theory, one could combine the advantages of midcourse interception with those of terminal intercept. An interceptor missile could be launched while a threat was still thousands of miles away, traveling in space over some large distance itself and then reentering the atmosphere and restarting its rocket boosters to attack the offensive threat. Such a system would combine the range of midcourse defenses—only one base, or perhaps two, of interceptor missiles would be needed—with the benefits of atmospheric discrimination of warheads from most decoys that characterize terminal defenses.

This idea has been pursued before. The Bush administration briefly investigated an endo-exo system as one possible part of its proposed Global Protection against Limited Strikes (GPALS) missile defense in the early 1990s.[46] The endo-exo idea, and GPALS, was shelved when the Clinton administration came to office. But in any event the necessary technology is probably still rather distant in the future.

An endo-exo interceptor would face many challenges of its own. It would require many radars to guide the low-altitude intercepts, because the range of any one radar would be limited by the curvature of the earth. To intercept an object at 30 miles above the earth's surface, for example, a radar would have to be located within roughly 300 miles of the engagement zone to be able to observe the process, so at least a dozen radars would be required to defend the continental United States alone. An endo-exo system would also require rocket motors that could be turned off and then turned back on when the interceptor reentered the atmosphere. It would also require very good guidance and synchronization, because the interceptor missile would have to be launched many minutes before intercept and directed to the appropriate region. It should be possible to synchronize the arrival of the threat and interceptor if the threat was an isolated warhead, or a warhead accompanied by nearby decoys, but this approach might not work against a larger "threat cloud" such as that created by a more advanced, MIRVed missile.

Finally, an endo-exo system might not work against decoys that could mimic a warhead's flight within the atmosphere or against warheads designed to maneuver upon atmospheric reentry. This latter problem becomes severe when an incoming warhead reaches a point 25 miles above the earth's surface. At that point, the density of the atmosphere is sufficient to allow warheads equipped with simple aerodynamic features to maneuver by exploiting the effects of air resistance. To cope with incoming warheads that have even limited maneuver, the interceptor rocket would need to be fast and maneuverable itself. Despite these challenges, an endo-exo system may have enough promise to merit further research in the years ahead.[47]

Boost-Phase Defenses

To make it much tougher for an enemy to defeat an NMD system with fairly simple countermeasures, and to provide defense for regions outside of North America, the United States could develop capabilities for shooting down missiles during their boost phase. At that point, the enemy ICBM—essentially a large, full gas tank—would be highly vulnerable and easy to see and hit. It would also not have had the chance to dispense decoys or countermeasures because these devices would not yet be up to the speeds needed for intercontinental trajectories and would slow down if the missile released them within the atmosphere. Although an advanced enemy could build fast-burn ICBMs to counter such a boost-phase defense system, these types of ICBMs are much harder to master than the missiles that North Korea, Iraq, and Iran are now developing.[48]

There are two main types of boost-phase defense that the United States could realistically develop within a decade. One, a system using interceptor missiles based at sea or on land or possibly in the air, has been prominently promoted by physicist Richard Garwin and others. It has also received support from a number of former Clinton administration Pentagon officials and from Governor George Bush during the 2000 presidential campaign. However, as of the start of 2001, the Pentagon had no program intended to investigate or develop a boost-phase defense. The second type of boost-phase defense, known as the airborne laser, is an existing Pentagon program—though it is being designed to provide theater missile defense. However, that distinction is somewhat artificial, in that boost-phase defenses that would work against shorter-range missiles would generally also work against longer-range rockets. Whether or not ABL is used as a boost-phase NMD defense, a similar system surely could be.

Boost-Phase Interceptor Missiles Based on Earth or in Its Atmosphere

Earth-based boost-phase interceptor missiles could be based on land, ships, or even on airplanes or unmanned aircraft.

BOOST-PHASE DEFENSES ON LAND OR AT SEA. Boost-phase interceptor missiles based on land or ships would be moderately large, extremely fast-burn rockets that would be fired very quickly after an enemy launch was detected. They would catch up, and then collide, with the enemy ICBM while it was still in its boost phase—within the atmosphere or just outside it.[49]

The coverage zone of any earth-based boost-phase defense would extend perhaps 500 miles beyond the location of the interceptor missile base and not much further. That is because the interceptors would have only two to three minutes to make their intercepts. (They might be launched a minute or minute and a half after the enemy ICBM was fired—once their accompanying radar had identified and begun to track the missile—and would accelerate for seventy to one hundred seconds before cruising at roughly 5 miles, or 8 kilometers, per second thereafter).[50]

The limited geographical reach of earth-based boost-phase interceptors means they could not play much of a role in defending the United States against an ICBM attack from China or Russia. Missiles launched from central and western China or most of Russia and headed over the North Pole would be beyond the range of interceptors based, say, near the Korean Peninsula or in the Arctic or Pacific oceans because the ICBMs would have completed their boost phase long before interceptors could reach them. In theory, if properly positioned, earth-based boost-phase defenses could be used to shoot down some Chinese missiles headed at Taiwan or Japan. But they would be very expensive devices to use in such missions and would almost certainly not be produced or deployed in sufficient numbers to constitute a serious counter to a Chinese short-range missile force numbering in the hundreds of weapons. In addition, short-range missiles have such quick boost phases that they would be very hard if not impossible to intercept while still burning.

One drawback to the boost-phase defense concept is that, by hitting the rocket rather than the warhead, the latter would not necessarily be destroyed. The warhead could then continue onward, possibly detonating—and, most likely, at least scattering radioactive, chemical, or biological material where it landed. However, since the rocket would have been hit before completing its boost phase, the warhead would almost certainly not have enough speed to reach densely populated parts of North America. If launched from North Korea, the warhead would most likely land in arctic waters or the tundra of Russia, Alaska, or Canada. Its chances of landing near a city would be less than one in a thousand. If launched from the

Middle East, it could land in Europe, but even there, the chances of it hitting within a heavily populated region would be quite modest—roughly several percent. While far from an ideal situation, chances are low that many individuals would lose their lives. By the standards of nuclear war, that is a relatively benign prospect on the whole. Nonetheless, the possibility of casualties is a liability of most boost-phase systems.

Another liability, limited in severity but nonetheless real, is that boost-phase defenses must work very quickly—so quickly, in fact, that national command authorities could not realistically be consulted during an actual engagement. Thus, predelegation would be essential—and a military officer would have to take responsibility for determining if a given country's launch was legitimate (say a space vehicle) or threatening. This concern can be overblown, since the most likely scenario in which NMD would be relevant is during a crisis or war, when there would be little need to presuppose friendly intent on the part of an adversarial country launching a large rocket. But it should at least be acknowledged. It could, in a worst case, lead to the downing of a space launch vehicle and the loss of its payload. Since such a payload would presumably not include people, the damage would probably be only financial, and the United States could probably compensate the aggrieved party if doing so was appropriate. But nonetheless this is a complicating dimension of the technology.

Boost-phase NMD could be deployed near the Korean Peninsula, Middle East, and other potential trouble spots provided appropriate basing on land or at sea was available—and defensible. Sea-based boost-phase defenses would presumably require escort from surface combatants and perhaps even aircraft; land-based defenses would require soldiers capable of fending off a commando strike against the base. Both types would need to be hardened electronically and physically against the possibility of attack, perhaps by cruise missiles. Ship-based systems would benefit further from their mobility; land-based systems would benefit from the likelihood that interceptor missiles would be based in underground, hardened silos. But even so, vulnerabilities could not be ruled out entirely. That is one reason why a limited, two-tiered defense system may make sense, as we argue in chapter 6—a single tier may be destroyed or otherwise circumvented by a clever adversary. It is also another reason why a power such as Russia or China should not fear boost-phase defenses. Not only are they unable to work against missiles launched from deep within a large country's territory, but they could be subject to direct attack and neutralization from a state with numerous cruise missiles or other advanced technologies.

Unless the détente process accelerates on the Korean Peninsula, a boost-phase system would most likely be based in northeastern Asia initially, either on barges in the Sea of Japan or on land in the general vicinity of Vladivostok, Russia. Deployments focused on the Middle East could follow, perhaps in 2010 or thereafter (though there is some chance that they might be considered sooner, depending on the evolution of the Iranian and Iraqi intermediate-range missile threats to Europe).

Given the size of Iran, defending against a missile launch by that country would require two boost-phase interceptor bases. One would have to be north of Iran—in the Caspian Sea, Turkmenistan, or possibly Kazakhstan or Uzbekistan. The other would be below it, in the Persian Gulf, Sea of Oman, or possibly Oman, Saudi Arabia, or the United Arab Emirates. Iraqi missiles might be defended against by a base in eastern Turkey, which could also defend the United States (and large parts of Europe) against launches from certain parts of Iran.[51]

The limited geographic scope of earth-based boost-phase defenses is at once one of the concept's greatest strengths and also its greatest weakness. It would be a strength because it would not, and could not, threaten the deterrent of a large country such as Russia—making it more likely that Moscow will ultimately agree to modify the ABM Treaty to permit a limited national missile defense. However, basing a defense on foreign territory, especially that of a non-ally, would raise questions about its dependability in wartime. Land-based boost-phase systems would be difficult to move if new threats developed. Sea-based boost-phase systems would not be useful against missiles from all potential threats, since not all are near international or friendly waters. (Air-based boost-phase systems, discussed below, would be impractical to operate over large countries, particularly those with advanced air defenses.)

Such a boost-phase system does, however, appear within reach technologically—possibly on roughly the time horizon of the Clinton administration's planned C1 capability, and almost certainly as fast as the C2 system could be fielded. It would require a new interceptor of extremely high speed, but that could be built without radically new types of technologies. Missiles like the Trident II or D5 were built within a decade, and this boost-phase missile likely could be as well (though the challenges would admittedly be different in its case, relating more to speed than to precise guidance).[52] Indeed, even in the early 1980s a major U.S. defense contractor was proposing a missile that could reach ICBM-range speeds of seven kilometers per second in just fifty seconds of boosting, in contrast to boost times of seventy to one hundred seconds commonly foreseen for the slightly faster boost-phase interceptors.[53]

A boost-phase defense would not require a sophisticated sensor network on a par with what the Clinton administration's program requires. Its main infrared seeker would have such a hot target to home in on that it could use relatively inexpensive, simple, short-wavelength devices rather than the long-wavelength IR seeker needed on the midcourse interceptor system (to say nothing of the long-range radars the latter system needs).[54]

Nor would a boost-phase defense likely be as expensive as the NMD program now in the works. The rockets would probably be more expensive than those envisioned for the Clinton administration's planned system (about $18 million apiece, according to the latest estimates of the Congressional Budget Office). But they would probably not be on a par with the most expensive ICBMs and submarine-launched ballistic missiles (SLBMs), which are much larger systems. (The MX, for example, cost more than $100 million a copy, or about six times the cost of an interceptor in the Clinton administration's proposed system.)[55] The rest of the NMD technology—which accounts for about two-thirds of the cost of the administration's C1 proposal, and three-fourths of the cost of C3[56]—would be far simpler for boost-phase defense.

As for operating costs, they will also likely be lower for boost-phase defense. Such a defense would not require as sophisticated a sensor or battle-management capability as the Clinton NMD architecture—even TMD radars might suffice. But it could require spending at least several tens of millions a year on several ships or on the infrastructure and security for a land base.

Boost-phase defenses would require modifying the ABM Treaty. But the changes might be portrayed as less fundamental, because as noted, they would not challenge Russia's deterrent—and the treaty's purpose is to reassure Russia and the United States about their nuclear deterrents vis-à-vis each other. Most boost-phase defenses would not provide comprehensive national missile defense against all threats, but defense only against certain threats launched from certain regions.

Boost-phase defenses could in theory be reconfigured to work against an offensive missile after it had left the atmosphere and stopped burning fuel. But that would require better sensors as well as testing.[57] Such a system would also be just as vulnerable to simple decoys as any other midcourse defense. Thus, this potential feature of boost-phase defenses seems unlikely to negate the technology's basic benefits.

AIRBORNE BOOST-PHASE INTERCEPTOR MISSILES. Boost-phase defenses could also hypothetically be based on unmanned, long-endurance aircraft and flown in orbits over enemy territory. This approach would presumably only work during wartime, when the United States could establish air supremacy, and only against countries of modest size with mediocre air defense capabilities. Although the interceptors could be flown at high altitude, even countries like North Korea and Iraq could probably find ways to threaten them in the absence of U.S. fighter cover for the planes hosting the interceptors.

But this approach could still have benefits. It could add an extra element of redundancy to missile-defense efforts. It could also make use of slower, smaller, cheaper interceptors than boost-phase defenses operating from sea level.[58] Perhaps most of all, it may be the only practical boost-phase defense against missiles launched from Iran, since it is far from clear that any country north of Iran would be willing to host a U.S. missile-defense base on its soil.

Airborne Laser

The airborne laser (ABL) involves more futuristic technology. It would use chemical fuel to generate an intense beam of light that would be aimed at an offensive rocket's outer surface, weakening it and causing it to rupture unless the attacker could find ways to shield the rocket or reduce the energy absorbed by any one part of its skin. The Pentagon currently envisions that, at any time, two ABL aircraft would operate near the likely launch points of enemy missiles and above the clouds at about 40,000 feet altitude. Each plane would be capable of firing twenty shots before returning to the ground for more chemical fuel.

The Air Force plans to flight test the ABL in 2003, and if that test is successful, to enter into engineering manufacturing and development the next year; initial operating capability would be in 2007 and the full capability of seven aircraft would be available in 2009. The ABL program schedule seems likely to slip, however, given that high-powered lasers are a fundamentally new type of technology. The program remains essentially in the laboratory experimental stage today, a point the Clinton administration's director for Defense Department Operational Test and Evaluation, as well as the department's director of defense research and engineering, emphasized.[59] For example, even though progress has been made in dealing with the effects of atmospheric turbulence on the laser beam (by deforming the laser mirror to compensate for that turbulence), the Pentagon still does not have a sufficiently powerful laser of the size and weight needed to operate aboard an aircraft.

If and when the ABL is available, it would likely have a range of no more than several hundred miles. That would mean that ABL, like other earth-based boost-phase defenses, could only defend against missiles launched from relatively close by and could not realistically defend against a Russian or Chinese attack from most parts of those countries.

How effective ABL will prove in practice against the threats it is designed to handle is unclear. No one knows for certain how vulnerable the system might be to countermeasures, such as reflective coatings on offensive missile bodies that reflect rather than absorb the laser's energy. The ABL aircraft is vulnerable to enemy air defenses, meaning it will be practical to use only where the United States can establish air dominance. The enormous expense of maintaining ABL planes and their escort aircraft on continuous patrol raises serious questions about whether the system could ever function as a national missile defense in a day-to-day, as opposed to crisis or wartime, role. And again, most fundamentally, it is not yet clear that the Pentagon will be able to make the ABL's basic concept work within the next decade.[60] For all these reasons, while vigorous research and development of the laser technology makes sense, we do not consider it an option for next-generation TMD or first-generation NMD systems.[61] It could, however, be part of an early second-generation of defenses, if current development timelines do not slip too much. Figure 4-4 depicts how the ABL works.

Layered and Space-Based Systems

To this point, we have talked about individual NMD architectures in isolation from one another. This largely reflects the fact that proponents of different architectures often portray their favored system as capable of providing a single layer of defense that would by itself be sufficient to perform the NMD mission. But these different architectures could be combined into a multitiered, or layered, defense against an enemy missile attack if the associated cost is deemed acceptable.

At the same time, we have not discussed the possibility of building futuristic defenses, such as space-based lasers. That omission is deliberate. This book focuses on NMD systems that the United States could reasonably

Figure 4-4. *How the Airborne Laser Works*

How the Airborne Laser Works

1. One of six **infrared search and track sensors** (IRSTs) detects a missile in its boost phase.

2. The IRST passes the track to the low-power **active-laser ranger**, which measures a ping off the missile to determine its exact distance.

3. The active-laser ranger sends this information to the **illuminator lasers**, which travel . . . [via a] tube and through the nose turret. They calculate the missile's sweet spot — generally its fuel tank — and measure disturbance pockets in the intervening atmosphere.

4. The system uses this information to bend and distort a deformable mirror in the beam control system. It then opens a valve to unleash the mixture of hydrogen peroxide, chlorine and iodine, which generates the **high-energy laser.**

5. The kill beam travels down its 12.5-inch tube. . . . When it reaches the swiveling **nose turret**, it expands to about 5 feet in diameter before it is unleashed on the missile.

6. As the kill beam moves through the atmosphere, the distortion pockets in the atmosphere focus it like a contact lens. By the time it hits its target, the beam will return to its original 12.5-inch diameter. The beam is invisible to the human eye.

IN THE THEATER
The system will fly at 40,000 feet with a fighter escort and target theater ballistic missiles.

Two pilots

IRST

IRSTs (two on each side)

Beam control system

Four crew consoles

Bulkhead protects crew from chemicals

IRST

ED

USAF

12.5 inches   5 feet   12.5 inches

Source: "How the Airborne Laser Works," *Defense News*, November 27, 2000, p. 8, artwork and text by Nathaniel Levine, basic airplane rendering by Team ABL. Reprinted by permission.

expect to deploy within the next decade or so. The Pentagon does not expect to be able to deploy space-based lasers before 2020. The obstacles to perfecting space-based lasers are considerable and are likely to remain daunting even with much higher research and development expenditures. Not only would lightweight lasers and automated tracking and aiming technology be needed, as is the case for ABL, but so would inexpensive space-launch capabilities and long-term durability of materials and fuels—and huge yet lightweight mirrors the likes of which have never even been built for use on earth.[62] It is possible that the United States might put interceptor missiles in space sooner—but doubtful that they could be deployed as first-generation NMD within the next ten years.

"Thick," Layered Defenses

A layered approach to national missile defense has two potential advantages. First, a layered defense might be less likely to fail because the strengths of one layer could offset the weaknesses of others. As a result, warheads that penetrated one layer might be picked off by another. (Of course, layering would not provide much protection if none of the layers worked very well.) Second, if each layer were sufficiently large and effective, it is possible that a layered defense would be capable of protecting against far larger attacks than any single NMD architecture could do on its own. In theory, the "thicker" the defense—that is, the greater the number of layers and capability per layer—the greater the protection.

The possibility of building layered defenses has attracted considerable attention. During the Clinton administration, Secretary of Defense William Cohen spoke of boost-phase systems and Aegis capabilities as NMD technologies that could complement, rather than replace, the administration's proposed midcourse NMD system. Moreover, many Republican missile defense enthusiasts favor building a thick, layered defense. It is impossible to say with certainty what such a defense might look like. There are many possibilities. It could be a midcourse NMD architecture more ambitious than the Clinton plan (in the number of interceptors) combined with boost-phase and select TMD programs. Or it could consist of an Aegis-style midcourse system plus boost-phase interceptors and the ABL. And it might eventually involve spaced-based defense. During the 2000 presidential campaign, for example, then-governor Bush expressed interest in robust defenses that included space-based weapons.[63]

Global Protection against Limited Strikes

One possible NMD architecture that combines layered defense with space-based defense is the GPALS system that the Bush administration proposed in the early 1990s. That design included 1,000 space-based "brilliant pebbles," or orbiting interceptor missiles that could home in on offensive missiles while they were still in their boost phase. It also included 750 ground-based interceptors at a total of six sites for midcourse intercepts. Depending on how an enemy attacked, such a defense might be capable of shooting down 100 to 200 warheads with no more than several warheads getting through. A defense of this size could be needed to defend against an unauthorized Russian launch that involved all the warheads on a given submarine or within a given ICBM field.

GPALS would be very expensive, easily exceeding $100 billion and probably costing $150 billion if one scales from cost estimates of the Clinton architecture.[64] Half of its capabilities—the land-based interceptors that would work in the midcourse phase of an enemy missile's flight—would run the same risk of being useless against a missile force armed with good countermeasures that the Clinton administration's system would face. Finally, its space-based elements might not be developed as quickly as its ground-based ones.

However, the space-based interceptors might be able to provide boost-phase defense. Moreover, it might be possible to put them into orbits of inclination that made them useful against North Korea, Iran, and Iraq without threatening the Russian or Chinese deterrents—a concept promoted by former CIA director James Woolsey and known as "burros."[65] The verification difficulties associated with convincing Russia and China that the burros interceptors were not deployed over their territories, and that they could not be quickly repositioned, would be considerable, however.

The sheer scale of a GPALS system is also daunting. And even if successfully built and deployed, its space-based assets would probably be worthless against an enemy that could develop "fast-burn" rockets that would stop firing below fifty miles' altitude or so.[66]

Limited, Layered Systems

Layered defenses need not be thick. One could also imagine deploying a limited, layered defense that combined boost-phase capability with a

Table 4-2. *Estimated Acquisition Costs of Selected NMD Systems*

Billions of 2001 dollars

System	Total research, development, construction, and production cost
Clinton C1 capability	25
Clinton C2 capability	40
Clinton C3 capability	50
Aegis system	20
Boost-phase interceptors	15
Airborne laser	10
GPALS	150
Limited two-tier system	35

small U.S.-based system. European nations might collectively deploy one such similar system on their continent. Table 4-2 provides cost estimates for this and other NMD systems. The idea behind this system would be to provide as reliable protection as possible against a launch of a small number of enemy missiles, without threatening the larger deterrents of Russia or even China.[67]

Conclusion

The NMD system the Clinton administration proposed building has a major weakness: because it must work in the vacuum of outer space, where even light decoys would travel at the same speed as heavy warheads, it could almost surely be defeated by reasonably sophisticated enemy missiles. It might even be defeated by a relatively unsophisticated threat. A more promising technology, at least against small countries such as North Korea, Iraq, and even Iran, would appear to be boost-phase defense that would be based near the potential enemy country and used to shoot down threatening missiles early in their flight. This system's chief disadvantage is that it must be based in the right place ahead of time. But the geographic limitations of earth-based boost-phase defense may also be an important diplomatic and strategic strength, because they make it incapable of seriously threatening deterrents from physically large countries such as Russia and China.

The International Politics of Missile Defense

THE DECISION ON WHETHER to proceed with national missile defense involves more than assessing the threat and evaluating the feasibility of competing architectures. It also involves weighing the consequences that a national missile defense (NMD) deployment might have on international politics and America's interests abroad. It is not overstating things to say that missile defense has become, perhaps even more than it deserves to be, a matter of great interest around the globe. It is also true that a U.S. decision to deploy a national missile defense could cause more harm than good for U.S. security. For example, Americans might be worse off with a deployed NMD system if the price is a Russian decision to reverse some arms cuts and suspend collaborative work with the United States on consolidating and securing its oversized and aging nuclear stockpile.

A quick scan of newspaper headlines might suggest that national missile defense pits the United States against the rest of the world. Russia and China view themselves as potential targets of a U.S. NMD system and typically voice views ranging from deep skepticism to outright hostility to the idea. Many of America's NATO allies oppose it, and those that do not hope the issue will go away. But on closer inspection the image of unified world opposition fades, and a much more complex picture emerges. Russia acknowledges that the spread of ballistic missile technology poses a threat and says it might support some types of missile defense. America's

European allies tend to criticize missile defense, but their objections will likely diminish to the extent that Russia's concerns can be addressed. Other friends and allies—such as Israel, Japan, South Korea, Taiwan, Australia, and a few others—quietly or publicly support U.S. efforts to develop theater missile defense (TMD) and often also NMD.

Countries differ in how they evaluate missile defense not just because they have different relations with the United States but also because they inhabit different strategic environments. Moscow, with its thousand long-range ballistic missiles, looks at missile defense differently than China with only twenty. Israeli leaders who saw their country hit by Scud missiles in the 1991 Persian Gulf War, and Japanese officials who saw North Korea fire a long-range missile over their heads, think differently about defenses than German officials who see no threat. Because countries see missile defense through the prisms of their own national interests and regional threat assessments, it may be possible to craft a missile defense policy that garners substantial international support.

Why should the United States care how the international community might react? It is not because other countries should have a veto over American foreign policy or because the United States is trying to win the Miss Congeniality award. Rather, the United States needs to consider international reaction because other countries, whether Americans like it or not, can make the United States pay a strategic, military, and diplomatic price for building a missile defense. It is important to know what this price might be so Americans can decide whether they want to pay it—and whether there are some viable missile defense concepts that would keep it as low as possible.

Russia

Discussions about the international consequences of missile defense typically focus on Russia for understandable reasons. Russia not only possesses a nuclear arsenal equal to America's, but the two are partners to the Anti-Ballistic Missile (ABM) Treaty, which bars both countries from building national missile defenses. If the United States builds an NMD system, it will have to persuade Moscow to renegotiate the treaty or invoke its legal right to withdraw from the treaty on six months' notice.

That may be a Hobson's choice because Russia officially opposes modifying the ABM Treaty. Moscow insists that the treaty is crucial to preserving strategic stability and preventing a new arms race. Yet Moscow's behavior and strategic interests suggest that its opposition to modifying the treaty may not be immutable.

The mixed signals coming from Moscow explain why the Clinton administration believed that it might be possible to negotiate changes to the ABM Treaty. Russian officials had held discussions with the first Bush administration on the possibility of amending the treaty to permit national missile defense, talks the Clinton administration later halted. Then at the 1997 Helsinki summit Russian president Boris Yeltsin once again agreed to discuss modifying the ABM Treaty. The Clinton administration recognized that official Russian statements praising the importance of the ABM Treaty might simply be part of Moscow's bargaining strategy. And the administration calculated that Moscow knew the proposed U.S. system would not threaten its nuclear deterrent and would find negotiating small changes to the treaty preferable to watching the United States walk away from it entirely.

As a result, in early 2000, U.S. officials proposed to their Russian counterparts changing the treaty just enough to allow the United States to deploy one hundred interceptor missiles (the so-called C1 capability), and then beginning a second round of negotiations after March 2001 and the inauguration of a new American president on more far-reaching treaty modifications.[1] Many observers expected the administration to seek to persuade Russia to accept this proposal by giving Moscow something it wanted: deep cuts in both sides' nuclear arsenals. President Clinton never offered such a grand bargain, however, at least in part because senior U.S. military officials opposed cutting the U.S. strategic nuclear arsenal below 2,000 warheads.[2]

Without anything to offer Moscow, the talks on modifying the ABM Treaty—which might well have failed in any event—went nowhere. At the Moscow summit in June 2000, Russian president Vladimir Putin rebuffed the Clinton proposal. While acknowledging a "dangerous and growing threat" from weapons proliferation, Putin reaffirmed that for Russia the ABM Treaty was the "major key point in the whole strategic balance and for maintaining security." In a direct shot at the proposed U.S. missile defense, he insisted, "We're against having a cure which is worse than the disease."[3]

To drive the point home, Putin made a whirlwind diplomatic tour of European and Asian capitals in the weeks following the summit to criticize the Clinton administration's proposed NMD system. But in doing so, he muddied the waters about his ultimate goals. Not only did he acknowledge that the emerging ballistic missile powers posed a real threat, he proposed that Russia, the European Union, and NATO work together to build a pan-European missile defense.[4] The vagueness of Putin's proposal—in the days following the announcement Russian officials scrambled to flesh out his plan—along with the fact that he had not mentioned it at the Moscow summit, led some to dismiss it as a clumsy ploy aimed at splitting Europe from the United States.[5] Russia's ideas remained vague even in early 2001. At a minimum, though, Putin has conceded the basic principles behind the U.S. push for a missile defense.

If Russia acknowledges that the threat is real and is willing to consider missile defenses under some circumstances, why then refuse to renegotiate the ABM Treaty? Moscow's formal position is that NMD will threaten its nuclear deterrent. Indeed, many Russians believe that is the U.S. goal. As one general put it, the U.S. claim that it needs missile defense to protect itself from North Korea, Iran, or Iraq is "an argument for the naïve or the stupid. . . . This system will be directed against Russia and against China."[6] According to this view, the U.S. decisions to expand NATO, bomb Serbia during the Kosovo war, and criticize Moscow for the Chechnya war all demonstrate Washington's desire to establish what Defense Minister Igor Sergeyev calls "strategic domination."[7]

President Putin's acknowledgment that the emerging ballistic missile powers do pose a potential threat indicates that not all Russian officials insist on viewing U.S. motives as quite so sinister or domineering. Just as important, many Russian officials understand that no missile defense the United States is likely to build during the next decade will threaten their nuclear deterrent. Russia's nuclear forces would overwhelm even the most advanced version of the Clinton administration's proposed system (the C3 capability, with 250 interceptors and hence a realistic capacity to intercept fewer than 100 warheads). Earth-based boost-phase systems would pose no threat at all, and as chapter 4 discusses, space-based defenses remain many years away.

Russian officials might be engaging in worst-case analysis and worrying that the United States could launch a surprise first strike and use its missile defense to pick off any straggler warheads fired in a retaliatory attack. Even assuming U.S. officials were willing to gamble that Moscow would not fire on warning, before U.S. missiles could hit, Russian scientists express great confidence that its second strike, though perhaps small, would penetrate any U.S. defense.[8] It is possible that Russia's silo-based intercontinental ballistic missiles (ICBMs) might be its only nuclear forces to survive a surprise U.S. attack—and that even they might suffer attrition of up to 80 percent or so. Under a START II or START III framework, that could translate into no more than a couple hundred surviving warheads. But that is still far more than the number that might be defeated by the Clinton administration's proposed C3 capability.[9] It is also an enormous deterrent, given the power of nuclear weapons. As Sergei Ivanov, the secretary of Russia's Security Council and the man reputed to be Putin's closest national security adviser, publicly observed, even a Russian arsenal with 1,500 nuclear warheads "will be ample to penetrate through the national ABM system . . . the Americans hypothetically are going to create over the next 20–25 years."[10] Moreover, Russian scientists know that they can defeat the planned U.S. system with simple countermeasures that they probably already possess.

All that said, Russia is still worried. Not all of its officials may have the same confidence in Russian countermeasures that its scientists probably do. Russians also fear that once the United States has a global infrastructure for tracking missile trajectories and guiding interceptors to them, it could easily expand its defense—either in violation of treaty commitments, or after abrogating a future, modified version of the ABM Treaty and whatever numerical limits it imposed.[11] Their concern is probably most closely tied to the sophistication and scope of U.S. sensor capabilities—meaning the so-called C2 and C3 capabilities, which include numerous x-band radars and space-based infrared system (SBIRS) satellites.

Russia is also worried about the threat that missile defense poses to its international status. During the past decade Russia has given up its empire, ceded much of its former territory, and watched its economy collapse. Its last remaining claim to great power status is that it is America's equal as a nuclear superpower. Modifying the ABM Treaty would end that equality; Moscow cannot afford to launch an ambitious missile defense effort. As a former Soviet diplomat puts it, "If Russia were to simply withdraw from its position of nuclear equality with the U.S., it would fundamentally alter the global security landscape we have known for more than half a century. We would become a second-tier power, like France, or Britain."[12] Some would argue that the global security landscape has already been altered in this way (if not more drastically), but Russia may cling to vestiges of superpowerdom for as long as it can anyhow.

At the same time, Russia's refusal to renegotiate the ABM Treaty reflects the fact that thus far the United States has not given it a reason to agree. The Clinton administration's strategy in dealing with Moscow on the ABM Treaty emphasized the "here's-what-you-can-do-for-me"; it was silent on "here's-what-I-can-do-for-you." By contrast, saying "nyet" to the Clinton administration served Putin's domestic political interests. It enabled him to build favor with the Russian elite as well as ordinary Russians by portraying himself as a staunch defender of Russian interests who refused to give in to the demands of an overbearing America. Much of Putin's initial rhetoric as Russian president affirmed Russia's continued greatness even amid economic and budgetary woes, and his initial opposition to a U.S. NMD might be best understood as part of that broader political approach. Finally, the test failures that plagued the Clinton administration's proposed NMD system relieved any pressure Putin might have faced to cut a deal on the ABM Treaty before the United States withdrew.

All this suggests that the Clinton administration's failure to reach agreement with Moscow tells us little about the Bush administration's chances to strike a deal. Given Russia's strategic position, it might be willing to modify the ABM Treaty. Much depends on the kinds of modifications the United States insists on and what it offers in return. Moscow's bottom line is hard to discern; it may well be that Putin himself has not yet decided what it would take to make a deal.

What is clear is that the United States has an interest in striking a deal on the ABM Treaty or otherwise mitigating Russian objections to a missile defense. Although Moscow cannot stop a U.S. decision to deploy, it could respond by taking steps with relatively little effort that would negate other U.S. goals and potentially leave the United States less secure. To begin with, Russia could retaliate by abrogating other arms control treaties. Putin himself has vowed that Russia "will withdraw not only from the Start II treaty, but from the whole system of treaties on the limitation and control of strategic and conventional weapons."[13] The commander of Russia's Strategic Rocket Forces similarly warned that Russia would pull out of the Intermediate-Range Nuclear Forces (INF) Treaty if the United States proceeded with building an NMD system.[14]

Whether Moscow would go so far as to abrogate all arms control treaties is questionable. Any decision to abrogate the INF Treaty, which required the Soviet Union (and subsequently Russia) and the United States to eliminate all medium-range missiles, would alienate European capitals at a time when Moscow is interested in securing European support for its troubled economy. But a decision to abrogate the START treaties, or to adhere to them only selectively, might have considerable appeal. Doing so would allow Moscow to backtrack on its pledge to eliminate MIRVed missiles, which would enable it to maintain a much larger nuclear arsenal without incurring substantially greater costs. This obviously runs counter to both countries' commitments to cut their nuclear forces.

Perhaps an end to the START process would not in and of itself be too high a price to pay for effective missile defense; that point can be debated. But the damage might not stop there. Russia might resist any future U.S. suggestions to reduce nuclear alert levels. Indeed, it might even place its missile force on a higher state of alert than is the case today—possibly, for example, surging more of its troubled submarine fleet to sea despite a danger of accidents in order to increase the odds that some vessels would survive any preemptive U.S. strike. Moscow might take this step to give itself a hedge against the possibility that the United States succeeded in building a highly effective national missile defense and began contemplating a first strike. This is not to suggest that Russian officials would see such a possibility as likely; they almost certainly would not. But then again, U.S. officials would not look with equanimity on a Russian decision to expand its nuclear capabilities vis-à-vis those of the United States. So it would not be surprising if a country like Russia went the extra mile to assure itself of a robust deterrent against a former rival—even if doing so entailed dangers to the United States and itself.

Third, Moscow might respond by refusing to cooperate on other issues that matter to the United States. An obvious candidate would be nonproliferation. Russia might choose to expand its nuclear and ballistic-missile ties to countries such as North Korea and Iran. It could go as far as to sell them countermeasures that could defeat any midcourse U.S. interceptors. Moscow could also block U.S. efforts at the UN Security Council and make common cause with other U.S. critics.

Perhaps worst of all, Russia could suspend bilateral programs designed to downsize and secure its dilapidated nuclear facilities—increasing the odds that nuclear weapons and nuclear materials could fall into the wrong hands through bribery or theft. Although Nunn-Lugar and related efforts have helped Russia consolidate and secure most of its nuclear weapons, the same cannot be said for excess nuclear materials including plutonium and highly enriched uranium. Moreover, many Russian weapons scientists remain in a state of limbo, temporarily employed by U.S.-Russian or other similar programs but not yet possessing sustainable employment in the post–Soviet economy. So there is a great deal more to do. Alas, many Russians already see these collaborative threat-reduction programs as a clever disguise for U.S. espionage and would be happy to see them stopped. Such sentiment could snowball in the wake of a U.S. withdrawal from the ABM Treaty.[15]

These are the risks. Can the United States minimize them?[16] There are probably ways to reduce Russian anger, and Russia's reactions, in the face of a U.S. NMD deployment. Certainly, designing a missile architecture that poses minimal threat, or even potential threat, to Russia's deterrent is critical. Further steps the United States might take range from offering deeper cuts in nuclear forces and even beginning some of them unilaterally, to taking most or all of its nuclear forces off alert, to otherwise minimizing the threat Russia feels from the West. That latter goal might be served by delaying any consideration of NATO expansion to the Baltics or Ukraine for a significant number of years. Greater economic support for Russia, including not simply loans but grants or debt forgiveness, may also be appropriate if and when President Putin implements an economic reform plan with good prospects of success. Such aid should be given even if Russia continues its low-grade war in Chechnya. Although Moscow's chosen military tactics there have been excessively brutal, its basic cause in Chechnya is not unreasonable, and in any case the conflict should not be allowed to impede progress on all other dimensions of the West's extremely important relationship with Russia. After all, helping Russia strengthen its economy may be the best means of preventing other possible Chechnya-style conflicts within the federation and of reducing the risks that Russia's nuclear weapons or materials could be stolen or purchased by foreign elements. Together, these types of measures may improve the general U.S.-Russian relationship and alleviate Russian security fears sufficiently to convince Moscow that an American NMD system should not be viewed as threatening or even unfriendly.

China

Like Russia, China staunchly opposed the Clinton administration's proposed NMD system and its efforts to revise the ABM Treaty.[17] Chinese officials insisted that "any amendment, or abolishing of the [ABM] treaty, will bring a halt to nuclear disarmament now between the Russians and the Americans, and in the future will halt multilateral disarmament as well."[18] In December 1999, the UN General Assembly overwhelmingly approved a nonbinding resolution that China cosponsored with Russia and Belarus calling for the preservation of the ABM Treaty and urging nations to resist pressures to build national missile defenses.[19] In July 2000, China joined with Russia to issue a joint statement that described the Clinton administration's proposed NMD system as having "the most grave adverse consequences not only for the security of Russia, China and other countries, but also for the security of the United States and global strategic stability."[20]

If anything, Beijing opposes a U.S. national missile defense even more vehemently than Moscow does. The reasons are simple: China is more vulnerable to a missile defense in technical terms, and it is more likely to wind up in conflict with the United States based on strategic realities. As discussed above, Russia will almost certainly be able to overwhelm any missile defense the United States builds during the next decade or two. China, however, possesses only about twenty missiles that can reach American soil. Thus, the Clinton administration's NMD system, though limited relative to the Russian nuclear arsenal, could, in theory, nullify the Chinese nuclear deterrent. (Again, an earth-based boost-phase system would not threaten China's ICBM force, with the possible exception of any missiles based near its coast.) U.S. assurances that the Clinton system was aimed at North Korea, Iran, and Iraq rather than China did not reassure Beijing. As one Chinese official put it, "That doesn't matter, the consequences are still terrible for us."[21]

It is understandable, then, that China views missile defense with alarm. Having had some type of nuclear deterrent—even if not a highly survivable one—against the United States for decades, Beijing would naturally regret running a risk of losing it as a matter of general principle. China has always shown restraint in its strategic nuclear aspirations, but it probably values its ability to strike the other nuclear powers as, if nothing else, an important symbol of its great-power status and deterrent of last resort against the improbability of any direct foreign aggression. Nation-states do not like to be defanged of military capabilities by countries they do not trust.[22]

And China's interest in being able to deter the United States is not hypothetical. The two countries' differences over Taiwan mean that a direct military confrontation is always possible. China clearly hopes that the United States would elect to stay out of any conflict between Beijing and Taipei. But the United States probably would not.

Although the U.S. policy on whether to aid Taiwan is deliberately murky and would undoubtedly be influenced by the circumstances under which a conflict began, U.S. policy leans toward intervention. Nonetheless, there is enough uncertainty in the U.S. position that the simple existence of a Chinese nuclear capability against the United States might help dissuade Washington from intervening militarily. At least, that is Beijing's hope. Witness the famed 1995 comment by a senior Chinese general to a former American envoy: "In the end, you care more about Los Angeles than you do about Taipei."[23] Whether that was an intemperate remark by one Chinese official, or something closer to official policy, is unclear. In any case, China would naturally have grave reservations—whether or not its leaders ever really thought they would use nuclear weapons in a Taiwan crisis—about a U.S. NMD system large and capable enough that it could theoretically intercept the entire Chinese deterrent.[24] Even if China knew it would never be so foolish as to consider launching an ICBM at the United States during a war over Taiwan, it might be troubled by the perception that it had lost coercive leverage over Washington. From a U.S. perspective, that might be all well and good—except that China would probably not allow the situation to stand and would take steps to restore the impression that it had a viable nuclear capability against the United States.

At the same time, China's views on NMD are intertwined with its views on TMD—in part because the same U.S. defense systems are sometimes discussed as candidates for carrying out both missions. Again, the core issue is Taiwan. China believes its theater-range missiles can help to prevent Taipei from declaring independence. Beijing's ability to seize Taiwan in an amphibious invasion is highly dubious, and likely to remain that way—even if U.S. armed forces did not participate in any conflict. China might use submarines to blockade the island, but the U.S. Navy, teamed with Taiwan's own armed forces, could break it, perhaps inflicting considerable losses on China's navy in the process.[25] Ballistic missiles may therefore be Beijing's best coercive instrument, as its decision to fire missiles near Taiwan in 1995 and 1996 suggested. Taiwan's president Lee Teng-hui subsequently refrained from provocative actions until 1999; in 2000, Taiwan's new president, Chen Shui-bien, also backed off his party's pro-independence stance when he took office.

A missile's perceived coercive utility explains why China has been deploying some 50 of them a year along its coast near Taiwan.[26] It now stations at least 200 ballistic missiles, presumed to be armed with conventional warheads, in range of Taiwan and apparently intends to triple that force within five years.[27] Taiwan has some Patriot PAC-2 missile defenses, but these systems can defend an area of only about five to ten miles on a dimension, meaning that each military base or city requires a separate system for its protection. This is a losing proposition; even though Taiwan is a rather small island, it would take dozens if not hundreds of radars and missile batteries to protect all of its cities, key economic infrastructure, and military bases. If China wished to strike Taiwan today, it could do so with a high probability that most missiles would reach their targets.

But what would that accomplish? Chinese missiles are not highly accurate and would make poor weapons for hitting key military infrastructure, assuming that they would be deployed only with conventional warheads. They are too inaccurate to do much damage to airfields, ports, or other such infrastructure, and will remain that way for many years to come (even advanced ballistic missiles are not nearly as accurate as cruise missiles or airplanes). They are accurate enough to strike cities and sow terror—though as chapter 3 points out, conventionally tipped missiles are not extremely devastating weapons. If detonated near reasonably well-built buildings, they would be unlikely to cause their collapse. Unless one detonated at a busy intersection or amid a crowd, casualties per missile would probably number no more than a couple dozen on average. To be sure, multiplied by 200 missiles, that translates into a substantial toll in dead and injured. But by the standards of war, it is rather limited. So China's desire to build up its missile force further, while counter to Taiwan's interests, is not without a certain logic given Beijing's perceived need to prevent Taipei from slipping entirely out of its grasp. As much as Washington may not like the buildup, it is unlikely the United States and Taiwan can fully counter it.

It is largely because China wants to protect or even expand its ability to threaten Taiwan with theater missiles that it opposes the sale of U.S. TMD systems to Taiwan. The United States, however, has not ruled out selling Taipei improved defense systems in the future—a point the Clinton administration emphasized to Beijing.[28] Theater high-altitude area defense (THAAD) would greatly improve Taipei's defensive capabilities; even Patriot PAC-3 and Navy area defense (also known as Navy lower tier) would be marked improvements over the Patriots that Taiwan now has. Probably the most difficult system for the Chinese to swallow is the Navy theater-wide (NTW) defense. It is the most capable, most prestigious, and most expensive (assuming that Aegis-class ships need to be purchased as well).

Even THAAD and NTW would have great difficulty defending Taiwan against a dedicated Chinese attack, however—as would a boost-phase

NMD system used in a TMD mode. The first issue is sheer numbers; to shoot down 200 missiles the United States or Taiwan would need to fire at least 400 interceptors, and probably many more, as chapter 2 discusses. Even then a dozen or more missiles might penetrate the defense given the likely reliabilities of the interceptors. But the situation is worse than that for the defense. China could concentrate its attack on one part of Taiwan or the other and force the local defenses to fire all their missiles (what the military calls "getting Winchestered"); nothing would be left to shoot down subsequent Chinese missiles. China could also use bomblets that would disperse ordance before the interceptor missile could do its job.

Although it is sometimes trumpeted as a savior, NTW would not solve these problems. Taiwan is too large for a single ship wielding NTW defense to protect the entire island from Chinese attack. Additional ships could be deployed, but individually and collectively they would be vulnerable to getting Winchestered. Also, as chapter 4 notes, NTW, like any midcourse interceptor, is vulnerable to countermeasures, which China probably possesses and will likely improve in the future. Finally, and perhaps most simply, the short-range missiles that China could fire from bases closest to Taiwan might never leave the atmosphere, which means that NTW, which must intercept warheads in space, would be powerless to stop them. Similarly, NMD boost-phase interceptors, even if deployed near Taiwan, could probably not react quickly enough to reach the short-range missiles during their short burn times.

So believing that Taiwan could gain a reliable, leakproof shield against Chinese missiles is illusory. But it might be able to limit damage with TMD. It could also stand a chance of shooting down a limited Chinese missile attack, something Beijing might be tempted to try. And it could at least symbolically help Taipei make a statement that it was not going to be easily intimidated by Beijing.

Indeed, the symbolism probably matters more than the military issues in other ways. Greater collaboration between American and Taiwanese military officials would be needed if Taiwan acquired advanced TMD. That collaboration would itself raise Taiwan's international stature. To some, it could have the trappings of partially rekindling the U.S.-Taiwan military alliance that Washington ended in the 1970s. China would fear that Taiwan would gain confidence in the dependability of an American military response under such circumstances, increasing its likelihood of declaring independence and reducing Beijing's coercive leverage far more than any TMD system would probably be able to.[29]

China's military and political calculations, then, make it likely that it will be an implacable critic of any U.S. foray into national missile defense and any U.S. sales of TMD to friends and allies in East Asia. But so what? The United States does not owe China the right to strike the American homeland, or the territory of U.S. friends and allies, with its ballistic missiles. This view is not confined to the right wing of the American political spectrum; centrist thinkers like the editorial board of the *Washington Post* also make this argument.[30] That NMD and TMD threaten Beijing's interests is not reason enough to stop the programs, and China's expressions of displeasure by themselves are unlikely to persuade Americans to drop the idea of missile defense.[31]

The decisive question is whether China could and would retaliate in ways that could counter or even outweigh the benefits of having missile defense. China clearly has the means. Like Russia, it can make its displeasure felt in many ways. The most obvious response, and one apparently judged highly likely by U.S. intelligence analysts, would be to accelerate its current nuclear modernization program, outfitting its missiles with multiple warheads and advanced countermeasures.[32] Beijing could also take a step that it has not, to date, and place its own nuclear forces on a high state of alert to reduce their vulnerability to preemptive attack. Regrettably, that would also increase the likelihood of an accidental, unauthorized, or erroneous launch.

Beijing could also attempt to put pressure on the United States by expanding production of its medium-range missiles, which are more numerous and cheaper to build, to put American friends such as Taiwan and Japan at risk. It could explore means for delivering nuclear warheads or other weapons of mass destruction against the United States in other ways—with cruise missiles launched from unmarked merchant ships, or by special agents in the United States (most probably armed with biological agents), or through some other approach. Given Beijing's resources, it could probably succeed with at least one such effort.

Another tack China could take would be to increase support for Iran and Pakistan's nuclear and missile programs, thereby increasing the threat the United States faces. Indeed, it may already have begun doing so.[33] China could also sell countermeasure technology to any country seeking to penetrate a midcourse antimissile system. From Beijing's vantage point, such steps might force the United States to expend more of its missile-defense efforts on building a reliable shield against such smaller threats rather than against its own arsenal. China might even help North Korea build a bigger missile arsenal to force the United States to deploy more boost-phase interceptors near North Korea, which could divert funds from possible work on developing other NMD systems—such as a space-based boost-phase defense of greater potential use against China.

Finally, to the extent it was prepared to practice "linkage," China could retaliate by becoming more disagreeable on other issues that matter to Washington. To some extent it has already begun doing so. The UN Conference on Disarmament's effort to negotiate a multilateral treaty to stop the production of fissile material has foundered over Beijing's insistence that the talks focus on controlling space-based weapons, which might form part of a future missile defense system.[34] China might conceivably block U.S. initiatives in other multilateral organizations, including the World Trade Organization. Of potentially greatest concern to American domestic economic interests, Beijing might steer government contracts away from American firms to bring pressure to bear on Washington. Perhaps worst of all, China might end its efforts to help convince North Korea to cooperate with the United States and South Korea in the security sphere and to open up its society. It is not clear how much influence Beijing has over Pyongyang, but for a very long time it has had considerable access to North Korean leaders, who probably take its counsel seriously.

Given the importance that Beijing places on retaining a nuclear deterrent and preserving its ability to attack Taiwan, its willingness to punish the United States if its interests are harmed should not be doubted. For that reason, the United States stands to gain little by engaging in an offensive-defensive competition with Beijing. Even though the United States could afford such an arms race far more easily than China, there is little reason to believe it would wind up with a defense capable of defeating a modernized and expanded Chinese arsenal. The effort to build a defense against China or to eliminate China's ability to threaten Taiwan will not produce a lasting U.S. advantage and could well harm U.S. security. As one Chinese official put it, "Instead of enhancing your security, your security policy will be further compromised. The United States will play the role of a fire brigade. Rushing from one place to another to extinguish fires."[35] China's own ability to rush about from one place to another—and most notably, to Taiwan—might be slowed somewhat if a nuclear competition with the United States diverts resources away from modernizing its conventional military power. But then again, such a competition might lead China to increase overall defense spending in a belief that all-out military competition with the United States had become likely.

The bottom line is that Beijing's objections should not dissuade the United States from deploying TMD or NMD, either for itself or its allies. China is using missiles in a strident way vis-à-vis Taiwan. It also stubbornly refuses to acknowledge the right of the United States to defend itself against the potential long-range missile forces of countries such as Iraq and North Korea with extremist political systems and aggressive recent histories.

By the same token, however, the United States should not pursue goals that are excessive and unattainable. The United States, which faces missile threats from a wide range of actors around the world, should purchase whatever TMD systems it considers necessary and effective regardless of Beijing's possible objections. But it should be more circumspect in its TMD sales to Taiwan, since excessive sales could give Taiwan a sense of impunity that could lead it to take provocative actions and could also spark an action-reaction arms race spiral between China and Taiwan without guaranteeing Taiwan any net protection in the end. Sales of advanced Patriot systems, and possibly someday THAAD, probably make more sense than sales of the high-profile NTW system (THAAD may work better than NTW too, given that it is less vulnerable to decoys). Washington should also do what is possible to deploy an NMD system that does not threaten China's deterrent. Although many Americans might desire a shield against a possible Chinese ICBM attack, it almost certainly cannot be achieved given China's ability to take measures to defeat it. Even worse, the act of trying to build an NMD capability against China would worsen U.S.-China relations significantly, while increasing the odds that China would help the likes of North Korea gain the technical capability to overcome whatever U.S. missile defense system is built.

America's Friends and Allies

America's friends and allies are often described as opposing U.S. proposals to build a national missile defense. Although majority opinion is clearly against the Clinton administration's proposed approach, and skeptical of NMD in general, the story is more complex. America's NATO allies are mostly hostile to the idea, but significant differences exist across European capitals. At the same time, American allies in Asia tend to support defenses—and they are strong supporters of theater defenses, which they see as important to their own security. The same holds true for U.S. friends in the Mideast and Persian Gulf. Again, these differences primarily reflect the different strategic environments that countries inhabit. And in pushing ahead with a missile defense deployment that balances the desire to gain protection on the one hand against the possibility of provoking Russian or Chinese responses that would degrade U.S. and allied security on the other, U.S. officials need to keep these differences in mind.

The NATO Allies

The NATO allies include eighteen countries, and 300 million people, so it is misleading to speak of a single "allied view" on national missile defense. Most NATO governments believe that NMD is a bad idea.[36] Many of their citizens agree, though Canadians are an exception to this generalization.[37] However, anti-NMD sentiment is not very strong among European publics—the current NMD debate has not generated nearly the interest that nuclear debates did in Europe in the 1980s.[38]

The depth of opposition within NATO to national missile defense varies from country to country. France and Germany are perhaps the most skeptical of missile defense, while Britain has tried to avoid publicly criticizing U.S. plans.[39] Indeed, while the British Foreign Office opposes national missile defense, the Ministry of Defence is more sympathetic.[40] William Hague, the leader of the opposition Conservative Party, has endorsed U.S. plans to build an NMD system.[41] So do some prominent individuals and groups in Britain.[42] Among NATO allies, Britain takes its security responsibilities in the Persian Gulf the most seriously, perhaps explaining why it supports or at least tolerates the idea that missile defenses against the likes of Iran and Iraq may be desirable. Again, U.S. allies' willingness to countenance NMD depends largely on how acute they assess the global ballistic missile threat to be—and especially how acute they consider the threat to their own territory.

European critics have attacked U.S. national missile defense plans on many fronts. Four criticisms are common. A British scholar, Charles Grant, explained them well. First, Europeans

are more sanguine than the Americans about the potential threat: North Korea is a long way from Europe, while Iran seems to be becoming democratic. Second, they regard the ABM Treaty as a cornerstone of international disarmament agreements, and they do not want the U.S. to provoke the Russians by disregarding it. Third, if NMD prompted Russia and China to improve their ABM systems, the British and French deterrents could be devalued. Fourth, they worry that if the U.S. had NMD, and Europe had no equivalent, their security could be "de-coupled:" rogue states might try to blackmail Europe rather than the U.S.[43]

Few Europeans (or Canadians) subscribe to all these criticisms, which are not all consistent or necessarily correct, and some of which, in the words of one European analyst, are more "Pavlovian" than thoughtful.[44] For example, if North Korea and Iran have no hostile intent, then Europe has little reason to fear that an American decision to build a national missile defense will make it a target of blackmail.[45] It may also come as a surprise to many Europeans to discover that Europe and the continental United States are essentially equidistant from North Korea. (Alaska and Hawaii are much closer.) If a North Korean ICBM can reach New York or Washington, it can reach London or Paris; if it can reach Seattle, it can reach Vancouver. Finally, the common complaint that missile defense could "decouple" European security from the United States by making Americans feel so well protected that they no longer need trouble themselves about the security of their allies is a bit bizarre. Americans are indeed somewhat worried about the long-range missile threat—but it is hardly their only, or even their main, security worry. Therefore, deploying a defense against that possible threat will surely not radically reshape their overall view about global security, or the desirable role of the United States in its various alliances. Overall, NMD would probably strengthen coupling somewhat since Americans would have less reason to fear for their own security when they came to the aid of an ally.

NATO complaints about missile defense do, however, highlight two important concerns for the United States. The first is that the allies' objections to national missile defense will largely stand or fall on how Washington handles relations with Moscow (assuming that their perception of the missile threat does not change substantially in the years ahead). European and Canadian governments greatly value stable ties with Russia, and a rash decision by Washington to leave the ABM Treaty will probably strain U.S. relations with allied governments while possibly poisoning their publics' attitudes on the issue. Conversely, as French foreign minister Hubert Vedrine has noted, a negotiated agreement with Moscow would likely deflate European and Canadian opposition, even if it did not eliminate it entirely.[46] (This argument cuts both ways, however; Russians know that if they object to U.S. NMD, the NATO allies will probably take their side, reducing the pressure on Moscow to cut a deal.)[47]

European attitudes toward missile defense are not just alliance issues. They are also critical to the U.S. ability to deploy the Clinton administration's planned NMD system. Any earth-based midcourse interceptor depends on overseas radar to track the flight of incoming missiles. The Clinton administration's proposed missile defense requires upgrading existing early warning radars at Fylingdales, England and Thule, Greenland (which is Danish territory) and eventually building new radars. Without these radars, Secretary of Defense William Cohen told the Senate in 2000, "You can't see the missiles coming. Therefore, your interceptors really are not worth very much."[48] (The Navy is reportedly investigating whether these early warning radars could instead be placed on ships, though sea-based radars would be costly and possibly vulnerable to attack).[49] But London and Copenhagen might block new construction if the United States decides to withdraw from the ABM Treaty. The British Parliament's Foreign Affairs Committee urged the British government to inform the United States that "it cannot necessarily assume unqualified U.K. cooperation with U.S. plans to deploy NMD in the event of unilateral U.S. abrogation of the ABM treaty."[50] The Danish government says it "continues to desire that the use of the Thule Radar does not contravene international agreements in force."[51] It has stated that it will take into account the views of Greenlanders, and Greenland's prime minister says Greenland will oppose upgrading the radar facility "if it resulted in increased tension and world destabilization."[52] Similarly, Canadian objections to NMD could complicate long-standing U.S.-Canada cooperation on North American Air Defense (NORAD).

The crucial question also arises of whether the United States can consider itself defended in a meaningful strategic sense if its security partners are not. The 1949 NATO Treaty obliges the United States to defend its allies in Europe and Canada. Beyond this legal obligation, the United States has powerful moral and strategic reasons to defend its allies, not the least of which is that tens of thousands of Americans live in NATO countries and are vulnerable to attack. As a result, the wisdom of leaving U.S. allies exposed and thereby making them a more tempting target for attack, as the Clinton administration's proposed NMD system would do, is questionable. To repeat a point chapter 3 makes, if a country is willing to threaten the United States directly—the prime justification for building a national missile defense—it would probably be willing to coerce the United States indirectly by threatening London or Paris.[53] That would be even more true if British or French troops were participating in a U.S.-led coalition that was waging war against a country such as Iraq, Iran, or North Korea.

The difficult question is how to protect Europe. (Virtually any NMD system that covers the United States will also cover Canada.) Geography limits the utility of TMD systems. Britain, for example, is 4,000 miles away from some points in southeastern Iran, or twice the range limit that applies to testing TMD systems. Even Italy is more than 2,000 miles away from the most distant parts of Iran. If European allies are to be protected against a future Iraqi or Iranian long-range missile force, some of them at least will need to buy a system that the United States would define as NMD—be it the Clinton administration's program, a related European system, or a boost-phase concept. That fact needs to be recognized in any modification of the ABM Treaty, since the treaty presently bans the transfer of strategic missile defense systems to third parties or the basing of such defenses on their territories.

A decision to defend Europe also raises the question of who should pay. European defense budgets are stagnant or falling, and Europeans are far less concerned than their American counterparts over potential conflicts in places like the Persian Gulf. Moreover, some worry that a push for missile defense will steal resources from the European Security and Defense Policy (ESDP), the European Union's effort to improve its collective capability to project conventional military force beyond its members' borders to places such as the Balkans. If would be regrettable if the ESDP were weakened because it is very much in the U.S. interest if done effectively and seriously. While European allies could, and probably should, increase defense spending (or cut excessive military manpower) to make that trade-off unnecessary, in reality such steps will remain politically difficult and perhaps unachievable.[54] Many Europeans recognize the trade-off between NMD and ESDP—and they resent the United States for risking the latter to promote the former.[55]

East Asia

America's friends and allies in East Asia for the most part do not share Europe's hostility toward a U.S. national missile defense. In the weeks leading up to the G-8 summit in July 2000, the Japanese government resisted pressure from other G-8 countries to criticize U.S. NMD plans. Its official position is admittedly short of direct support for NMD; to be precise, Tokyo "understands" the American interest in developing a national missile defense. But actions speak louder than words, and Japan is working with the United States to develop a possible TMD system that could be used to defend Japan.[56] Since advanced TMD systems could defend all of Japan's territory, Tokyo is moving toward accepting the legitimacy of the idea of national missile defense—at least for itself. If the potential missile threat to the American homeland becomes more concrete and acute, it is therefore hard to believe that Tokyo would oppose U.S. efforts to defend its national territory.

South Korea does not own missile defenses, owing to resource constraints and more immediate threats such as North Korean artillery, but it supports U.S. deployments of TMD on its territory. It may have some concerns about offending China with TMD, but that has not stopped it from allowing U.S. Patriot deployments against the North Korean missile threat.[57] Seoul appears ambivalent about NMD, given its desire to promote good relations with China, Russia, and North Korea. But during a March 2001 visit to Washington, South Korean president Kim Dae Jung acknowledged that in principle missile defenses could be an important element of an allied response to missile proliferation. Taiwan has not taken a formal position on national missile defense. But it is believed to support the U.S. effort. It certainly supports the general notion of missile defense for itself and American forces in the East Asia region, even if its immediate concerns focus more on TMD than on U.S. NMD. Taiwan has Patriot PAC-2 missile defenses and would like to acquire more advanced TMD.

Further south, Australian officials privately assured the Clinton administration that the United States could use a key satellite relay station that the two countries operate jointly at Pine Gap in central Australia as part of its NMD system.[58] The facility would play a crucial role in the U.S. ability to provide early warning of a missile attack.

This greater receptivity to an American decision to deploy a national missile defense reflects the different strategic situation East Asian countries face. For most of them, the prospect of a missile attack is not a theoretical possibility but a threat that exists here and now. South Korea and Taiwan are already within reach of short-range ballistic missiles from North Korea and China. North Korea's decision in August 1998 to test-fire a long-range version of its Taepo Dong-1 missile over Japan drove home to the Japanese people their vulnerability to a North Korean attack. Australia does not currently face a pressing ballistic missile threat, but it has a long history of working closely with the United States on defense matters. The Pine Gap facility played a key role during the Persian Gulf

War in detecting the launch of Iraqi Scud missiles (though NMD is admittedly a different matter).

An important question, of course, is whether support in Asia for a U.S. NMD system will persist if Russia and China escalate their rhetorical war against it. Australian support is not axiomatic. Officials in the opposition Labor Party criticized the governing Liberal-National Party for agreeing to work with the United States, arguing that doing so will poison Canberra's relations with Beijing and possibly provoke China into targeting Australia with its long-range missiles. Should the Labor Party come to power—Australia's next general election is scheduled for October 2001—it may halt cooperation with the United States on missile defense.[59] It was a Labor government, however, that allowed the United States to use the Pine Gap facility to track Iraqi Scud missile launches during the Gulf War.

Support—or at least "understanding"—for a U.S. NMD deployment is likely to be more robust in Japan. Thus far, Japanese political parties seem unruffled by Beijing's denunciations of national missile defense and its criticisms of Tokyo for collaborating with the United States on NTW. No doubt the vivid memory of North Korea's Taepo Dong launch and its arsenal of medium-range No Dong missiles explains Japan's stance. But then again, Japan's support for a U.S. NMD system and interest in working jointly on TMD systems might evaporate in the absence of a North Korean threat. Japan is currently less inclined and less likely to build TMD to defend itself against China—though that could change depending on future Chinese behavior and the evolution of Japanese security thinking. (In any event, Japan is unlikely to deploy its own NTW system to help defend Taiwan; current interpretations of the Japanese constitution would prevent an active Japanese role in such a conflict, even if Tokyo did elect to provide logistical and base support to U.S. forces taking part.)

As for South Korea, its views are likely to be heavily influenced by its budding rapprochement with Pyongyang. Should that continue, Kim Dae Jung at some point may consider the likelihood of the North developing long-range missiles small enough that he would oppose U.S. efforts to deploy a system aimed at a potential North Korean threat if still in office at the time. But a good deal of ground still has to be covered on the peninsula before that is the case—and even if it is, South Korea is hard-headed enough about security that it may still support U.S. NMD on other grounds (such as the possibility of Mideast threats).

In summary, Washington's conduct of missile defense diplomacy with Moscow and Beijing will shape how its European and Asian allies react. If the United States succeeds in diminishing Russian and Chinese objections, or failing that, is perceived to have made reasonable efforts to accommodate them, allied reaction is likely to be less negative and in some cases even supportive. But if Washington acts presumptively and unilaterally—especially if the threat appears to be declining—it is likely to fuel existing allied opposition and possibly even destroy the support it already has.

South Asia

The prospect that the United States will deploy a national missile defense has also prompted speculation about its consequences for South Asia. In the view of many experts, including many U.S. intelligence analysts, the Indian subcontinent is the region most likely to experience nuclear warfare.[60] Indeed, before President Clinton traveled to India and Pakistan in mid-2000, he called the Indian subcontinent "the most dangerous place in the world today."[61] Many critics argue that a U.S. national missile defense will only make matters worse.

The reasons to worry about the Indian subcontinent are plain. India and Pakistan have fought three wars in their history, and the chief source of those conflicts, the divided state of Kashmir, remains as contested as ever. Pakistan's active support for Kashmiri insurgents continues to inflame tensions between the two countries. They fought another border war in 1999, the so-called Kargil conflict—only a year after both went overtly nuclear, with India testing five nuclear devices and Pakistan claiming to have tested six.[62]

As serious as the Indo-Pakistani nuclear rivalry is for the countries and peoples involved, is it relevant to the U.S. missile defense debate? After all, India and Pakistan are geographically and geostrategically rather isolated in the world; none of the other nuclear powers has come to their aid in past conflicts, none has a security treaty with them, and with the exception of China, none has ever fought either one. Moreover, with the cold war over, the United States is far less likely to inject its armed forces into South Asian disputes as it did in 1971, for example, when it deployed an aircraft carrier to the Indian Ocean during the Indo-Pakistani war to reassure Pakistan and discourage India and its ally, the Soviet Union.

However, NMD critics and even the U.S. intelligence community point to at least one possible linkage between U.S. missile defense deployments and South Asia: a domino effect beginning with China and then extending to India and Pakistan.[63] The logic is as follows. China will respond to U.S. TMD and NMD deployments by expanding its nuclear arsenal. New Delhi might respond to the Chinese buildup with one of its own—and that could convince Pakistan to build and deploy a larger arsenal than it otherwise might. In short, if Americans decide to protect themselves they could intensify an arms race among countries that are too close to the brink of war for comfort—not to mention too poor to afford an arms race without further impoverishing their own peoples.

These fears cannot be fully dismissed, but they do appear overwrought. Even if China expands its arsenal more than it would otherwise in response to a U.S. NMD deployment, that may not affect India very much. China had a nuclear arsenal for more than three decades before India overtly pursued its own, suggesting that any linkage is indirect. More important, even its Hindu nationalist government, as well as most of its major schools of strategic thought, do not favor outright competition with China in the nuclear sphere. Most Indians wish to maintain a certain moral high ground in their nuclear posture, even if they have sacrificed much of it with their recent tests.[64] Furthermore, India cannot easily afford an arms competition, and it is hard to see the potential utility of nuclear weapons in any future disputes with Beijing. The balance of forces in this Indian debate could change over time, but it would have to change quite a bit to make the numerical size of China's nuclear force decisive in New Delhi's nuclear force planning decisions.[65] As for India's competition with Pakistan, the two have been aggressively developing ballistic missile technology in the absence of any U.S. missile defense system, and that competition is likely to persist regardless of what the United States decides on missile defense. In sum, a U.S. NMD deployment may drive up nuclear force levels in China and South Asia a bit, but it is unlikely to precipitate anything resembling a self-perpetuating arms race.

Some supporters of U.S. missile defense offer an entirely different take on the impact such programs might have on South Asian stability. They argue that such defenses, particularly sea-based missile defense, would make the region safer. If a crisis erupted on the subcontinent, the United States could deploy a sea-based missile defense off the coast of India and Pakistan and pledge to shoot down any missiles that were fired.[66] This idea has immediate appeal. Who wouldn't want to be able to shoot down a nuclear-armed missile as it headed to New Delhi (a city of 10 million people) or Islamabad (1 million people)?

Unfortunately, geography and physics get in the way. New Delhi and Islamabad are only about 300 miles from each other's territories; both are at least 700 miles from the sea. An offensive ballistic missile would cover 300 miles in less than five minutes (figure 2-1). Make the generous assumption that it would take the U.S. ship only a minute to learn of the offensive missile's launch and to fire its interceptor. Even the most advanced sea-based missile interceptors now envisioned could travel no more than 600 miles in the next four minutes. (This calculation assumes roughly a minute for acceleration and a final speed of almost three miles per second). So the interceptor would arrive on the scene too late to make a difference. Moreover, the attacker has the option of firing its missiles on a depressed trajectory, speeding their flight and limiting their time outside the atmosphere, the only place where they could be intercepted by NTW. In short, Pakistan and India are too big for a sea-based system to work against most of their missiles.

Missile defense proponents have also argued that the United States should sell TMD technology to India or Pakistan. It is true that each country could use a combination of Patriot and THAAD systems to cover most of its territory against ballistic-missile attack by the other, assuming that neither had advanced countermeasures capable of defeating an endoatmospheric TMD. However, it is also true that neighboring countries have natural geographic advantages—and lots of options—in how they threaten each other. It could become a very expensive proposition to defend their territories against short-range and medium-range missiles, most of which could be configured to fly primarily within the atmosphere, from the other. An attacker would also have the option of using cruise missiles or airplanes to deliver weapons. Defenses of key cities may be deemed prudent at some point, but it is doubtful that TMD technologies on the drawing board will allow India or Pakistan affordable routes to thorough national protection.

No More Disarmament?

U.S. plans for missile defense interest not only the nuclear powers but also the broader international community. As noted earlier, the UN General Assembly has passed a resolution urging that the ABM Treaty be respected and the planned U.S. deployment of national missile defenses canceled. Critics regularly complain that NMD really stands for "no more disarmament" and that defenses will encourage rather than discourage nuclear and missile proliferation.[67] One can debate the desirability of certain disarmament efforts, but anything that encouraged proliferation would be undesirable from the perspective of the United States and most other countries.

These criticisms reflect a firm belief abroad that the U.S. commitment to arms control is fading. Many foreign critics point to the Senate's 1999 rejection of the Comprehensive Test Ban Treaty as proof. They ask, not unreasonably, why the United States refused the opportunity to turn the informal ban on nuclear testing into a binding one, making it easier to detect clandestine nuclear explosions, and (ironically enough) locking in U.S. nuclear superiority. And while Americans can methodically list the problems with the test ban treaty, that does not change the point that much of the rest of the world needs to be persuaded that the United States remains interested in reducing stockpiles of nuclear weapons—as it is required to do under the Nuclear Non-Proliferation Treaty.

In fact, missile defenses and arms reductions are not mutually exclusive, so there is no reason why the United States must abandon its long-standing commitments to reduce the numbers and visibility of nuclear weapons just because it decides to deploy an NMD system.[68] True, a missile defense deployment done badly could push Moscow to reverse course on cutting its arsenal and prompt Beijing to expand its nuclear modernization program above and beyond what it already plans. But that is an argument against doing missile defense badly—rapidly building a large, multilayered defense with little consideration for other countries' security interests—rather than an argument against missile defense itself. Indeed, a "grand bargain" in which Washington and Moscow trade deep cuts in offensive nuclear weapons for modifications of the ABM Treaty seems much more likely than the "grand disaster" in which the two return to cold-war-like patterns of arms competition.

The same can be said for the impact that missile defense might have on nonproliferation. It is true, as one French ambassador argued, that an American administration that declares the ABM Treaty "outdated and irrelevant . . . must also be prepared to hear some countries apply the same logic to all of international law, including, in the first place, the Nuclear Non-Proliferation Treaty."[69] But the United States faces a potential threat because countries such as North Korea and Iraq are already trying to skirt the international prohibition on developing nuclear weapons. Nor is the United States on unreasonable ground in believing that a bilateral treaty fashioned during the cold war to limit the superpower rivalry of the day must adapt to post–cold war circumstances. And if Washington and Moscow do succeed in negotiating a grand bargain that trades deep cuts in offensive nuclear weapons for NMD, the effect would be to invigorate the nonproliferation cause.

That said, real concerns persist. Besides the potential threat that a precipitate deployment of a large-scale, multilayered NMD system poses to existing arm control agreements, there are other major worries. First, the U.S. ability to work with other countries to pressure potential proliferators—as the Clinton administration did, successfully, in regard to North Korea in the 1990s—could be eroded if Washington is seen as derelict in its arms control responsibilities. Second, and probably most important of all, the U.S. ability to continue cooperative threat reduction activities with Russia—securing, downsizing, and converting its enormous weapons of mass destruction capabilities—could be put at risk by a wanton NMD deployment. In that case, critics would be right that the cure would probably be worse than the disease.

The broader lesson is that national missile defense can serve U.S. and global security interests. But for that to be the case, the United States must embed its NMD program within a broader strategy for reducing nuclear weapons and curbing proliferation. That is not because traditional arms control agreements or smooth relations with Russia are more important than missile defense. Rather, it is because the United States could wind up less secure, rather than more secure, as a result of a wrongheaded and precipitous NMD deployment. To approach missile defense solely as an issue of defending American territory, the rest of the world be damned, will increase the odds that dangerous countries will get their hands on nuclear weapons, reduce the odds of securing and downsizing Russia's dilapidated and dangerous nuclear archipelago, and otherwise likely increase the scale of direct physical threats to American citizens and territory.

It is far better to make the case that missile defense does not mean relinquishing the hope of slashing nuclear stockpiles—and that it also can help prevent the further spread of nuclear weapons by ensuring that the United States will remain willing to defend its allies so that they need not acquire nuclear weapons of their own. But is that really possible? Can the United States devise a missile defense deployment that both defends the country and its allies from attack while also being compatible with lower arms levels and greater international stability?

CHAPTER SIX

Missile Defense
and
American Security

SHOULD THE UNITED STATES build a national missile defense? Critics have advanced many thoughtful arguments for saying no: the threat to the United States comes from only a handful of countries, most of which are probably not now close to having operational intercontinental missiles; the United States cannot yet build a fully functioning NMD system; enemies could attack the United States in ways that do not require long-range missiles; and NMD could jeopardize arms control and related efforts such as the Nunn-Lugar cooperative threat reduction program intended to secure nuclear warheads and materials within Russia.

But in the end five facts stand out. First, ballistic missile technology, including long-range missile technology, is spreading to more countries. It is possible that Iran, Iraq, or North Korea will acquire the ability to strike the United States in this decade, perhaps having given little advance warning of its ability to do so. Second, the technology for shooting down enemy missiles is no longer the stuff of science fiction—particularly when matched against the small long-range missile arsenals that countries such as Iraq, Iran, or North Korea could plausibly develop in the years ahead. Improved sensors, computers, and rocket technologies should soon make it possible to carry out high-reliability intercepts without the use of nuclear weapons. Third, the end of the cold war creates the opportunity to rethink the role of missile defense in U.S. security policy and in U.S.-Russian relations. As we argue later in this chapter, there should also be ways to mitigate China's most serious concerns about U.S. NMD—even if it does not prove possible, or necessary, to address all of Beijing's concerns.

Fourth, the intercontinental ballistic missile (ICBM) is nearly the only type of threat against which the United States has absolutely no defense today. Those who claim that an enemy "suitcase bomb" could circumvent any national missile defense often forget that the country already has several lines of possible defense against such weapons, including its intelligence services, Coast Guard, and customs agency. They also exaggerate the ease of building small, easily concealed nuclear weapons and overstate the ability of a foe to quickly gain coercive power from such weapons during a crisis or war.

Finally, nuclear deterrence, while reliable in most circumstances, may fail in certain types of crises or conflicts. For example, if in a future war caused by Iraqi or North Korean aggression, the United States and its allies elected to overthrow the offending regime, occupy its country, and reform its political institutions—similar to the successful approach of allied forces in World War II—the regime in question might threaten or even carry out an attack with weapons of mass destruction in an effort to save its skin or as a last-ditch act of defiance. Deterrence cannot be expected to work under such circumstances, since the threatened regime would already be facing annihilation even if it did not use WMD against the United States. And the prospect that deterrence might fail could weaken American resolve to respond to a crisis or shake the confidence that U.S. friends and allies have in American security guarantees—possibly even leading some to consider developing their own nuclear weapons.

Ultimately, there is no compelling reason for the United States to stand defenseless before the world, vulnerable to any and all missile attacks—and hence potentially less willing to defend its global interests and allies out of fear that doing so could make its population vulnerable to catastrophic reprisal. And it is difficult to believe it cannot find an approach to deploying NMD that will address the reasonable security concerns of Russia and China.

Of course, missile defense will not be a panacea for American national security. No NMD system will protect Americans against nuclear suitcase bombs—more accurately described as truck bombs or ship-based bombs, given that they would generally be quite large. Nor will a system address the threat from governments or terrorists using ships or possibly even the territory of nearby countries to launch cruise missiles or shorter-range ballistic missiles at the United States.[1] Washington should continue efforts to strengthen the ability of the Coast Guard, the Customs Service, and the intelligence community to detect and stop efforts to smuggle bombs into the United States. It should also deploy defenses against the shorter-range missile threat as events warrant, and make sure that no Anti-Ballistic Missile (ABM) Treaty modifications would bar it from doing so.[2]

The conclusion that national missile defense has a role to play in promoting American security raises a second, and equally important, question: what kind of defense should the United States build? As chapter 4 discusses, NMD architectures are not all created equal. They differ in potential capability, feasibility, strategic impact, development time, and cost. To put it even more bluntly, some could improve U.S. security, while others might degrade it on balance.

The key to assessing these trade-offs is to remember the fundamental purpose of national missile defense. It is not to build the most elaborate system possible or to trumpet U.S. technological and economic superiority. It is to make America, and its allies, more secure. Not all defenses would do that. As chapter 5 notes, any defensive deployment that ran roughshod over Russian and Chinese concerns could provoke a backlash that increased the nuclear threat to the United States and harmed other important American interests abroad. And Russia and China could almost surely defeat any missile defense the United States builds. Thus, while Moscow and Beijing do not deserve a veto over U.S. NMD plans, Washington must keep their core security interests—and their likely reactions to a deployment—in mind.

In our judgment, the way to maximize American security is to build a limited, two-tier national missile defense.[3] The first tier would consist of boost-phase interceptors, to be deployed near likely adversaries armed with long-range missiles, that would attempt to shoot down any such missiles early in their flight. They could be based on land, at sea, or in the air (in the latter case, probably only during crises or conflicts). The second tier would initially consist of a smaller version of the U.S.-based midcourse interceptor system the Clinton administration proposed building, based, however, in North Dakota rather than Alaska. Later, it might evolve into a system using more advanced long-range interceptors that could also intercept warheads as they returned to earth and reentered its atmosphere (these would be endo-exo interceptors).

The two tiers would offset each other's weaknesses and provide reasonably robust defense against the long-range missile threats that countries such as North Korea, Iran, or Iraq could likely pose during the next two decades. Construction of a working two-tier defense looks techno-logically feasible by the end of the decade. Equally important, a two-tier defense that emphasized boost-phase interceptors should be compatible with negotiating deep cuts in strategic nuclear forces with Russia, con-tinuing efforts to help Russia secure its nuclear weapons and materials, assuaging China's greatest concerns and thereby enhancing strategic sta-bility in Asia, and combating the proliferation of ballistic missiles and weapons of mass destruction. It should also provide good defense for key U.S. allies (though some may have to augment the protection offered by acquiring other NMD and TMD technologies of their own).

A Limited, Two-Tier National Missile Defense against "Rogue" Regimes

The analysis we have developed in this book suggests that three criteria should govern the choice of a specific missile defense architecture. First, force planning should be based on what we can reasonably expect tech-nology to accomplish during the next decade, not what we hope it might achieve decades from now. There is no sound reason to believe that the United States is on the verge of being able to defend itself against sophis-ticated and large-scale missile threats. Second, the United States needs a missile defense robust enough to defend against attacks from new ballis-tic missile states but not so robust as to provoke Russia and China into taking actions that undercut the broader causes of missile defense, nuclear security, and nonproliferation—especially since Washington can-not realistically develop a defense against Russian or Chinese missile forces in any event. Third, any national missile defense must also be an alliance missile defense. It must offer U.S. allies some element of protec-tion, otherwise the United States will remain vulnerable to blackmail.

In balancing these three criteria, we advocate a limited, two-tier defense capability for the United States within the ABM Treaty's original numerical limit of 200 interceptor missiles. The focus of the defense would not be the Russian or Chinese nuclear arsenal but possible attack by a country such as Iraq, North Korea, or Iran run by a regime that was tyrannical or extremely hostile to the United States, or both.

Under this proposal, the first one to two years of President George W. Bush's term should be devoted to conducting research and development for the necessary technologies, discussing deployment strategies with allies, and if possible negotiating necessary changes to the ABM Treaty with Russia—or at a minimum, going the extra mile in an attempt to do so, to mitigate any hostile reaction from Moscow that would result if the United States ultimately withdrew from the treaty. The United States should also consult with China, explaining its need for missile defense and its efforts to address those security concerns of the People's Republic that it finds valid and understandable. Then, as technology permitted and the threat warranted, deployment would begin, probably sometime between 2003 and 2005.

As noted, a total of 200 interceptors of all types would be allowed for the United States—the numerical ceiling in the original ABM Treaty. Up to 50 could be deployed in the United States; the rest would operate as a boost-phase defense—sea based, land based, and even aircraft based (especially if Iran turns out to present a threat). But initial deployments would certainly not have to bump up against these ceilings because none of the new ballistic missile powers is likely to build more than a handful of ICBMs if they build any at all; it is likely, then, that a capability on the order of 25 to 50 boost-phase interceptors and 25 U.S.-based interceptors could suffice for many years. Additional interceptors, above and beyond the ceiling of 200 for the United States, would be allowed for allies abroad, should they desire more protection than the U.S. boost-phase defenses (and theater missile defenses, or TMD) could provide. The treaty's prohibitions on nationwide and mobile defenses would also have to be eliminated to permit construction of this two-tier defense.

Some supporting sensor and battle management infrastructure would also have to be permitted, meaning that the ABM Treaty's strictures limiting many such technologies would need to be changed. Whether the limits would simply be eliminated, or modified to permit certain sensor capabilities, would be a matter for negotiation. They are most relevant to midcourse missile defense systems such as the one the Clinton administration proposed building. Given our modest expectations for such systems, and our belief that in the end decoy technology may thwart them, we would be prepared to accept some constraints on sensors as the price for getting a modified treaty. For example, the United States might be limited to a modest number of high-accuracy x-band radars, with specific geographic limitations that prevented them from monitoring most Russian intercontinental ballistic missile (ICBM) trajectories. It might not be desirable to ban space-based infrared system (SBIRS)-low, given the U.S. military's desire to use it for TMD as well as NMD. Moreover, SBIRS-low can also help discriminate some simple decoys—which may be all that a country such as North Korea or Iraq would prove capable of developing on its own. But if a ban on a technology such as SBIRS-low was necessary to convince Moscow to modify the ABM Treaty, we would be inclined to consider the idea seriously—at least for the next decade or so. In the future, when U.S.-Russian relations will have presumably progressed further and the problem of securing Russia's weapons of mass destruction may have been largely resolved, a deployment of SBIRS-low might become less strategically nettlesome and thus desirable (assuming that the threat from new powers had increased, warranting improved NMD capabilities).

Bans on testing theater missile defenses in ABM modes should be retained, as should the 1997 demarcation agreement between the United States and Russia. The United States is likely to build so many TMD interceptors in the years to come that, if the interceptors were to acquire NMD capability, the idea of a limited national missile defense could be quickly forfeited. Again, China or Russia could probably defeat any midcourse defense (likely Navy theater-wide, or NTW) with decoys—but they might not have confidence in that conviction and might instead react to such a U.S. "breakout" by taking many of the harmful steps we mention elsewhere. The concern is less acute for the airborne laser, since it is inherently a short-range system but applies directly to NTW and theater high-altitude area defense, or THAAD.

The First-Tier: Earth-Based Boost-Phase Defense

Why should the heart of any U.S. national missile defense be boost-phase interceptors based on land, at sea, or in the air? As chapter 4 discusses, boost-phase defense has two advantages in purely military terms over midcourse and terminal defenses: enemy missiles are the easiest to locate when their rocket motors are burning, and there are few countermeasures to foil a boost-phase intercept, since it is far harder to mimic or hide a large, burning rocket than a warhead traveling in the vacuum of space.

Earth-based boost-phase defenses also have a distinct diplomatic advantage: they would not threaten the basic viability of either the Russian or the Chinese nuclear deterrents. Regardless of whether they were deployed on land, sea, or air, boost-phase interceptors could only shoot down missiles launched within a few hundred miles of where they were based. Even if Moscow and Beijing's neighbors cooperated with the United States, boost-phase interceptors still could not get close enough to threaten Russian or Chinese nuclear weapons based in the interior of those countries.

Beijing and Moscow would have to be reassured that the boost-phase interceptors could not function as midcourse interceptors. That would require verifiable limits on testing. Beijing and Moscow could also deal with such a concern by planning to deploy decoys to fool any midcourse interceptors. They should be further reassured by the fact that boost-phase interceptors based near Mideast countries, even if hypothetically assumed to have midcourse intercept capabilities in violation of the revised treaty we propose, would simply not have enough time to catch up to ICBMs launched from most parts of China or Russia and headed toward the United States.

Admittedly, boost-phase NMD is no panacea. The most glaring problem is finding reliable basing for the defense near whatever countries may be threats. That problem would be exacerbated by the risk that the warhead from a missile intercepted in its boost phase might detonate when it landed. It could land anywhere along a swath several thousand miles long and several hundred miles wide, so the odds that it would come down near a city would be very small—comparable to the odds that space debris would land in populated regions. But the odds would not be zero, and in the case of a missile launched over Europe, they could be as high as a few percent.

The specific basing mode of a boost-phase system would vary with the country the United States was trying to defend against. The North Korean case is the most straightforward. Geography makes it possible to defend against missiles launched from North Korea using sea-based interceptors alone, though a land base on Russian soil near Vladivostok might be considered if Moscow were agreeable.

It would not be physically possible, however, to provide thorough protection against Mideast missiles from the open oceans. And it might not prove politically possible to find bases on land either. The case of Iraq would probably be solvable, because a missile defense base in eastern Turkey could cover launches from anywhere on Iraqi territory. Ankara's assent could not be taken for granted. But the closeness of the U.S.-Turkish security relationship, Turkey's long-standing willingness to allow U.S. aircraft to operate from Incirlik to conduct no-fly-zone operations over northern Iraq, and its interest in being defended from Iraqi missiles bode reasonably well for this idea. That said, Ankara undoubtedly would ask Washington for concessions in other policy areas in exchange for the right to operate a missile defense base on Turkish soil. That price probably would not be too high to pay for reliable missile defense against Saddam Hussein, should he (or a comparably ruthless successor) ever acquire an ICBM capability—but there will be a price nonetheless.

Iran is a much tougher case. The country is large enough that interceptor missiles would probably be needed both north and south of its territory. The southern location could probably be established. Options range from ships or perhaps even submarines in the Gulf of Oman (if they could be kept safe from Iranian attack) to land bases in Oman, the United Arab Emirates, Saudi Arabia, or possibly Qatar. But the northern base would be a huge challenge. Options include Turkmenistan, Kazakhstan, Uzbekistan, or the Caspian Sea. All three countries depend heavily on Russia for trade, travel, and other needs. They can be expected to give great weight to Moscow's concerns, again underscoring the importance of factoring Russian interests into U.S. missile defense calculations. Even with concerted efforts to address Russia's concerns, however, these former Soviet republics may refuse the United States access to their territory for a military base.

For these reasons, it may prove intractable to permanently deploy boost-phase defenses against Iranian missiles. The United States might need instead to develop and have ready airborne boost-phase interceptor missiles that it could deploy in the event of war. Thankfully, such missiles appear technologically within reach. In addition, during wartime scenarios—the most likely situations in which missile defenses might be needed—airborne defenses probably could be deployed in time to do the job, and well protected while on station. But this example nonetheless underscores the complexities of boost-phase defense, particularly should NMD someday be needed against Iran (or a country of comparable size and location).

How many boost-phase interceptors would be enough? Clearly, at least two, and probably three or four, would be desirable for each possible enemy missile for the reasons chapter 2 describes. Thus one must ask how many countries might be able to threaten the United States with long-range missiles, multiply by the expected number of missiles per country, and then multiply again by a factor of roughly three. Assuming a "reasonable worst case" of three possible threatening countries, four interceptors per missile, and up to a dozen ICBMs per country makes for a total of slightly less than 150 boost-phase interceptors. That is a rather conservative and cautious way of planning, from the point of view of the

United States. It assumes that Iran, Iraq, and North Korea could together have twice as many long-range missiles in the medium-term future as China does today (even though China's estimated annual defense expenditures of some $40 billion are four times their aggregate total). Moreover, it is unlikely that Iran, Iraq, or North Korea will be able to build more than a handful of nuclear weapons.

The United States probably would not need to deploy, or even build, 150 boost-phase interceptors, however. The odds that Iran, Iraq, and North Korea will all acquire long-range missile forces by 2015 or so are low. Our approach would allow for an expansion of the system if necessary. But it might wind up being sufficient to deploy just 25 to 50 boost-phase interceptors, and perhaps another 25 exoatmospheric interceptors as part of a second tier in the United States.

It would make sense for the United States to allow Russia and China access to its interceptor missile production facilities for purposes of verifying the output of those factories. This would not be an unprecedented step; Russia and the United States agreed to allow monitoring of some missile production sites in the START Treaty. But in this case the U.S. offer would be unilateral (unless Russia or China decided to build NMD interceptors at some future date). It would also be unconditional, in the sense that it would apply even if Russia did not agree to modify the ABM Treaty. It would be intended as a further demonstration of the U.S. desire to deploy missile defense in a nonthreatening manner.

Such boost-phase interceptors might eventually also be supplemented during a crisis by the airborne laser. The airborne laser (ABL) was initiated as a TMD system but may be capable in an NMD mode as well once it is fully developed—assuming that it is not easily defeated by countermeasures (such as a rotating rocket body), as some fear it will be.[4] Like airborne interceptors, ABL would only be useful under certain circumstances, notably in war. At other times its cost and need for continuous protection would probably preclude deployment. (Even its potential contribution in a crisis is questionable. Presidents may decide that dispatching ABL once tensions were high would be more likely to provoke an attack than to deter it by putting an adversary in a "use-them-or-lose-them" situation.)

How Russia and China would react to ABL is unclear. Even if ABL someday works well, its range limitations mean that Russia and China would not have to worry that it could destroy missiles launched from their territories or warheads in midcourse trajectory, so quantitative limits would be less important. But Moscow and Beijing might worry that ABL could exploit gaps in their air defenses or might be useful in conjunction with a U.S. first strike. So if Russia did insist on limiting ABL, the United States might agree—while asking for favorable "counting rules" that would treat each one as the equivalent of no more than a few interceptors (even though a single ABL is designed to have the capability to destroy up to twenty enemy missiles during one flight).

The Second Tier: A Small Midcourse Interceptor System

Although boost-phase defenses have appealing properties, they come with five significant disadvantages. First, they would have only a brief window of opportunity in which to shoot down a missile because rocket motors burn for no more than five minutes. Second, in most instances another country would have to agree to allow interceptors to be deployed on their territory; persuading them to do so and ensuring that they would not veto the use of the interceptors would be no mean feat. Third, if based on land, they would be vulnerable to political coup or insurrection in the host country. Fourth, even if the host country is politically stable, boost-phase defenses would be more vulnerable to attack than U.S.-based systems precisely because they are located overseas. Fifth, they must be based near a threatening country in advance; thus, they would be useless against attacks from an unsuspected country.

For these reasons, it would be prudent to supplement any boost-phase defenses with an interceptor system based on the territory of the United States. Such a second-tier defense would be positioned to attempt to destroy missiles that survived the first-tier boost-phase defense. It might also provide defense against a surprise ICBM launch from another region. Finally, it could defend against unauthorized or accidental launches from Russia or China, provided that the launches were limited in scope and did not involve sophisticated decoys. (Some thought should also be given to developing command-destruct mechanisms that would enable countries to destroy ICBMs in their first few minutes of flight; present technology probably makes it possible to build such mechanisms so that they are impervious to sabotage. But command-destruct mechanisms require more detailed technical and strategic analysis before we would propose fully relying upon them for this purpose.) It would have limitations of its own— most notably, its vulnerability to decoys, a weakness much greater than the sum total of the shortcomings of boost-phase defenses. But it would nonetheless provide a certain useful backup for the boost-phase systems.

The obvious candidate for such an interceptor is the one the Clinton administration proposed to build. However, that system should probably be modified in two crucial ways. First, the system should consist of a single site based in North Dakota rather than Alaska. Basing a national missile defense in Alaska would leave the northeastern portion of the United States poorly protected against a missile attack from the Middle East. It would also require immediately building a radar station on Shemya Island at the tip of the Aleutians. Building a radar on Shemya would take a great deal of time, given that the construction season lasts only three months—forcing the Bush administration to make premature decisions about beginning construction and withdrawing from the ABM Treaty.[5]

By contrast, a midcourse interceptor system based in North Dakota—where the United States deployed its lone Safeguard site a quarter century ago—could cover all but the westernmost islands in the Aleutian and Hawaiian island chains.[6] These islands would not be an inviting target for attack because they are extremely sparsely populated, and they would also have substantial protection from boost-phase defenses. Moreover, it does not make sense to weaken protection for tens of millions of U.S. citizens in the Northeast in order to provide a second layer of missile defense for several thousand Americans in western Alaska and Hawaii. But that moral quandary need not trouble us excessively, since the bottom line is that all American (and Canadian) populations would be protected in one way or another under our proposal.

The more hospitable construction conditions in North Dakota mean that the United States would not confront the question of whether to withdraw from the ABM Treaty for two to three years, even if it still aspired to have a defense working by 2006 or 2007. (The exact deployment date would depend on when a midcourse interceptor system proved itself under operational conditions and also on the evolution of the likely threat.) This would give the Bush administration more time to develop NMD technology and pursue NMD diplomacy with Moscow, Beijing, the allies, and other countries.

Second, rather than including up to 250 interceptor missiles, as the Clinton administration envisioned with its C3 capability, the North Dakota site should have no more than 50 missiles. The rationale for scaling back the number of interceptors is straightforward: the system should be geared to handle the very small-scale missile threat that North Korea, Iran, or Iraq could likely pose over the next two decades. There is simply no need for 250 interceptors to handle a potential threat from countries that lack the financial and technological resources needed to build more than a handful of missiles, let alone the warheads to match. At the same time, limiting the number of U.S.-based interceptors to 50 would probably be much more palatable to Russia and China. These numbers could be revisited in the future if necessary, but a ceiling of 50 U.S.-based interceptors would likely suffice for at least a decade.

A Deployment Timetable

When could the limited, two-tier system we are proposing be deployed? No one can say with certainty. The Defense Department does not currently have a boost-phase research program, and the Pentagon would need to overcome several significant technological hurdles to make such a system work. These obstacles do not seem insurmountable, however. Fast-burn rockets have been considered within technological reach for decades, and while practical engineering challenges would need to be addressed, the nature of the problem is less fundamental than for hit-to-kill or laser technology, each of which requires the United States to move into new technological frontiers. Some sensor challenges would need to be solved in making boost-phase interceptors, but infrared detectors—perhaps coupled with an active radar for finding the missile amid the rocket plume—should work. This type of defense could probably be developed and deployed within a few years.

The system the Clinton administration proposed building is further along in development today—but also would require more sophisticated technologies that have yet to be perfected. Midcourse interceptors always face a tougher task than boost-phase interceptors do, and while the Pentagon has been working intensively on the midcourse interceptor program for several years, the problems that plagued the first three tests (two of them outright failures) indicate that the 2005 deployment date was overly optimistic. That the Clinton administration proposed to deploy a working NMD system several years before the deployment of TMD systems such as THAAD and NTW, which are less technologically demanding, also suggests that the NMD deployment schedule was unrealistic. Even the current notional goal of 2006 or 2007 may be too quick. In short, the Pentagon's frequent argument that the Clinton system is the only viable near-term candidate for deployment does not seem correct.

There are advantages to slowing down deployment schedules. Besides allowing the Pentagon to get the technology right, a slower deployment schedule also makes sense for America's missile defense diplomacy. It provides time for proper negotiations on a revised ABM Treaty with Russia and for consultation with China. It also provides more time for discussions with U.S. allies. Under the Clinton administration's proposed timeline, the United States would defend its homeland earlier than it could help major allies defend theirs with advanced TMD systems such as THAAD and NTW. That is a recipe for dissension in the alliance; if Washington is right that the emergence of a long-range missile threat will leave it open to attack or blackmail, it makes little sense to plan on leaving U.S. allies undefended even as the United States protects itself. An aggressor could then blackmail, and paralyze, the United States almost as effectively by threatening Paris, Berlin, Rome, or Tokyo as by targeting U.S. territory.

Eventually, the U.S.-based interceptor missiles might be partially supplanted by endo-exo interceptors of the type chapter 4 discusses. These rockets would leave the atmosphere, fly to the region where warheads were projected to land, and intercept them there during their final approach to target. A central base of interceptors in North Dakota could provide coverage of the entire country, even against threats that included decoys, if the interceptors could reenter the atmosphere before trying to destroy a target. Between twenty-five and fifty miles in altitude, air is dense enough to filter out light decoys without blinding most infrared sensors needed by interceptor missiles, and without being heavy enough to allow maneuvering warheads to evade interceptors using aerodynamic fins. This system would require more radars—perhaps a dozen, distributed throughout the United States—than the Clinton system. But it would be consistent with the numerical limits on interceptors of a revised ABM Treaty as proposed above.

Revising the ABM Treaty

In pushing ahead with a limited, two-tier defense the United States should seek to work with Moscow to negotiate the necessary changes to the ABM Treaty. Among other changes, this would require excising article 1's flat prohibition against defenses designed to defend the national homeland. But that could be done while formally reaffirming the treaty's core principles: neither side should build a missile defense that would threaten the other's nuclear deterrent or that could be rapidly expanded to do so. Article 3 already permits the United States to base 100 interceptors at Grand Forks, and as noted the original treaty permitted a total of 200 interceptors distributed between two sites.

Washington and Moscow would also need to reach an understanding on the permissibility of boost-phase interceptors on land, at sea, or in the atmosphere. Article 5, which prohibits testing and deployment of sea-based and air-based ABM systems, would need to be revised. If Russia feared that the United States might use its sea-based boost-phase capability to track its nuclear submarines and shoot down its SLBMs, agreement could be reached restricting what locations the naval boost-phase platforms could operate in. And if Russia refused to relax the prohibition on air-based interceptors (even though it is simply implausible that a U.S. airborne laser could survive the Russian air defense system), the United States could still abide by the terms of the ABM Treaty simply by not testing it in its NMD mode even as it continued to develop and someday possibly deploy the system.[7] Even if designed and tested for TMD, it would likely work in an NMD mode as well, if based in the right location.

What a two-tier missile defense would give the United States, then, is an insurance policy against an attack by a new long-range ballistic-missile state. Admittedly, and thankfully, such an attack is unlikely and will remain unlikely. That hardly ends the argument though. Conventional war against North Korea or Iraq or Iran is also unlikely, but the United States structures a $300 billion per year defense budget largely around the possibility that war against one or more of those countries may occur nonetheless. Adding several billion dollars a year to that price tag (perhaps $30 billion to $35 billion spread over a decade) as a form of catastrophic insurance does not seem so preposterous when viewed in broad perspective. To look at it a different way, millions of Americans buy life insurance every year, even though their chances of dying in the next twelve months are slim. What drives the purchase of those insurance policies is not the probability of dying but the consequences.

The fact that a two-tier missile defense would function as an insurance policy raises the question of a moral hazard: would a U.S. government armed with even a limited shield use its sword more aggressively to impose its will on others? This possibility strikes fear in many NMD critics (especially those abroad) and encourages many NMD proponents. But both groups have it wrong. The United States is not vulnerable to long-range missile attack from Iran, Iraq, or North Korea now, yet is hardly indiscriminate about using force against those states. Indeed, when faced with an adversary possessing long-range missiles, whether armed with nuclear or biological warheads, any president would likely tread lightly for the simple reason that the missile defense system might not work—

and that, leaving aside the missile issue, war is an inherently dangerous and unpredictable enterprise.

Selling a Limited, Two-Tier Defense Abroad

We have emphasized throughout this book that any successful missile defense policy must anticipate how other countries, whether friend or foe, would react to a U.S. NMD deployment. But is there good reason to believe that the two-tier missile defense we are proposing would skirt the potential problems we have discussed?

We think the answer is yes. Consider Russia first. For all Moscow's public bluster, its opposition to missile defense and ABM Treaty modification probably is not immutable. One cause for optimism is that President Vladimir Putin conceded in June 2000 that the spread of long-range ballistic missile technology poses a threat when he proposed a joint NATO-Russian effort to build so-called nonstrategic missile defense. Russian officials have been vague about what this concept means, but they seemed at least initially to have in mind defenses along the lines of the boost-phase interceptors we are proposing.[8] The other cause for optimism is Russian self-interest. Moscow knows that a "just-say-nyet" policy risks creating precisely the outcome it presumably wants to avoid: U.S. withdrawal from the ABM Treaty. Should that happen, the United States would be legally free to build any missile defense it wanted, including one that could theoretically deny Russia a second-strike capability against the United States.

So there are reasons to believe that Russian leaders could be persuaded to live with a limited, two-tier defense. Indeed, it has cosmetic appeal; Moscow could portray boost-phase interceptors as consistent with President Putin's proposed defense plans. And the numerical limits of our proposal are in accord with those of the (original) ABM Treaty. Although important substantive changes would be needed, Moscow could emphasize the continuity between the old treaty regime and the new one.

Still, no one can expect Moscow to agree to modify the ABM Treaty without getting something in return. And what Washington should offer is deep cuts in both sides' nuclear stockpiles, a process that could even be kick-started by unilateral U.S. reductions. Washington should accept Moscow's proposal to reduce strategic nuclear arsenals to 1,000 to 1,500 warheads apiece. It should also act promptly and unilaterally to reduce the U.S. nuclear arsenal to the START II level of 3,500 warheads and remove from alert all warheads it plans to destroy under a START III agreement. Further dealerting steps could occur later. These steps would give Russia something it wants, but more important, send an unmistakable message to Moscow and the rest of the world that the United States is not seeking to gain a nuclear first-strike advantage by deploying a two-tier national missile defense.

These steps would not harm American national security. No one seriously contends that Russia is planning a deliberate first strike against the United States. Whatever residual threat Russia poses will fall as its arsenal shrinks. More to the point, the United States would retain robust and highly survivable capabilities against a wide range of possible target sets with 1,000 or 1,500 warheads.[9] If it wished, the United States could retain its ability to launch nuclear weapons from land, sea, and air with that number of weapons. Maintaining the triad probably becomes less efficient, as measured by cost per warhead, at such arsenal sizes, since the typical submarine or bomber would typically carry fewer warheads than today, and various economies of scale would be lost. But keeping the triad hardly becomes impossible, if indeed it is considered still necessary. The Pentagon expects to save $1.5 billion a year by going down to 2,500 warheads. It could save at least hundreds of millions of dollars more by going down to 1,000, even if it retained a triad.[10] These are not huge sums by the standards of defense spending, but they would help pay for missile defenses in the years to come.

Besides assuaging Moscow and reducing the number of Russian missiles aimed at American soil, deep cuts would offer another advantage. They would enable the United States to seize the moral high ground against critics who argue that its embrace of missile defense—together with the Senate's 1999 rejection of the Comprehensive Test Ban Treaty—means it has abandoned the cause of disarmament. (We favor the test ban treaty, though the entire missile defense and offensive arms agenda laid out here could be pursued even without its ratification.) Retaining the moral high ground on nuclear matters could help the United States work with its allies and neutrals to maintain pressure on countries like China and Russia to respect nonproliferation norms. Since the best antidote to missile and nuclear proliferation is prevention, such nonproliferation efforts are of critical importance—just as important as missile defense.

Of course, President Putin could beat President George W. Bush to the punch. Faced with an aging military infrastructure that Russia cannot afford to maintain—a point driven home dramatically by the sinking of the submarine *Kursk*—Putin could decide (according to some Russian news reports, he has already decided) to make a virtue out of necessity and unilaterally cut Russia's nuclear stockpile.[11] Such a step would rob the United States of the leverage and credit it would gain by making its own offer of deep cuts, though it would disprove the claim NMD critics frequently make that deep cuts and missile defense are mutually exclusive. Without a carrot with which to entice agreement, Washington could only hope that Moscow would decide on the merits that its interests are better served by having a modified ABM Treaty than by having no treaty at all. It might also point to the longer-term possibility of direct U.S.-Russian collaboration on TMD and NMD, including joint production or sales of technology from one country to the other at some future date.

Some might worry that, even if a limited NMD deployment did not prevent cutting offensive forces to 1,000 or 1,500 warheads, it could prevent any subsequent cuts below those levels, as well as efforts to eliminate nuclear weapons entirely. Two replies are in order. First, the notion of nuclear abolition is impractical and will remain infeasible as long as the Saddam Husseins of the world exist. Moreover, physical limitations on sensor technologies mean that it will not become possible to verify that nuclear weapons have been eliminated in any event.[12] So the realistic goal is not to go to zero but to go down to perhaps a few hundred warheads.

Second, the two-tier defense we are proposing is compatible with efforts to go down to a few hundred nuclear warheads. Boost-phase defenses do not threaten Russia's deterrent, and midcourse defenses are vulnerable to countermeasures it could surely build. To reassure Moscow, Washington might eventually want to agree to aggregate ceilings on offensive and defensive weapons, requiring the United States (or Russia) to trade off one type against the other in order to reassure each other. (Such a treaty could grant defensive weapons favorable counting rules—the important point would not be the precise details but the principle that a country deploying NMD should make additional cuts in its offensive forces as a sign of good faith.) But such a treaty regime should be acceptable. Of course, such treaties may someday become unnecessary if Russia and the United States remain on their fitful but still promising path toward a closer relationship.

We are optimistic that Russia will agree to modify the ABM Treaty along the lines we suggest if the United States offers deeper nuclear warhead cuts and other conciliatory gestures to Moscow. But Russia could allow the treaty to die. Oddly enough, that would be most likely if

Moscow concluded that a two-tier missile defense did not fundamentally threaten its security. In such a case, President Putin might see advantages, and few real costs, to saying nyet. On the diplomatic front, defending the sanctity of the ABM Treaty might enable him to seize the high ground on arms control, put Washington on the defensive, create a split between Europe and the United States, and preserve his nascent new relationship with China. Saying nyet could also serve Putin's domestic political interests. He could use it to portray himself as refusing to sacrifice Russia's interests to a hegemonic America. This scenario assumes some Machiavellian judgments on Putin's part, but they are hardly out of the question.

If Russia did refuse to give the United States the flexibility it needs on NMD, Washington would have to find a way to proceed with missile defense while still reassuring Russia (and other major powers) about its intentions. Proponents of treaty withdrawal argue that this can be done through so-called tacit arms control.[13] The United States would limit its own capabilities, keep Russia and China fully informed about its plans for missile defense, share technical data on the capabilities of defensive systems, and unilaterally accept intrusive verification procedures like those mentioned above for interceptor-missile production factories.

Tacit arms control is not far-fetched. It has worked in the past. In 1991, for instance, George Bush unilaterally pulled all U.S. short-range nuclear weapons out of Europe and Asia. A week later, Mikhail Gorbachev responded in kind. Moreover, even if Moscow and Washington agreed to modify the ABM Treaty, tacit arms control would likely play a major role in U.S.-Chinese relations. Washington could use the transparency that forms the heart of tacit arms control to reassure Beijing that its intentions are benign.

The possibility of tacit arms control should not be oversold, however. One problem is that Moscow would likely view a U.S. decision to withdraw from the ABM Treaty as a hostile act, hardly an auspicious foundation on which to build a new cooperative relationship. Another problem is that tacit arms control works best with unambiguous commitments that are costly to break. But proponents of tacit arms control like it in large part because it would enable the United States to change its commitments on missile defense as events warrant. Moreover, domestic political support for the kind of transparency that tacit arms control assumes may prove fragile or elusive. Critics would ask why the United States was sharing sensitive information with countries that pointed nuclear weapons at American cities and were under no reciprocal legal obligations.

The net result might be no arms control at all. Both Washington and Moscow should keep this in mind as they discuss the future of the ABM Treaty. It is still much better to modify that treaty, or to replace it, than to abandon it entirely.

What about China? Beijing knows—or will soon know, once the concept becomes better understood internationally—that the boost-phase system we are proposing cannot threaten its nuclear deterrent (unless they were surreptitiously given midcourse interception capabilities or China based its ICBMs along its coast). But given its understandable fears that a midcourse system, even one limited to 50 interceptors, could potentially nullify its deterrent, China will likely expand its plans to build a larger and more modern ICBM force. Although this outcome is not to be applauded, the United States could live with it. Even if China increased its missile force fivefold, the effect on the strategic balance between the two countries would be modest. Nor, as chapter 5 pointed out, would it likely touch off an unconstrained arms race in Asia.

Whatever its actions on the offensive-weapons front, China might find it unwise to flatly oppose any U.S. NMD program.[14] Even more than Moscow, Beijing would be at risk if the Bush administration abandoned the ABM Treaty. China's much smaller nuclear deterrent is more vulnerable to the kinds of defenses the United States could build. We do not believe that the United States could ultimately win an offense-defense arms race with China, in the sense of being able to reliably defend American territory against any and all Chinese nuclear threats. But China would hardly benefit from such an arms race itself, since it might have to expend substantial resources to maintain its confidence in the viability of its deterrent.

A modified ABM Treaty permitting a limited, two-tier U.S. NMD system offers China a less risky path. Although it is not Beijing's ideal solution, it would pose little threat to China's nuclear deterrent. Moreover, if Russia agreed to negotiate changes to the ABM Treaty that permitted a two-tier missile defense, Beijing would have formal assurance that the United States would not suddenly expand the midcourse interceptor system and build a thick defense. And U.S. acceptance of Russia's proposal to slash offensive nuclear forces would be a tangible gesture to not only Moscow but also Beijing that the United States is speaking in good faith when it says it seeks security and not nuclear dominance.

Nor would the two-tier NMD system we are proposing be particularly useful in a TMD mode for intercepting short-burning and low-flying missiles headed from China to Taiwan—even if the United States situated large numbers of its NMD interceptors near the Strait during a future crisis there. China's missiles would in effect be able to fly under the boost-phase interceptors, and in all likelihood they would also greatly outnumber the interceptors.

Defusing Chinese opposition to a two-tier defense would require deft U.S. diplomacy. At a minimum, the Bush administration would need to keep Beijing fully briefed on its talks with Moscow. But it should go a step further and engage in high-level political (not just military) talks designed to reassure Beijing about American intentions. U.S. officials should brief their Chinese counterparts on the two-tier defense system's capabilities. They should also explore possible confidence-building measures the two countries could take, such as sharing U.S. early warning data with China, that might diminish bilateral tensions.

U.S. diplomats should also carry a clear warning to Beijing: it risks endangering its strategic interests by continuing to provide missile proliferators with technical assistance. China may blame Washington for creating a crisis in strategic stability by pushing missile defense, but it has helped create the problem by aiding and abetting missile proliferation (even if it has also taken steps to help defuse recent crises on the Korean peninsula—a benefit of a cooperative U.S.-Chinese relationship that Americans should not forget). If ballistic missile technology spreads more rapidly than currently anticipated, the rhythm of American politics makes it likely that the United States will pursue more robust defenses without regard to China's concerns. And Washington needs to make clear that the United States will consider it a hostile act should Beijing sell countermeasure technology to the likes of Iran, Iraq, and North Korea.

At the same time, Washington must exercise caution on the matter of selling TMD systems to Taipei. Beijing emphatically opposes such sales. Pursued without restraint, they would create problems for the United States not only on national missile defense but also on the rest of the bilateral relationship. Washington should tread slowly. It should take into account how much advanced technology Taiwan's military could productively handle. Washington should also recognize that China's missile threat to Taiwan is sufficiently large that even substantial sales of U.S. TMD systems to Taiwan would not eliminate Beijing's coercive leverage against Taipei. Some response to China's missile buildup makes sense, if for no other reason than to discourage Beijing from thinking that it has prevailed in the test of wills on this matter and that it can threaten Taiwan more forcefully. But pursuit of a leakproof TMD shield for Taiwan would be illusory and incendiary.

The two-tier NMD system we are proposing should engender much greater support from American friends and allies. To begin with, it responds to their insistence that any U.S. NMD deployment take Russian interests into account. Even if Moscow refused to modify the ABM Treaty, Washington's willingness to preserve the treaty's core principle, emphasize a missile-defense technology that was nonthreatening to Moscow, and make deep cuts in offensive nuclear forces would change the terms of the debate. A limited, two-tier defense would also allay fears that the United States is leaving its friends and allies vulnerable while it protects itself. Boost-phase interceptors would destroy long-range ballistic missiles regardless of whether their ultimate destination was Paris or Peoria. Furthermore, the slower pace that we propose for deploying any defense allows time for NMD systems to be synchronized with TMD systems—meaning that U.S. allies could purchase THAAD or Navy theater-wide defenses about the time that the United States acquired its own defense, filling in any gaps in coverage of their territories from boost-phase systems. Finally, a limited, two-tier defense is compatible with deep cuts in offensive nuclear forces. Thus, America's allies would be reassured that the United States remains committed to arms control and nonproliferation.

Selling a Limited, Two-Tier Defense at Home

So a limited, two-tier defense might have political appeal abroad. But why should President Bush endorse such a proposal, and could he marshal political support for it at home? These are important questions to ask. After all, no NMD system is going to proceed over the president's objections, and many observers expect Bush to propose deploying missile defenses far more robust than the one we advocate. At the same time, presidential initiative alone cannot sustain an NMD program. Congress must agree to fund it rather than alternative defenses, Congress must go along with the cuts in offensive forces (including unilateral cutbacks and one-sided verification agreements), and two-thirds of the Senate must ultimately agree to give its advice and consent to a modified ABM Treaty if one is negotiated.

The main reason President Bush should endorse a limited, two-tier defense is that it is the only NMD architecture that will enable him to achieve his stated goals for missile defense without jeopardizing his objec-

tives in foreign policy more broadly. During the campaign, he emphasized that "our missile defense must be designed to protect all 50 states,
and our friends and allies, from missile attacks by rogue nations or accidental launches."[15] Contrary to the hopes of NMD enthusiasts, he did not
endorse any particular NMD architecture.[16] Equally important, he did
not commit himself to building a defense designed to counter China's
strategic missiles, even when pressed to do so.[17] Finally, unlike many
NMD enthusiasts, Bush did not reject the ABM Treaty. Instead, he said
repeatedly that he would prefer to negotiate changes with Russia "so as
to make our deployment of effective missile defenses consistent with the
treaty."[18] All of these objectives are consistent with our proposal for a
limited, two-tier defense.

NMD enthusiasts will argue that more robust defenses would also fulfill President Bush's explicit campaign promises while being more in keeping with what they take to be his unspoken intentions. Two points are
worth making. The first is that for the foreseeable future effective robust
defenses will be more an illusion than a reality. The United States almost
certainly will not be able to build robust defenses during the next ten to
twenty years that can blunt large-scale missile attacks. As chapter 4 discusses, the kinds of defenses that could be built with existing and foreseeable technology will in most circumstances be vulnerable to fairly straightforward countermeasures that a major military power could develop if
necessary. And while NMD enthusiasts hold out the prospect of Star
Wars–like space-based defenses, such systems are at least two decades off—
if not more. It hardly seems sensible to base policy decisions today on hopes
about what scientists might be able to achieve twenty years in the future.

The second point is that, unlike the limited, two-tier defense we advocate, robust defenses would torpedo President Bush's other foreign policy
goals. During the campaign he spoke of his twin desires to reduce the
number of U.S. and Russian nuclear weapons significantly and to increase
U.S. efforts to assist Moscow in dismantling as many of its weapons as
possible.[19] As we have argued, pushing ahead with robust defenses would
likely prompt Moscow to keep as many nuclear missiles as it can afford
and possibly terminate its participation in cooperative threat reduction
programs. Similarly, Bush vowed to strengthen America's alliance relations. But robust missile defenses are likely to strain U.S. relations with
Europe, especially in light of Bush's desire to reduce the U.S. military
commitment in the Balkans and in light of the divisions within the
Atlantic alliance over issues such as trade and global warming.

A limited, two-tier defense should also make sense to President Bush on cost grounds. Simply put, robust defenses will crowd out spending for other much-needed defense programs. During the campaign, Bush promised to increase military pay, fund more research and development, and improve military readiness. On top of this he faces pressure to spend more on procurement because the country needs to rebuild the weapons stocks that it acquired during the Reagan years and began to wear out during the Clinton years. These demands could require a real-dollar increase in annual defense spending of up to $50 billion. Yet Bush's overall campaign spending plans called for increasing defense spending by only about $5 billion a year. His ability to find extra dollars to fund robust missile defenses is further limited by his pledge to cut taxes, create private Social Security retirement accounts, and increase spending on some domestic programs.

Besides appealing to President Bush on policy grounds, a limited, two-tier NMD system should also appeal to him on political grounds. He won election in the narrowest and most controversial presidential vote in more than a century. Bitter feelings are likely to last for some time, hampering his ability to win congressional support for his policy initiatives. Making his challenge even more daunting is the fact that he faces a Congress in which Republicans have a numerical majority but not a working one. If he decides to pursue development of a robust missile defense in this conflict-ridden political climate he is likely to trigger a contentious battle that will absorb his time and political capital and that in the end he will likely lose.

Proponents of robust missile defenses insist, of course, that the domestic political landscape favors robust defenses. The facts are otherwise. True, in 1999, Congress overwhelmingly passed the National Missile Defense Act, which President Bill Clinton reluctantly signed into law. It declared that it was "the policy of the United States to deploy as soon as is technologically possible an effective National Missile Defense system capable of defending the territory of the United States against limited ballistic missile attack."[20] But many Democrats pointed to the act's conditions: that diplomatic and cost issues be considered before making any deployment. Subsequent events showed that the act was more a marriage of convenience—North Korea's test flight of the Taepo Dong in August 1998 had made it politically irresistible—than a meeting of the minds. By mid-2000 the domestic coalition that had pushed a reluctant President Clinton to embrace national missile defense had unraveled, at least for the time being, and a significant number of both Democrats and Republicans urged Clinton to hand the issue to his successor.

So missile defense sentiment on Capitol Hill now falls into three camps. At one extreme lie NMD enthusiasts who favor building "thick" defenses against the possibility of a Chinese attack or a large-scale accidental launch from Russia. At the other extreme lie arms control enthusiasts who doubt that national missile defense is desirable or feasible against any threat. But most members of Congress fall into a broad middle camp that favors missile defense—at least in theory and at least against relatively small countries run by extremist regimes—for a mix of policy and political reasons. These legislators, however, are not firmly committed to a particular architecture and are sensitive to the potential financial and diplomatic costs of any defensive deployment. They will determine the outcome of the NMD debate, and they are likely to oppose exorbitantly expensive deployments that strain America's alliance relations and needlessly escalate tensions with other major powers. Opposition to robust defenses will be especially intense if North Korea continues to moderate its behavior and agrees to halt its missile programs.

The American public reflects that same range of views. Despite frequent claims to the contrary, Americans have always been ambivalent about missile defense. (Polls repeatedly showed, for instance, that Americans were split on the merits of Ronald Reagan's Strategic Defense Initiative.)[21] Some are firm opponents or supporters. But most Americans fall into what might be called the movable middle. They favor missile defense but only if the financial and diplomatic costs are limited—and if a deployment does not prompt other countries to take steps that leave America less secure. When the Pew Research Center asked Americans in May 2000 if they supported missile defense, 52 percent said yes and 37 percent said no. When Pew asked if they favored missile defense if it "jeopardizes negotiations with the Russians aimed at further reducing the nuclear arsenals in both countries," the responses shifted: 55 percent said the "U.S. should hold off on developing a missile defense system" and 36 percent said go ahead. Equally important, Americans are not yet paying attention to the issue. Just 10 percent told Pew they had heard a lot about the NMD debate, while another 43 percent said they had heard only a little.[22] Those numbers increased during the presidential campaign, but not radically so; in the heat of the fall campaign, the two presidential candidates focused on bread-and-butter defense issues such as military pay and readiness rather than national missile defense.

All this suggests that it is good policy and good politics for the Bush administration to build a domestic political coalition in favor of a limited, two-tier missile defense.[23] And it is crucial that the administration not neglect the politics of missile defense at home while it pursues missile defense diplomacy abroad. Any effort to develop an NMD policy that appeals to the movable middle will alienate NMD enthusiasts on Capitol Hill. These are mainly conservative Republicans who would normally support a Republican president. But their passion on the issue makes it possible that they will try to derail any proposal for a limited, two-tier defense.

The Senate's 1999 rejection of the Comprehensive Test Ban Treaty makes it clear that the Bush administration should not take this threat lightly. As debate on the test ban treaty moved toward a close, sixty-two senators, including twenty-four out of fifty-five Republicans, signed a letter urging Majority Leader Trent Lott to postpone the vote.[24] The postponement never came. The test ban's most fervent opponents—all of whom are also NMD enthusiasts—made it clear that they would make Lott's life miserable if he allowed the treaty to be withdrawn.[25] Moreover, numerous senators, among them Jesse Helms (R-N.C.), James Inhofe (R-Okla.), and Jon Kyl (R-Ariz.), have already vowed to block any modification of the ABM Treaty, a treaty that Inhofe insists "shouldn't be in effect anyway."[26] They are not likely to reverse their opposition to treaty modifications just because a Republican White House might favor the idea.

This is not to say, however, that the prospect of the Senate approving a modified ABM Treaty (or a successor agreement) is hopeless. Although the Senate has become more willing to oppose presidential initiatives, it has not reverted to the pattern of the late nineteenth century when it rejected every major treaty put before it. The test ban treaty's defeat had as much to do with the Clinton administration's poor preparation and lobbying as it did with Republican opposition. The administration did not involve key senators in the treaty's negotiations. Once Clinton signed the treaty, he let it languish for three years. Nothing changed when it became clear there would be a vote. The administration did not shift into its famed "war room" mode, and the president gave no speeches to the nation on its behalf. His own laboratory directors, whose support had been taken for granted, blindsided the administration in congressional testimony just before the Senate vote when they questioned whether the U.S. nuclear arsenal could be maintained indefinitely without testing.

President Bush must not repeat the same mistake. He must commit his political capital to building support on Capitol Hill and with the

American public. The key to doing that is to target the movable middle. Any strategy that begins by targeting either of the extremes is doomed to failure. Hard-core NMD enthusiasts are unlikely to relinquish their unrealistic dreams of rendering nuclear weapons "impotent and obsolete," and their blessing is not needed to secure the center. Arms control enthusiasts are not powerful enough to win on their own, and if Russia agrees to modify the ABM Treaty their objections to deployment of an NMD system will fade anyway.

The key to capturing the movable middle is to frame the debate in blunt national interest terms: how can the United States deploy national missile defense so that it maximizes its security and that of its closest allies? Most Americans will support national missile defense if they can also have deep cuts in nuclear weapons and continued efforts to secure Russia's arsenal. That should be what the Bush administration promises to deliver.

To make a strategy based on the movable middle work, President Bush has to educate members of Congress and the American public about the issues at stake. That means giving major presidential speeches and radio addresses, as well as detailed briefings for opinion leaders. Mobilizing support for a limited, two-tier defense on Capitol Hill also requires starting a process of genuine consultations with members of Congress. When the administration begins negotiations with Moscow on modifying the ABM Treaty it should create a Senate observer group that at a minimum consists of the chair and ranking members of the Foreign Relations, Armed Services, and Intelligence committees. The Clinton administration used such an observer group to great effect on NATO enlargement.[27] Making senators a part of negotiations—something that did not happen with the test ban treaty—sensitizes them to key issues, injects their views into the process, and inclines them to support the finished product.

Defining the missile defense debate in terms of what advances America's national interest and moving forcefully to educate Americans about the stakes involved will not magically remove the political obstacles that President Bush would face with a limited, two-tier defense. Missile defense is controversial because it stokes deep fears of an arms race spiraling out of control, and it unleashes hopes for a technological relief from possible nuclear Armageddon. But if President Bush fails to master the substance as well as the politics of missile defense, a deeply divisive domestic debate is likely. Given the controversy that surrounded his election, it is not a debate he should want.

Anti-Ballistic Missile Treaty and Related Documents

TREATY BETWEEN THE UNITED STATES OF AMERICA
AND THE UNION OF SOVIET SOCIALIST REPUBLICS
ON THE LIMITATION OF
ANTI-BALLISTIC MISSILE SYSTEMS

Signed at Moscow May 26, 1972
Ratification advised by U.S. Senate August 3, 1972
Ratified by U.S. President September 30, 1972
Proclaimed by U.S. President October 3, 1972
Instruments of ratification exchanged October 3, 1972
Entered into force October 3, 1972

The United States of America and the Union of Soviet Socialist Republics, hereinafter referred to as the Parties,

Proceeding from the premise that nuclear war would have devastating consequences for all mankind,

Considering that effective measures to limit anti-ballistic missile systems would be a substantial factor in curbing the race in strategic offensive arms and would lead to a decrease in the risk of outbreak of war involving nuclear weapons,

Proceeding from the premise that the limitation of anti-ballistic missile systems, as well as certain agreed measures with respect to the limitation of strategic offensive arms, would contribute to the creation of more favorable conditions for further negotiations on limiting strategic arms,

Mindful of their obligations under Article VI of the Treaty on the Non-Proliferation of Nuclear Weapons,

Declaring their intention to achieve at the earliest possible date the cessation of the nuclear arms race and to take effective measures toward reductions in strategic arms, nuclear disarmament, and general and complete disarmament,

Desiring to contribute to the relaxation of international tension and the strengthening of trust between States,

Have agreed as follows:

Article I

1. Each Party undertakes to limit anti-ballistic missile (ABM) systems and to adopt other measures in accordance with the provisions of this Treaty.

2. Each Party undertakes not to deploy ABM systems for a defense of the territory of its country and not to provide a base for such a defense, and not to deploy ABM systems for defense of an individual region except as provided for in Article III of this Treaty.

Article II

1. For the purpose of this Treaty an ABM system is a system to counter strategic ballistic missiles or their elements in flight trajectory, currently consisting of:

(a) ABM interceptor missiles, which are interceptor missiles constructed and deployed for an ABM role, or of a type tested in an ABM mode;

(b) ABM launchers, which are launchers constructed and deployed for launching ABM interceptor missiles; and

(c) ABM radars, which are radars constructed and deployed for an ABM role, or of a type tested in an ABM mode.

2. The ABM system components listed in paragraph 1 of this Article include those which are:

(a) operational;

(b) under construction;

(c) undergoing testing;

(d) undergoing overhaul, repair or conversion; or

(e) mothballed.

ARTICLE III

Each Party undertakes not to deploy ABM systems or their components except that:

(a) within one ABM system deployment area having a radius of one hundred and fifty kilometers and centered on the Party's national capital, a Party may deploy: (1) no more than one hundred ABM launchers and no more than one hundred ABM interceptor missiles at launch sites, and (2) ABM radars within no more than six ABM radar complexes, the area of each complex being circular and having a diameter of no more than three kilometers; and

(b) within one ABM system deployment area having a radius of one hundred and fifty kilometers and containing ICBM silo launchers, a Party may deploy: (1) no more than one hundred ABM launchers and no more than one hundred ABM interceptor missiles at launch sites, (2) two large phased-array ABM radars comparable in potential to corresponding ABM radars operational or under construction on the date of signature of the Treaty in an ABM system deployment area containing ICBM silo launchers, and (3) no more than eighteen ABM radars each having a potential less than the potential of the smaller of the above-mentioned two large phased-array ABM radars.

ARTICLE IV

The limitations provided for in Article III shall not apply to ABM systems or their components used for development or testing, and located within current or additionally agreed test ranges. Each Party may have no more than a total of fifteen ABM launchers at test ranges.

ARTICLE V

1. Each Party undertakes not to develop, test, or deploy ABM systems or components which are sea-based, air-based, space-based, or mobile land-based.

2. Each Party undertakes not to develop, test or deploy ABM launchers for launching more than one ABM interceptor missile at a time from

each launcher, not to modify deployed launchers to provide them with such a capacity, not to develop, test, or deploy automatic or semi-automatic or other similar systems for rapid reload of ABM launchers.

ARTICLE VI

To enhance assurance of the effectiveness of the limitations on ABM systems and their components provided by the Treaty, each Party undertakes:

(a) not to give missiles, launchers, or radars, other than ABM interceptor missiles, ABM launchers, or ABM radars, capabilities to counter strategic ballistic missiles or their elements in flight trajectory, and not to test them in an ABM mode; and

(b) not to deploy in the future radars for early warning of strategic ballistic missile attack except at locations along the periphery of its national territory and oriented outward.

ARTICLE VII

Subject to the provisions of this Treaty, modernization and replacement of ABM systems or their components may be carried out.

ARTICLE VIII

ABM systems or their components in excess of the numbers or outside the areas specified in this Treaty, as well as ABM systems or their components prohibited by this Treaty, shall be destroyed or dismantled under agreed procedures within the shortest possible agreed period of time.

ARTICLE IX

To assure the viability and effectiveness of this Treaty, each Party undertakes not to transfer to other States, and not to deploy outside its national territory, ABM systems or their components limited by this Treaty.

ARTICLE X

Each Party undertakes not to assume any international obligations which would conflict with this Treaty.

ARTICLE XI

The Parties undertake to continue active negotiations for limitations on strategic offensive arms.

ARTICLE XII

1. For the purpose of providing assurance or compliance with the provisions of this Treaty, each Party shall use national technical means of verification at its disposal in a manner consistent with generally recognized principles of international law.

2. Each Party undertakes not to interfere with the national technical means of verification of the other Party operating in accordance with paragraph 1 of this Article.

3. Each Party undertakes not to use deliberate concealment measures which impede verification by national technical means of compliance with the provisions of this Treaty. This obligation shall not require changes in current construction, assembly, conversion, or overhaul practices.

ARTICLE XIII

1. To promote the objectives and implementation of the provisions of this Treaty, the Parties shall establish promptly a Standing Consultative Commission, within the framework of which they will:

(a) consider questions concerning compliance with the obligations assumed and related situations which may be considered ambiguous;

(b) provide on a voluntary basis such information as either Party considers necessary to assure confidence in compliance with the obligations assumed;

(c) consider questions involving unintended interference with national technical means of verification;

(d) consider possible changes in the strategic situation which have a bearing on the provisions of this Treaty;

(e) agree upon procedures and dates for destruction or dismantling of ABM systems or their components in cases provided for by the provisions of this Treaty;

(f) consider, as appropriate, possible proposals for further increasing the viability of this Treaty; including proposals for amendments in accordance with the provisions of this Treaty;

(g) consider, as appropriate, proposals for further measures aimed at limiting strategic arms.

2. The Parties through consultation shall establish, and may amend as appropriate, Regulations for the Standing Consultative Commission governing procedures, composition and other relevant matters.

ARTICLE XIV

1. Each Party may propose amendments to this Treaty. Agreed amendments shall enter into force in accordance with the procedures governing the entry into force of this Treaty.

2. Five years after entry into force of this Treaty, and at five-year intervals thereafter, the Parties shall together conduct a review of this Treaty.

ARTICLE XV

1. This Treaty shall be of unlimited duration.

2. Each Party shall, in exercising its national sovereignty, have the right to withdraw from this Treaty if it decides that extraordinary events related to the subject matter of this Treaty have jeopardized its supreme interests. It shall give notice of its decision to the other Party six months prior to withdrawal from the Treaty. Such notice shall include a statement of the extraordinary events the notifying Party regards as having jeopardized its supreme interests.

ARTICLE XVI

1. This Treaty shall be subject to ratification in accordance with the constitutional procedures of each Party. The Treaty shall enter into force on the day of the exchange of instruments of ratification.

2. This Treaty shall be registered pursuant to Article 102 of the Charter of the United Nations.

DONE at Moscow on May 26, 1972, in two copies, each in the English and Russian languages, both texts being equally authentic.

FOR THE UNITED STATES OF AMERICA:
RICHARD NIXON
President of the United States of America

FOR THE UNION OF SOVIET SOCIALIST REPUBLICS:
L. I. BREZHNEV
General Secretary of the Central Committee of the CPSU

PROTOCOL TO THE TREATY BETWEEN THE UNITED STATES OF AMERICA AND THE UNION OF SOVIET SOCIALIST REPUBLICS ON THE LIMITATION OF ANTI-BALLISTIC MISSILE SYSTEMS

Signed at Moscow July 3, 1974
Ratification advised by U.S. Senate November 10, 1975
Ratified by U.S. President March 19, 1976
Instruments of ratification exchanged May 24, 1976
Proclaimed by U.S. President July 6, 1976
Entered into force May 24, 1976

The United States of America and the Union of Soviet Socialist Republics, hereinafter referred to as the Parties,

Proceeding from the Basic Principles of Relations between the United States of America and the Union of Soviet Socialist Republics signed on May 29, 1972,

Desiring to further the objectives of the Treaty between the United States of America and the Union of Soviet Socialist Republics on the Limitation of Anti-Ballistic Missile Systems signed on May 26, 1972, hereinafter referred to as the Treaty,

Reaffirming their conviction that the adoption of further measures for the limitation of strategic arms would contribute to strengthening international peace and security,

Proceeding from the premise that further limitation of anti-ballistic missile systems will create more favorable conditions for the completion of work on a permanent agreement on more complete measures for the limitation of strategic offensive arms,

Have agreed as follows:

ARTICLE I

1. Each Party shall be limited at any one time to a single area of the two provided in Article III of the Treaty for deployment of anti-ballistic

missile (ABM) systems or their components and accordingly shall not exercise its right to deploy an ABM system or its components in the second of the two ABM system deployment areas permitted by Article III of the Treaty, except as an exchange of one permitted area for the other in accordance with Article II of this Protocol.

2. Accordingly, except as permitted by Article II of this Protocol: the United States of America shall not deploy an ABM system or its components in the area centered on its capital, as permitted by Article III(a) of the Treaty, and the Soviet Union shall not deploy an ABM system or its components in the deployment area of intercontinental ballistic missile (ICBM) silo launchers as permitted by Article III(b) of the Treaty.

ARTICLE II

1. Each Party shall have the right to dismantle or destroy its ABM system and the components thereof in the area where they are presently deployed and to deploy an ABM system or its components in the alternative area permitted by Article III of the Treaty, provided that prior to initiation of construction, notification is given in accord with the procedure agreed to in the Standing Consultative Commission, during the year beginning October 3, 1977, and ending October 2, 1978, or during any year which commences at five year intervals thereafter, those being the years of periodic review of the Treaty, as provided in Article XIV of the Treaty. This right may be exercised only once.

2. Accordingly, in the event of such notice, the United States would have the right to dismantle or destroy the ABM system and its components in the deployment area of ICBM silo launchers and to deploy an ABM system or its components in an area centered on its capital, as permitted by Article III(a) of the Treaty, and the Soviet Union would have the right to dismantle or destroy the ABM system and its components in the area centered on its capital and to deploy an ABM system or its components in an area containing ICBM silo launchers, as permitted by Article III(b) of the Treaty.

3. Dismantling or destruction and deployment of ABM systems or their components and the notification thereof shall be carried out in accordance with Article VIII of the ABM Treaty and procedures agreed to in the Standing Consultative Commission.

Article III

The rights and obligations established by the Treaty remain in force and shall be complied with by the Parties except to the extent modified by this Protocol. In particular, the deployment of an ABM system or its components within the area selected shall remain limited by the levels and other requirements established by the Treaty.

Article IV

This Protocol shall be subject to ratification in accordance with the constitutional procedures of each Party. It shall enter into force on the day of the exchange of instruments of ratification and shall thereafter be considered an integral part of the Treaty.

DONE at Moscow on July 3, 1974, in duplicate, in the English and Russian languages, both texts being equally authentic.

FOR THE UNITED STATES OF AMERICA:
RICHARD NIXON
President of the United States of America

FOR THE UNION OF SOVIET SOCIALIST REPUBLICS:
L. I. BREZHNEV
General Secretary of the Central Committee of the CPSU

September 26, 1997

MEMORANDUM OF UNDERSTANDING RELATING TO THE TREATY BETWEEN THE UNITED STATES OF AMERICA AND THE UNION OF SOVIET SOCIALIST REPUBLICS ON THE LIMITATION OF ANTI-BALLISTIC MISSILE SYSTEMS OF MAY 26, 1972

The United States of America, and the Republic of Belarus, the Republic of Kazakhstan, the Russian Federation and Ukraine, hereinafter referred to for purposes of this Memorandum as the Union of Soviet Socialist Republics (USSR) Successor States,

Recognizing the importance of preserving the viability of the Treaty Between the United States of America and the Union of Soviet Socialist

Republics on the Limitation of Anti-Ballistic Missile Systems of May 26, 1972, hereinafter referred to as the Treaty, with the aim of maintaining strategic stability,

Recognizing the changes in the political situation resulting from the establishment of new independent states on the territory of the former USSR,

Have, in connection with the Treaty, agreed as follows:

Article I

The United States of America, the Republic of Belarus, the Republic of Kazakhstan, the Russian Federation, and Ukraine, upon entry into force of this Memorandum, shall constitute the Parties to the Treaty.

Article II

The USSR Successor States shall assume the rights and obligations of the former USSR under the Treaty and its associated documents.

Article III

Each USSR Successor State shall implement the provisions of the Treaty with regard to its territory and with regard to its activities, wherever such activities are carried out by that State, independently or in cooperation with any other State.

Article IV

For purposes of Treaty implementation:

(a) the term "Union of Soviet Socialist Republics" shall mean the USSR Successor States;

(b) the terms "national territory" and "territory of its country" when used to refer to the former USSR shall mean the combined national territories of the USSR Successor States, and the term "periphery of its national territory" when used to refer to the former USSR shall mean the periphery of the combined national territories of those States; and

(c) the term "capital" when used to refer to the capital of the Union of Soviet Socialist Republics in Article III of the Treaty and the Protocol thereto of July 3, 1974, shall continue to mean the city of Moscow.

Article V

A USSR Successor State or USSR Successor States may continue to use any facility that is subject to the provisions of the Treaty and that is currently located on the territory of any State that is not a Party to the Treaty, with the consent of such State, and provided that the use of such facility shall remain consistent with the provisions of the Treaty.

Article VI

The USSR Successor States shall collectively be limited at any one time to a single anti-ballistic missile (ABM) system deployment area and to a total of no more than fifteen ABM launchers at ABM test ranges, in accordance with the provisions of the Treaty and its associated documents, including the Protocols of July 3, 1974.

Article VII

The obligations contained in Article IX of the Treaty and Agreed Statement "G" Regarding the Treaty shall not apply to transfers between or among the USSR Successor States.

Article VIII

The Standing Consultative Commission, hereinafter referred to as the Commission, shall function in the manner provided for by the Treaty and the Memorandum of Understanding Between the Government of the United States of America and the Government of the Union of Soviet Socialist Republics Regarding the Establishment of a Standing Consultative Commission of December 21, 1972, as well as by the Regulations of the Commission, which shall reflect the multilateral character of the Treaty and the equal legal status of the Parties in reaching decisions in the Commission.

Article IX

1. This Memorandum shall be subject to ratification or approval by the signatory States, in accordance with the constitutional procedures of those States.

2. The functions of the depositary of this Memorandum shall be exercised by the Government of the United States of America.

3. This Memorandum shall enter into force on the date when the Governments of all the signatory States have deposited instruments of ratification or approval of this Memorandum and shall remain in force so long as the Treaty remains in force.

4. Each State that has ratified or approved this Memorandum shall also be bound by the provisions of the First Agreed Statement of September 26, 1997, Relating to the Treaty Between the United States of America and the Union of Soviet Socialist Republics on the Limitation of Anti-Ballistic Missile Systems of May 26, 1972, and the Second Agreed Statement of September 26, 1997, Relating to the Treaty Between the United States of America and the Union of Soviet Socialist Republics on the Limitation of Anti-Ballistic Missile Systems of May 26, 1972.

DONE at New York City on September 26, 1997, in five copies, each in the English and Russian languages, both texts being equally authentic.

FOR THE UNITED STATES OF AMERICA:
MADELEINE ALBRIGHT

FOR THE REPUBLIC OF BELARUS:
I. ANTONOVICH

FOR THE REPUBLIC OF KAZAKHSTAN:
K. TOKAYEV

FOR THE RUSSION FEDERATION:
Y. PRIMAKOV

FOR UKRAINE:
H. UDOVENKO

September 26, 1997

Standing Consultative Commission

First Agreed Statement Relating to the Treaty between the United States of America and the Union of Soviet Socialist republics on the Limitation of Anti-Ballistic Missile Systems of May 26, 1972

In connection with the provisions of the Treaty Between the United States of America and the Union of Soviet Socialist Republics on the Limitation of Anti-Ballistic Missile Systems of May 26, 1972, hereinafter referred to as the Treaty, the Parties to the Treaty have, within the framework of the Standing Consultative Commission, reached agreement on the following:

1. Land-based, sea-based, and air-based interceptor missiles, interceptor missile launchers, and radars, other than anti-ballistic missile (ABM) interceptor missiles, ABM launchers, or ABM radars, respectively, shall be deemed, within the meaning of paragraph (a) of Article VI of the Treaty, not to have been given capabilities to counter strategic ballistic missiles or their elements in flight trajectory and not to have been tested in an ABM mode, if, in the course of testing them separately or in a system:

(a) the velocity of the interceptor missile does not exceed 3 km/sec over any part of its flight trajectory;

(b) the velocity of the ballistic target-missile does not exceed 5 km/sec over any part of its flight trajectory; and

(c) the range of the ballistic target-missile does not exceed 3,500 kilometers.

2. The Parties have additionally agreed on reciprocal implementation of the confidence-building measures set forth in the Agreement on Confidence-Building Measures Related to Systems to Counter Ballistic Missiles Other Than Strategic Ballistic Missiles of September 26, 1997.

3. This Agreed Statement shall enter into force simultaneously with entry into force of the Memorandum of Understanding of September 26, 1997, Relating to the Treaty Between the United States of America and the Union of Soviet Socialist Republics on the Limitation of Anti-Ballistic Missile Systems of May 26, 1972.

Done at New York City on September 26, 1997, in five copies, each in the English and Russian languages, both texts being equally authentic.

FOR THE UNITED STATES OF AMERICA:
STANLEY RIVELES

FOR THE REPUBLIC OF BELARUS:
S. AGURTSOU

FOR THE REPUBLIC OF KAZAKHSTAN:
K. ZHANBATYROV

FOR THE RUSSIAN FEDERATION:
V. KOLTUNOV

FOR UKRAINE:
O. RYBAK

COMMON UNDERSTANDINGS RELATING TO THE FIRST AGREED STATEMENT OF SEPTEMBER 26, 1997, RELATING TO THE TREATY BETWEEN THE UNITED STATES OF AMERICA AND THE UNION OF SOVIET SOCIALIST REPUBLICS ON THE LIMITATION OF ANTI-BALLISTIC MISSILE SYSTEMS OF MAY 26, 1972

I

The term "interceptor missile," as used in the First Agreed Statement of September 26, 1997, shall refer to any missile subject to the provisions of paragraph (a) of Article VI of the Treaty if such a missile:

(a) has been developed by a Party as a missile to counter ballistic missiles other than strategic ballistic missiles; or

(b) has been declared by a Party as a missile to counter ballistic missiles other than strategic ballistic missiles; or

(c) has been tested by a Party even once with the use of a ballistic target-missile.

With respect to subparagraphs (a), (b), or (c), such a missile shall be considered an interceptor missile in all its launches.

II

The provisions of paragraph 1 of the First Agreed Statement of September 26, 1997, do not supersede or amend any provision of the

Agreed Statement of November 1, 1978, and do not alter the meaning of the term "tested in an ABM mode" as that term is used in the Treaty, including the Agreed Statement of November 1, 1978.

III

The Parties have agreed that, for the purposes of the First Agreed Statement of September 26, 1997, the velocity of an interceptor missile as well as the velocity of a ballistic target-missile shall be determined in an earth-centered coordinate system fixed in relation to the Earth.

IV

The Parties have agreed that, for the purposes of the First Agreed Statement of September 26, 1997, the velocity of space-based interceptor missiles shall be considered to exceed 3 km/sec.

These Common Understandings shall be considered an attachment to the First Agreed Statement of September 26, 1997, and shall constitute an integral part thereof.

September 26, 1997

STANDING CONSULTATIVE COMMISSION

SECOND AGREED STATEMENT RELATING TO THE TREATY BETWEEN THE UNITED STATES OF AMERICA AND THE UNION OF SOVIET SOCIALIST REPUBLICS ON THE LIMITATION OF ANTI-BALLISTIC MISSILE SYSTEMS OF MAY 26, 1972

In connection with the provisions of the Treaty Between the United States of America and the Union of Soviet Socialist Republics on the Limitation of Anti-Ballistic Missile Systems of May 26, 1972, hereinafter referred to as the Treaty, the Parties to the Treaty,

Expressing their commitment to strengthening strategic stability and international security,

Emphasizing the importance of further reductions in strategic offensive arms,

Recognizing the fundamental significance of the Treaty for the above objectives,

Recognizing the necessity for effective systems to counter ballistic missiles other than strategic ballistic missiles,

Considering it their common task to preserve the Treaty, prevent its circumvention and enhance its viability,

Relying on the following principles that have served as a basis for reaching this agreement:

—the Parties are committed to the Treaty as a cornerstone of strategic stability;

—the Parties must have the option to establish and to deploy effective systems to counter ballistic missiles other than strategic ballistic missiles, and such activity must not lead to violation or circumvention of the Treaty;

—systems to counter ballistic missiles other than strategic ballistic missiles may be deployed by each Party which will not pose a realistic threat to the strategic nuclear force of another Party and which will not be tested to give such systems that capability;

—systems to counter ballistic missiles other than strategic ballistic missiles will not be deployed by the Parties for use against each other; and

—the scale of deployment—in number and geographic scope—of systems to counter ballistic missiles other than strategic ballistic missiles by any Party will be consistent with programs for ballistic missiles other than strategic ballistic missiles confronting that Party;

Have, within the framework of the Standing Consultative Commission, with respect to systems to counter ballistic missiles other than strategic ballistic missiles with interceptor missiles whose velocity exceeds 3 km/sec over any part of their flight trajectory, hereinafter referred to as systems covered by this Agreed Statement, reached agreement on the following:

1. Each Party undertakes that, in the course of testing, separately or in a system, land-based, sea-based, and air-based interceptor missiles, interceptor missile launchers, and radars, of systems covered by this Agreed Statement, which are not anti-ballistic missile (ABM) interceptor missiles, ABM launchers, or ABM radars, respectively:

(a) the velocity of the ballistic target-missile will not exceed 5 km/sec over any part of its flight trajectory; and

(b) the range of the ballistic target-missile will not exceed 3,500 kilometers.

2. Each Party, in order to preclude the possibility of ambiguous situations or misunderstandings related to compliance with the provisions of the Treaty, undertakes not to develop, test, or deploy space-based interceptor missiles to counter ballistic missiles other than strategic ballistic missiles, or space-based components based on other physical principles, whether or not part of a system, that are capable of substituting for such interceptor missiles.

3. In order to enhance confidence in compliance with the provisions of the Treaty, the Parties shall implement the provisions of the Agreement on Confidence-Building Measures Related to Systems to Counter Ballistic Missiles Other Than Strategic Ballistic Missiles of September 26, 1997, hereinafter referred to as the Confidence-Building Measures Agreement, with respect to systems covered by this Agreed Statement and not subject to the Confidence-Building Measures Agreement on the date of its entry into force. Each such system shall become subject to the provisions of the Confidence-Building Measures Agreement no later than 180 days in advance of the planned date of the first launch of an interceptor missile of that system. All information provided for in the Confidence-Building Measures Agreement shall initially be provided no later than 30 days after such a system becomes subject to the provisions of the Confidence-Building Measures Agreement.

4. In order to ensure the viability of the Treaty as technologies related to systems to counter ballistic missiles other than strategic ballistic missiles evolve, and in accordance with Article XIII of the Treaty, the Parties undertake to hold consultations and discuss, within the framework of the Standing Consultative Commission, questions or concerns that any Party may have regarding activities involving systems covered by this Agreed Statement, including questions and concerns related to the implementation of the provisions of this Agreed Statement.

5. This Agreed Statement shall enter into force simultaneously with entry into force of the Memorandum of Understanding of September 26, 1997, Relating to the Treaty Between the United States of America and the Union of Soviet Socialist Republics on the Limitation of Anti-Ballistic Missile Systems of May 26, 1972.

DONE at New York City on September 26, 1997, in five copies, each in the English and Russian languages, both texts being equally authentic.

FOR THE UNITED STATES OF AMERICA:
STANLEY RIVELES

FOR THE REPUBLIC OF BELARUS:
S. AGURTSOU

FOR THE REPUBLIC OF KAZAKHSTAN:
K. ZHANBATYROV

FOR THE RUSSIAN FEDERATION:
V. KOLTUNOV

FOR UKRAINE
O. RYBAK

COMMON UNDERSTANDINGS RELATING TO THE SECOND AGREED STATEMENT OF SEPTEMBER 26, 1997, RELATING TO THE TREATY BETWEEN THE UNITED STATES OF AMERICA AND THE UNION OF SOVIET SOCIALIST REPUBLICS ON THE LIMITATION OF ANTI-BALLISTIC MISSILE SYSTEMS OF MAY 26, 1972

I

The term "interceptor missile," as used in the Second Agreed Statement of September 26, 1997, shall refer to any missile subject to the provisions of paragraph (a) of Article VI of the Treaty if such a missile:

(a) has been developed by a Party as a missile to counter ballistic missiles other than strategic ballistic missiles; or

(b) has been declared by a Party as a missile to counter ballistic missiles other than strategic ballistic missiles; or

(c) has been tested by a Party even once with the use of a ballistic target-missile.

With respect to subparagraphs (a), (b), or (c), such a missile shall be considered an interceptor missile in all its launches.

II

The Parties have agreed that, for the purposes of the Second Agreed Statement of September 26, 1997, the velocity of an interceptor missile as well as the velocity of a ballistic target-missile shall be determined in an earth-centered coordinate system fixed in relation to the Earth.

III

The Parties have agreed that for the purposes of the Second Agreed Statement of September 26, 1997, the velocity of space-based interceptor missiles shall be considered to exceed 3 km/sec.

IV

For systems to counter ballistic missiles other than strategic ballistic missiles with interceptor missiles whose velocity exceeds 3 km/sec over any part of their flight trajectory, that become subject to the Confidence-Building Measures Agreement in accordance with paragraph 3 of the Second Agreed Statement of September 26, 1997, the Parties understand that, in connection with the provisions of paragraph 2(b) of Section IV of the Confidence-Building Measures Agreement, detailed information on such systems shall be provided in a form and scope as agreed upon by the Parties.

These Common Understandings shall be considered an attachment to the Second Agreed Statement of September 26, 1997, and shall constitute an integral part thereof.

September 26, 1997

Agreement on Confidence-Building Measures Related to Systems to Counter Ballistic Missiles other than Strategic Ballistic Missiles

The States that have signed this Agreement, hereinafter referred to as the Parties,

Desiring to promote reciprocal openness, greater trust between the Parties, and the preservation of strategic stability,

Declaring their intention to implement, on a reciprocal basis, confidence-building measures with respect to systems to counter ballistic missiles other than strategic ballistic missiles,

Have agreed as follows:

I. General Provisions

1. Systems subject to this Agreement shall be: for the United States of America—the Theater High-Altitude Area Defense (THAAD) System and the Navy Theater-Wide Theater Ballistic Missile Defense Program, known to the other Parties by the same names; for the Russian Federation—the S-300V system, known to the United States of America as the SA-12 system; for the Republic of Belarus—the S-300V system, known to the United States of America as the SA-12 system; for Ukraine—the S-300V system, known to the United States of America as the SA-12 system; and other systems as agreed upon by the Parties in the future.

2. The Parties shall conduct an initial exchange of information and notifications, as provided for in this Agreement, no later than 90 days after entry into force of this Agreement, reflecting the status as of the date of its entry into force, and update this information annually, unless otherwise agreed. Information shall be updated reflecting the status as of January 1 of each year and provided no later than April 1 of each year.

II. Notifications

1. Each Party shall provide notifications to the other Parties of test ranges and other test areas where launches of interceptor missiles of systems subject to this Agreement will take place. Notifications of test ranges and other test areas shall include the names of ranges (test areas) and their locations. Such notifications shall be provided either within 30 days after entry into force of this Agreement, or no later than 90 days in advance of the first launch of an interceptor missile of a system subject to this Agreement at each test range (test area).

2. Each Party shall provide notification to the other Parties of each launch of an interceptor missile of systems subject to this Agreement, if during that launch a ballistic target-missile is used. In this connection:

(a) an interceptor missile launch notification shall specify the name of the test range (test area) where the interceptor missile launch will take place; the type (designation) of the interceptor missile; the planned date of the interceptor missile launch; the planned launch point of the interceptor missile (geographic coordinates; for air-based systems the geographic coordinates of the projection of the planned launch point of the interceptor missile onto the Earth's surface shall be specified); the planned launch point of the ballistic target-missile (geographic coordinates);

(b) each interceptor missile launch notification shall be provided no later than 10 days in advance of the planned date of the interceptor missile launch and shall be effective for seven days beginning with the planned date of that launch; and

(c) if the launch of the interceptor missile will not occur or has not occurred within the specified 7-day period, the Party that planned to carry out the launch of the interceptor missile shall provide a notification thereof no later than 24 hours after the expiration of the 7-day period. Such a notification shall state that the interceptor missile launch has not occurred and shall either specify a new launch date, which will establish the beginning of a new 7-day period, or state that a notification of a new launch date will be made in accordance with the procedure specified in subparagraph (b) of this paragraph.

III. Demonstrations of Systems and Observations of Tests

Any Party may on a voluntary basis arrange, for any other Party or Parties, a demonstration of its systems or their components subject to this Agreement or an observation of their tests. In each specific case, the participating Parties shall agree in advance on the purpose of, and the arrangements for, such demonstrations and observations.

IV. Assurances

Each Party shall provide assurances that it will not deploy systems subject to this Agreement in numbers and locations so that these systems could pose a realistic threat to the strategic nuclear force of another Party. The measures used to provide such assurances shall include:

1. Each Party shall provide to the other Parties, in a form and scope as agreed upon by the Parties, an assessment of the programs with respect to the development, testing and deployment of ballistic missiles, other than strategic ballistic missiles, confronting that Party.

2. For each of its systems subject to this Agreement, each Party shall provide the following information:

(a) the name, type (designation), and basing mode of the system as well as of its interceptor missiles, launchers, and associated radars;

(b) the general concept of operation; the status of plans and programs; and, in addition, for systems in testing, the number of systems it plans to possess; the information shall be provided in a form and scope as agreed upon by the Parties;

(c) the class and type of basing platform:

(i) for land-based systems: the number of launchers in a battalion;

(ii) for sea-based systems: the class and type of each ship, and the number of launchers on a ship of that class capable of launching interceptor missiles of each type;

(iii) for air-based systems: the type of each aircraft, and the number of interceptor missiles each aircraft is capable of carrying;

(d) the number of interceptor missiles of a fully loaded launcher.

3. For components of each of its systems subject to this Agreement, each Party shall provide the following information:

(a) for a completely assembled interceptor missile: the number of stages, the length, the maximum diameter, the type of propellant (solid or liquid), maximum velocity demonstrated during launches, and the length and diameter of the interceptor missile launch canister;

(b) for the interceptor missile launcher: the maximum number of interceptor missiles of a fully loaded launcher; and

(c) for the radar: the frequency band (in designations adopted by the International Telecommunication Union) and potential, expressed as a value that is not exceeded by the radar's potential. The potential of a radar shall mean the product of its mean emitted power in watts and its antenna area in square meters.

V. Additional Voluntary Measures

Each Party may provide on a voluntary basis any other information or any other notifications not specified elsewhere in this Agreement. The topics, amount, and time frame for such information and notifications shall be such as each Party determines.

VI. Implementation of the Agreement

1. To promote the objectives and implementation of the provisions of this Agreement, the Parties, within the framework of the Standing

Consultative Commission established in accordance with the Treaty Between the United States of America and the Union of Soviet Socialist Republics on the Limitation of Anti-Ballistic Missile Systems of May 26, 1972, shall consider:

(a) issues concerning implementation of the obligations assumed under this Agreement, as well as related situations which may be considered ambiguous; and

(b) amendments to the provisions of this Agreement and other possible proposals on further increasing its viability.

2. The Parties shall use the Nuclear Risk Reduction Center channels or the equivalent government-to-government communications links for providing the notifications and for exchanging the information provided for in Sections II, IV and V of this Agreement.

VII. CONFIDENTIALITY

Each Party undertakes not to release to the public the information provided pursuant to this Agreement except with the express consent of the Party that provided such information.

VIII. ENTRY INTO FORCE AND DURATION

This Agreement shall enter into force simultaneously with entry into force of the First Agreed Statement of September 26, 1997, Relating to the Treaty Between the United States of America and the Union of Soviet Socialist Republics on the Limitation of Anti-Ballistic Missile Systems of May 26, 1972, and the Second Agreed Statement of September 26, 1997, Relating to the Treaty Between the United States of America and the Union of Soviet Socialist Republics on the Limitation of Anti-Ballistic Missile Systems of May 26, 1972, and shall remain in force so long as either of those Agreed Statements remains in force.

DONE at New York City on September 26, 1997, in five copies, each in the English and Russian languages, both texts being equally authentic.

FOR THE UNITED STATES OF AMERICA:
STANLEY RIVELES

FOR THE REPUBLIC OF BELARUS:
S. AGURTSOU

FOR THE REPUBLIC OF KAZAKHSTAN:
K. ZHANBATYROV

FOR THE RUSSIAN FEDERATION:
V. KOLTUNOV

FOR UKRAINE:
O. RYBAK

September 26, 1997
New York City

STATEMENT BY THE UNITED STATES OF AMERICA ON PLANS WITH RESPECT TO SYSTEMS TO COUNTER BALLISTIC MISSILES OTHER THAN STRATEGIC BALLISTIC MISSILES

The United States of America states that, with regard to systems to counter ballistic missiles other than strategic ballistic missiles, it has no plans:

(a) before April 1999 to test, against a ballistic target-missile, land-based, sea-based or air-based interceptor missiles whose velocity exceeds 3 km/sec over any part of their flight trajectory;

(b) to develop such systems with interceptor missiles whose velocity over any part of their flight trajectory exceeds 5.5 km/sec for land-based and air-based systems or 4.5 km/sec for sea-based systems; or

(c) to test such systems against ballistic target-missiles with multiple independently targetable reentry vehicles or against reentry vehicles deployed or planned to be deployed on strategic ballistic missiles.

Excerpts from the
DCI National Intelligence Estimate

PRESIDENT'S SUMMARY
EMERGING MISSILE THREATS TO
NORTH AMERICA DURING THE NEXT 15 YEARS

Secret NOFORN Rel CAN
PS/NIE 95-19
November 1995

No country, other than the major declared nuclear powers, will develop or otherwise acquire a ballistic missile in the next 15 years that could threaten the contiguous 48 states and Canada.

—Among Third World countries hostile to the United States, North Korea has the most advanced ballistic missile program. One of its missiles in development, the Taepo Dong 2, is assessed to have a range of 4,000 to 6,000 kilometers. A 6,000-kilometer range would be sufficient to strike portions of Alaska and the far western portion of the Hawaiian Island chain (more than 1,000 kilometers west of Honolulu).

—North Korea is unlikely to obtain the technological capability to develop a longer range operational ICBM. North Korea would have to overcome significant hurdles to complete such a program, particularly given the political and economic uncertainties and technological challenges it faces. For such an ICBM, North Korea would have to develop new propulsion and improved guidance and control systems and conduct a flight test program. We have no evidence that Pyongyang has begun or intends to begin such a program, and we think we would detect propulsion system development.

Ballistic missile programs of other countries are focused on regional security concerns and are not expected to evolve into threats to North America during the period of this estimate.

—We have no evidence Iran wants to develop an ICBM. Even if Tehran wanted to, we assess that it would not be able to do so before 2010 because it lacks the economic resources and technological infrastructure.

—Iraq's ability to develop an ICBM is severely constrained by international sanctions and the intrusive U.N. inspections and monitoring regime. Should these programs end, Baghdad could develop the technology and infrastructure necessary for an ICBM program. But even with substantial foreign assistance, it would require at least 15 years to develop an operational ICBM.

—Three countries not hostile to the United States—India, Israel and Japan—could develop ICBMs within as few as five years if they were motivated, but we judge that they are unlikely to make the necessary investment during the period of this estimate.

We are likely to detect any indigenous long-range ballistic missile program many years before deployment.

—Developmental flight-testing normally would provide a minimum of five years warning before deployment. We would probably see other indicators of an ICBM program, particularly propulsion related development efforts, two to 10 years before the first flight test—seven to 15 years before deployment.

—Foreign assistance is a wild card that can sometimes permit a country to solve difficult developmental problems relatively quickly. Such external assistance can hinder our ability to predict how soon a system will become operational.

—Any country with a capability to produce space boosters could almost certainly use the same facilities and personnel to produce most ICBM components. However, a development program for a space launch vehicle (SLV) by a potentially hostile state with nuclear ambitions would be a key indicator of a potential ICBM program.

We expect countries that currently have ICBMs will not sell them. Each of the countries either is a Missile Technology Control Regime

(MTCR) member or has agreed to abide by its terms and recognizes that transfer of an intercontinental range missile would show blatant disregard for the regime. Also, countries probably would be concerned that any missiles sold might some day be turned against them.

Similarly, we do not believe any country with space launch vehicles will sell them. Furthermore, if a country were to purchase an SLV, converting it to an ICBM would involve technological obstacles roughly as challenging as those involved in an indigenous ICBM program.

We see no indications, and think it unlikely, that any potentially hostile nation will develop submarine-launched ballistic missiles over the period of this estimate.[1] Launching ballistic missiles from surface vessels or aircraft is so technically challenging as to be a highly unlikely approach.

CRUISE MISSILES

By 2005, several countries, including some hostile toward the United States, probably will acquire land-attack cruise missiles (LACMs) with ranges of hundreds of kilometers. A cruise missile attack on North America by a Third World country, using ships (or possibly aircraft) off the coast as launch platforms, would be technically feasible. However, we think such an act is unlikely because of the perceived difficulty of ensuring mission success. It is extremely unlikely any Third World country would acquire submarine-launched LACMs and use them against North America because of the technological sophistication required and the difficulty of deploying submarines far from home port.

Because of the size and nature of cruise missile systems, as well as the hard-to-detect signatures associated with flight testing, LACM development programs can be easily hidden, thus limiting our confidence in early detection.

EXPORT CONTROLS

The MTCR significantly limits the availability of missiles, components, and related technology. We project it will continue to serve as a substantial barrier to countries interested in acquiring ballistic missiles, but some leakage of components and critical technologies will likely continue. Because of their relatively greater dual-use nature, technology and components applicable to LACMs will proliferate more widely than those for ballistic missiles.

Unauthorized or Accidental Launch

We conclude that the current threat to North America from unauthorized or accidental launch of Russian or Chinese strategic missiles remains remote and has not changed significantly from that of the past decade. However, we are less confident about the future, in view of the fluid political situations in both countries. If there were a severe political crisis in either country control of the nuclear command structure could become less certain, increasing the possibility of an unauthorized launch. Nevertheless the possibility would remain quite low.

Note

1. India is planning submarine-launched ballistic missiles (SLBM) with a 300-km range for deployment by 2010.

Excerpts from the
1998 Rumsfeld Commission Report

REPORT OF THE COMMISSION TO ASSESS THE
BALLISTIC MISSILE THREAT TO THE UNITED STATES
. . . .

II. EXECUTIVE SUMMARY
A. CONCLUSIONS OF THE COMMISSIONERS

The nine Commissioners are unanimous in concluding that:

—Concerted efforts by a number of overtly or potentially hostile nations to acquire ballistic missiles with biological or nuclear payloads pose a growing threat to the United States, its deployed forces and its friends and allies. These newer, developing threats in North Korea, Iran and Iraq are in addition to those still posed by the existing ballistic missile arsenals of Russia and China, nations with which the United States is not

Members of The Commission to Assess the Ballistic Missile Threat to the United States were nominated by the Speaker of the U.S. House of Representatives, the Majority Leader of the U.S. Senate and the Minority Leaders of the U.S. Senate and the U.S. House of Representatives and appointed by the Director of Central Intelligence. The Honorable Donald H. Rumsfeld, Chairman, Dr. Barry M. Blechman, General Lee Butler, U.S. Air Force (Ret.), Dr. Richard L. Garwin, Dr. William R. Graham, Dr. William Schneider, Jr., General Larry D. Welch, U.S. Air Force (Ret.), Dr. Paul D. Wolfowitz, The Honorable R. James Woolsey.

now in conflict but which remain in uncertain transitions. The newer bal-listic missile-equipped nations' capabilities will not match those of U.S. systems for accuracy or reliability. However, they would be able to inflict major destruction on the U.S. within about five years of a decision to acquire such a capability (10 years in the case of Iraq). During several of those years, the U.S. might not be aware that such a decision had been made.

—The threat to the U.S. posed by these emerging capabilities is broader, more mature and evolving more rapidly than has been reported in estimates and reports by the Intelligence Community.

—The Intelligence Community's ability to provide timely and accurate estimates of ballistic missile threats to the U.S. is eroding. This erosion has roots both within and beyond the intelligence process itself. The Community's capabilities in this area need to be strengthened in terms of both resources and methodology.

—The warning times the U.S. can expect of new, threatening ballistic missile deployments are being reduced. Under some plausible scenarios—including re-basing or transfer of operational missiles, sea- and air-launch options, shortened development programs that might include testing in a third country, or some combination of these—the U.S. might well have lit-tle or no warning before operational deployment.

Therefore, we unanimously recommend that U.S. analyses, practices and policies that depend on expectations of extended warning of deploy-ment be reviewed and, as appropriate, revised to reflect the reality of an environment in which there may be little or no warning.

B. The Commission and Its Methods

The Commissioners brought to their task the perspectives of former senior policymakers from outside the Intelligence Community who have decades of experience and a variety of views as users of the Intelligence Community's products. We shared an informed understanding of intelli-gence processes. In making our assessment, we took into account not only the hard data available, but also the often significant gaps in that data. We had access to both data and experts drawn from the full array of departments and agencies as well as from sources throughout the Intelligence Community. We also drew on experts from outside that Community and on studies sponsored by the Commission. Our aim was to ensure that we were exposed to a wide range of opinion and to the greatest possible depth and breadth of analysis.

We began this study with different views about how to respond to ballistic missile threats, and we continue to have differences. Nevertheless, as a result of our intensive study over the last six months we are unanimous in our assessment of the threat, an assessment which differs from published intelligence estimates.

This divergence between the Commission's findings and authoritative estimates by the Intelligence Community stems primarily from our use of a somewhat more comprehensive methodology in assessing ballistic missile development and deployment programs. We believe that our approach takes more fully into account three crucial factors now shaping new ballistic missile threats to the United States:

—Newer ballistic missile and weapons of mass destruction (WMD) development programs no longer follow the patterns initially set by the U.S. and the Soviet Union. These programs require neither high standards of missile accuracy, reliability and safety nor large numbers of missiles and therefore can move ahead more rapidly.

—A nation that wants to develop ballistic missiles and weapons of mass destruction can now obtain extensive technical assistance from outside sources. Foreign assistance is not a wild card. It is a fact.

—Nations are increasingly able to conceal important elements of their ballistic missile and associated WMD programs and are highly motivated to do so.

C. New Threats in a Transformed Security Environment

The Commission did not assess nuclear, biological and chemical weapons programs on a global basis. We considered those countries about which we felt particular reason to be concerned and examined their capabilities to acquire ballistic missiles armed with weapons of mass destruction.

All of the nations whose programs we examined that are developing long-range ballistic missiles have the option to arm these, as well as their shorter range systems, with biological or chemical weapons. These weapons can take the form of bomblets as well as a single, large warhead.

The knowledge needed to design and build a nuclear weapon is now widespread. The emerging ballistic missile powers have access to, or are pursuing the acquisition of, the needed fissile material both through domestic efforts and foreign channels.

As our work went forward, it became increasingly clear to us that nations about which the U.S. has reason to be concerned are exploiting a dramatically transformed international security environment. That environment provides an ever-widening access to technology, information and expertise that can be and is used to speed both the development and deployment of ballistic missiles and weapons of mass destruction. It can also be used to develop denial and deception techniques that seek to impede U.S. intelligence gathering about the development and deployment programs of those nations.

1. Geopolitical Change and Role for Ballistic Missiles

A number of countries with regional ambitions do not welcome the U.S. role as a stabilizing power in their regions and have not accepted it passively. Because of their ambitions, they want to place restraints on the U.S. capability to project power or influence into their regions. They see the acquisition of missile and WMD technology as a way of doing so.

Since the end of the Cold War, the geopolitical environment and the roles of ballistic missiles and weapons of mass destruction have both evolved. Ballistic missiles provide a cost-effective delivery system that can be used for both conventional and non-conventional weapons. For those seeking to thwart the projection of U.S. power, the capability to combine ballistic missiles with weapons of mass destruction provides a strategic counter to U.S. conventional and information-based military superiority. With such weapons, these nations can pose a serious threat to the United States, to its forward-based forces and their staging areas and to U.S. friends and allies.

Whether short- or long-range, a successfully launched ballistic missile has a high probability of delivering its payload to its target compared to other means of delivery. Emerging powers therefore see ballistic missiles as highly effective deterrent weapons and as an effective means of coercing or intimidating adversaries, including the United States.

2. Russia

With regard to Russia, the principal cloud over the future is lingering political uncertainty. Despite enormous changes since the break-up of the Soviet Union, Russia is in an uncertain, in some ways precarious, transition. It may succeed in establishing a stable democracy allied with the

West in maintaining peace and extending freedom. Or it may not. Or it might be torn by internal struggles for an extended period. In its present situation, accurate U.S. intelligence estimates are difficult to make.

Russia continues to pose a ballistic missile threat to the United States, although of a different character than in the past. The number of missiles in its inventory is likely to decline further compared with Cold War levels in that large numbers of Soviet strategic missiles deployed in the 1970s and 1980s are scheduled to be retired. Still, Russian ballistic missile forces continue to be modernized and improved, although the pace of modernization has been slowed from planned schedules by economic constraints. The Russian ballistic missile early warning system and nuclear command and control (C2) system have also been affected by aging and delays in planned modernization. In the context of a crisis growing out of civil strife, present early warning and C2 weaknesses could pose a risk of unauthorized or inadvertent launch of missiles against the United States.[1]

With the Cold War ended, the likelihood of a deliberate missile attack on the U.S. from Russia has been greatly lessened but not entirely eliminated. However, Russia's leaders issued a new national security policy in 1993 that places greater reliance on nuclear deterrence, very likely in response to Russia's economic difficulties and decline in its conventional military capabilities. At the same time, the risk of an accident or of a loss of control over Russian ballistic missile forces—a risk which now appears small—could increase sharply and with little warning if the political situation in Russia were to deteriorate.

Also, quite apart from these risks, Russia poses a threat to the U.S. as a major exporter of enabling technologies, including ballistic missile technologies, to countries hostile to the United States. In particular, Russian assistance has greatly accelerated Iran's ballistic missile program.

3. China

As in the case of Russia, China's future is clouded by a range of uncertainties. China, too, is going through a transition, but one which has been going on for 20 years. The improvement in Sino-U.S. relations, interrupted in 1989, has resumed. Although the U.S. and China are developing a more cooperative relationship, significant potential conflicts remain, and China is less constrained today by fear of Russia than it once was by fear of the Soviet Union. Taiwan is an obvious potential flashpoint. Other flashpoints could arise as China pursues its drive for greater influence in

Asia and the Western Pacific. Even now China has conflicts with several of its neighbors, some of which could involve the U.S. in a confrontation.

China is modernizing its long-range missiles and nuclear weapons in ways that will make it a more threatening power in the event of a crisis. China's 1995–96 missile firings in the Taiwan Strait, aimed at intimidating Taiwan in the lead-up to its presidential election, provoked a sharp confrontation with the United States. For example, a pointed question was posed by Lt. Gen. Xiong Guang Kai, a frequent spokesman for Chinese policy, about U.S. willingness to trade Los Angeles for Taipei. This comment seemed designed to link China's ballistic missile capabilities with its regional priorities.

China also poses a threat to the U.S. as a significant proliferator of ballistic missiles, weapons of mass destruction and enabling technologies. It has carried out extensive transfers to Iran's solid-fueled ballistic missile program. It has supplied Pakistan with a design for a nuclear weapon and additional nuclear weapons assistance. It has even transferred complete ballistic missile systems to Saudi Arabia (the 3,100-km-range CSS-2) and Pakistan (the 350-km-range M-11).

The behavior thus far of Russia and China makes it appear unlikely, albeit for different reasons—strategic, political, economic or some combination of all three—that either government will soon effectively reduce its country's sizable transfer of critical technologies, experts or expertise to the emerging ballistic missile powers.

4. Countries With Scud-Based Missile Infrastructures

The basis of most missile developments by emerging ballistic missile powers is the Soviet Scud missile and its derivatives. The Scud is derived from the World War II–era German V-2 rocket. With the external help now readily available, a nation with a well-developed, Scud-based ballistic missile infrastructure would be able to achieve first flight of a long-range missile, up to and including intercontinental ballistic missile (ICBM) range,[2] within about five years of deciding to do so. During several of those years the U.S. might not be aware that such a decision had been made. Early production models would probably be limited in number. They would be unlikely to meet U.S. standards of safety, accuracy and reliability. But the purposes of these nations would not require such standards. A large force armed with scores of missiles and warheads and meeting higher operational standards would take somewhat longer to test, produce and deploy. But meanwhile, even a few of the simpler missiles could be highly effective for the purposes of those countries.

The extraordinary level of resources North Korea and Iran are now devoting to developing their own ballistic missile capabilities poses a substantial and immediate danger to the U.S., its vital interests and its allies. While these nations' missile programs may presently be aimed primarily at regional adversaries, they inevitably and inescapably engage the vital interests of the U.S. as well. Their targeted adversaries include key U.S. friends and allies. U.S. deployed forces are already at risk from these nations' growing arsenals. Each of these nations places a high priority on threatening U.S. territory, and each is even now pursuing advanced ballistic missile capabilities to pose a direct threat to U.S. territory.

a. North Korea

There is evidence that North Korea is working hard on the Taepo Dong 2 (TD-2) ballistic missile. The status of the system's development cannot be determined precisely. Nevertheless, the ballistic missile test infrastructure in North Korea is well developed. Once the system is assessed to be ready, a test flight could be conducted within six months of a decision to do so. If North Korea judged the test to be a success, the TD-2 could be deployed rapidly. It is unlikely the U.S. would know of such a decision much before the missile was launched. This missile could reach major cities and military bases in Alaska and the smaller, westernmost islands in the Hawaiian chain. Light-weight variations of the TD-2 could fly as far as 10,000 km, placing at risk western U.S. territory in an arc extending northwest from Phoenix, Arizona, to Madison, Wisconsin. These variants of the TD-2 would require additional time to develop and would likely require an additional flight test.

North Korea has developed and deployed the No Dong, a medium-range ballistic missile[3] (MRBM) using a scaled-up Scud engine, which is capable of flying 1,300 km. With this missile, North Korea can threaten Japan, South Korea and U.S. bases in the vicinity of North Korea. North Korea has reportedly tested the No Dong only once, in 1993. The Commission judges that the No Dong was operationally deployed long before the U.S. Government recognized that fact. There is ample evidence that North Korea has created a sizable missile production infrastructure, and therefore it is highly likely that considerable numbers of No Dongs have been produced.

In light of the considerable difficulties the Intelligence Community encountered in assessing the pace and scope of the No Dong missile program, the U.S. may have very little warning prior to the deployment of the Taepo Dong 2.

North Korea maintains an active WMD program, including a nuclear weapon program. It is known that North Korea diverted material in the late 1980s for at least one or possibly two weapons. North Korea's ongoing nuclear program activity raises the possibility that it could produce additional nuclear weapons. North Korea also possesses biological weapons production and dispensing technology, including the capability to deploy chemical or biological warheads on missiles.

North Korea also poses a major threat to American interests, and potentially to the United States itself, because it is a major proliferator of the ballistic missile capabilities it possesses—missiles, technology, technicians, transporter-erector-launchers (TELs) and underground facility expertise—to other countries of missile proliferation concern. These countries include Iran, Pakistan and others.

b. Iran

Iran is placing extraordinary emphasis on its ballistic missile and WMD development programs. The ballistic missile infrastructure in Iran is now more sophisticated than that of North Korea, and has benefited from broad, essential, long-term assistance from Russia and important assistance from China as well. Iran is making very rapid progress in developing the Shahab 3 MRBM, which like the North Korean No Dong has a range of 1,300 km. This missile may be flight tested at any time and deployed soon thereafter.

The Commission judges that Iran now has the technical capability and resources to demonstrate an ICBM-range ballistic missile, similar to the TD-2 (based on scaled-up Scud technology), within five years of a decision to proceed—whether that decision has already been made or is yet to be made.

In addition to this Scud-based long-range ballistic missile program, Iran has acquired and is seeking major, advanced missile components that can be combined to produce ballistic missiles with sufficient range to strike the United States. For example, Iran is reported to have acquired engines or engine designs for the RD-214 engine, which powered the Soviet SS-4 MRBM and served as the first stage of the SL-7 space-launch vehicle. Iran is known to have an interest in even more advanced engines. A 10,000 km-range Iranian missile could hold the U.S. at risk in an arc extending north-east of a line from Philadelphia, Pennsylvania, to St. Paul, Minnesota.

Iran has also developed a solid-fueled rocket infrastructure; it already produces short-range solid-fueled rockets. It is seeking long-range missile technology from outside sources, purportedly for a space-launch vehicle. Both contribute directly to Iran's ballistic missile technology base. Iran is known to rely heavily on imports of missile technology from foreign sources, particularly Russia and North Korea. These imports have allowed Iran's missile programs to proceed swiftly, and they can be incorporated into Iran's domestic infrastructure as well.

Iran is developing weapons of mass destruction. It has a nuclear energy and weapons program which aims to design, develop and, as soon as possible, produce nuclear weapons. The Commission judges that the only issue as to whether or not Iran may soon have or already has a nuclear weapon is the amount of fissile material available to it. Because of significant gaps in our knowledge, the U.S. is unlikely to know whether Iran possesses nuclear weapons until after the fact. While Iran's civil nuclear program is currently under International Atomic Energy Agency (IAEA) safeguards, it could be used as a source of sufficient fissile material to construct a small number of weapons within the next 10 years if Iran were willing to violate safeguards. If Iran were to accumulate enough fissile material from foreign sources, it might be able to develop a nuclear weapon in only one to three years. Iran also has an active chemical weapon development and production program and is conducting research into biological weapons.

c. Iraq

Iraq has maintained the skills and industrial capabilities needed to reconstitute its long-range ballistic missile program. Its plant and equipment are less developed than those of North Korea or Iran as a result of actions forced by United Nations (U.N.) Resolutions and monitoring. However, Iraq has actively continued work on short-range (under 150 km) liquid- and solid-fueled missiles, programs allowed by the U.N. Resolutions. Once U.N.-imposed controls are lifted, Iraq could mount a determined effort to acquire needed plant and equipment, whether directly or indirectly. Such an effort would allow Iraq to pose an ICBM threat to the United States within 10 years. Iraq could develop a shorter range, covert, ship-launched missile threat that could threaten the United States in a very short time.

Iraq had a large, intense ballistic missile development and production program prior to the Gulf War. The Iraqis produced Scuds and then modified Scud missiles to produce the 600-km–range Al Hussein and 900-km–range Al Abbas missiles. The expertise, as well as some of the equipment and materials from this program remain in Iraq and provide a strong foundation for a revived ballistic missile program.

Prior to the invasion of Kuwait in 1990, Iraq could have had nuclear weapons in the 1993–1995 time frame, although it still had technical hurdles to overcome. After the invasion of Kuwait, Iraq began a crash program to produce a nuclear device in six to nine months based on highly enriched uranium removed from the safeguarded reactor at Tuwaitha. Iraq has the capability to reconstitute its nuclear weapon program; the speed at which it can do so depends on the availability of fissile material. It would take several years to build the required production facilities from scratch. It is possible that Iraq has hidden some material from U.N. Special Commission (UNSCOM) inspection or that it could acquire fissile material abroad (from another "rogue" state, for example). Iraq also had large chemical and biological weapons programs prior to the war and produced chemical and biological warheads for its missiles. Knowledge, personnel and equipment related to WMD remain in Iraq so that it could reconstitute these programs rapidly following the end of sanctions.

5. India

India is developing a number of ballistic missiles from short-range to those with ICBM-class capabilities, along with a submarine-launched ballistic missile (SLBM) and a short-range, surface ship-launched system. India has the infrastructure to develop and produce these missiles. It is aggressively seeking technology from other states, particularly Russia. While it develops its long-range ballistic missiles, India's space-launch vehicles provide an option for an interim ICBM capability. India has detonated several nuclear devices, and it is clear that it is developing warheads for its missile systems. India has biological and chemical weapons programs. Since the Pakistani nuclear tests, India has announced its intention to increase its spending on missiles and nuclear weapons.

India's program to develop ballistic missiles began in 1983 and grew out of its space-launch program, which was based on Scout rocket technology acquired from the United States. India currently has developed and deployed the Prithvi short-range ballistic missile[4] (SRBM), and is developing longer range, liquid- and solid-fueled missiles. They include the Prithvi II SRBM, the Agni, Agni-Plus and Agni-B intermediate-range ballistic missiles[5] (IRBMs), a sea-launched ballistic missile and an SLBM, the Sagarika.

India detonated a nuclear device in 1974, conducted a test series in May 1998, and it is clear that it is developing warheads for its missile systems. Indian leaders recently declared that India has developed nuclear weapons for deployment on the Prithvi SRBM and the Agni Plus MRBM.

India has acquired and continues to seek Russian, U.S. and Western European technology for its missile programs. Technology and expertise acquired from other states, particularly from Russia, are helping India to accelerate the development and increase the sophistication of its missile systems. For example, Russian assistance is critical to the development of the Indian SLBM and its related submarine. But India is rapidly enhancing its own missile science and technology base as well. Many Indian nationals are educated and work in the U.S., Europe and other advanced nations; some of the knowledge thereby acquired returns to the Indian missile program. While India continues to benefit from foreign technology and expertise, its programs and industrial base are now sufficiently advanced that supplier control regimes can affect only the rate of acceleration in India's programs. India is in a position to supply material and technical assistance to others.

6. Pakistan

Pakistan's ballistic missile infrastructure is now more advanced than that of North Korea. It will support development of a missile of 2,500-km range, which we believe Pakistan will seek in order to put all of India within range of Pakistani missiles. The development of a 2,500-km missile will give Pakistan the technical base for developing a much longer range missile system. Through foreign acquisition, and beginning without an extensive domestic science and technology base, Pakistan has acquired these missile capabilities quite rapidly. China and North Korea are Pakistan's major sources of ballistic missiles, production facilities and technology.

Pakistan currently possesses nuclear-capable M-11 SRBMs acquired from China, and it may produce its own missile, the Tarmuk, based on the M-11. In 1998, Pakistan tested and deployed the 1,300-km-Ghauri

MRBM, a version of the North Korean No Dong, and the Commission believes Pakistan has acquired production facilities for this missile as well.

Pakistan possesses nuclear weapons that employ highly-enriched uranium and conducted its first nuclear weapon test series in May 1998. A new Pakistani nuclear reactor has been completed that could be used for the production of plutonium. In addition to its nuclear weapons, Pakistan has biological and chemical weapons programs.

Chinese assistance has been crucial to Pakistan's nuclear weapons program. India and Pakistan are not hostile to the United States. The prospect of U.S. military confrontation with either seems at present to be slight. However, beyond the possibility of nuclear war on the subcontinent, their aggressive, competitive development of ballistic missiles and weapons of mass destruction poses three concerns in particular. First, it enables them to supply relevant technologies to other nations. Second, India and Pakistan may seek additional technical assistance through cooperation with their current major suppliers—India from Russia, Pakistan from North Korea and China—because of the threats they perceive from one another and because of India's anxieties about China, combined with their mounting international isolation. Third, their growing missile and WMD capabilities have direct effects on U.S. policies, both regional and global, and could significantly affect U.S. capability to play a stabilizing role in Asia.

D. A New Non-Proliferation Environment

Since the end of the Cold War a number of developments have made ballistic missile and WMD technologies increasingly available. They include:

—A number of nations have chosen not to join non-proliferation agreements. Some participants in those agreements have cheated.

—As global trade has steadily expanded, access has increased to the information, technology and technicians needed for missile and WMD development.

—Access to technologies used in early generations of U.S. and Soviet missiles has eased. However rudimentary compared to present U.S. standards, these technologies serve the needs of emerging ballistic missile powers.

—Among those countries of concern to the U.S., commerce in ballistic missile and WMD technology and hardware has been growing, which may make proliferation self-sustaining among them and facilitate their ability to proliferate technology and hardware to others.

Some countries which could have readily acquired nuclear weapons and ballistic missiles—such as Germany, Japan and South Korea—have been successfully encouraged not to do so by U.S. security guarantees and by non-proliferation agreements. Even though they lack such security guarantees, other countries have also joined non-proliferation agreements and abandoned development programs and weapons systems. Some examples are Argentina, Brazil, South Africa and the former Soviet republics of Belarus, Kazakhstan and Ukraine.

1. Increased Competence of and Trade Among Emerging Ballistic Missile Powers

Conversely, there are other countries—some of which are themselves parties to various non-proliferation agreements and treaties—that either have acquired ballistic missile or WMD capabilities or are working hard to do so. North Korea, Iran and Iraq, as well as India and Pakistan, are at the forefront of this group. They now have increased incentives to cooperate with one another. They have extensive access to technology, information and expertise from developed countries such as Russia and China. They also have access through commercial and other channels in the West, including the United States. Through this trade and their own indigenous efforts, these second-tier powers are on the verge of being able to provide to one another, if they have not already done so, the capabilities needed to develop long-range ballistic missiles.

2. U.S. as a Contributor to Proliferation

The U.S. is the world's leading developer and user of advanced technology. Once it is transferred by the U.S. or by another developed country, there is no way to ensure that the transferred technology will not be used for hostile purposes. The U.S. tries to limit technology transfers to hostile powers, but history teaches that such transfers cannot be stopped for long periods. They can only be slowed and made more costly, and even that requires the cooperation of other developed nations. The acquisition and use of transferred technologies in ballistic missile and WMD programs has been facilitated by foreign student training in the U.S., by wide dissemination of technical information, by the illegal acquisition of U.S. designs and equipment and by the relaxation of U.S. export control policies. As a result, the U.S. has been and is today a major, albeit unintentional, contributor to the proliferation of ballistic missiles and associated weapons of mass destruction.

3. Motives of Countries of Concern

Recent ballistic missile and nuclear tests in South Asia should not be viewed as merely a sharp but temporary setback in the expanding reach of non-proliferation regimes. While policymakers may try to reverse or at least contain the trends of which these tests are a part, the missile and WMD programs of these nations are clearly the results of fundamental political calculations of their vital interests. Those nations willing and able to supply dangerous technologies and systems to one another, including Russia, China and their quasi-governmental commercial entities, may be motivated by commercial, foreign policy or national security interests or by a combination thereof. As noted, such countries are increasingly cooperating with one another, perhaps in some instances because they have reciprocal needs for what one has and the other lacks. The transfer of complete missile systems, such as China's transfer to Saudi Arabia, will continue to be available. Short of radical political change, there is every reason to assume that the nations engaged in these missile and WMD development activities will continue their programs as matters of high priority.

4. Readier Market Access to Technology

In today's increasingly market-driven, global economy, nations so motivated have faster, cheaper and more efficient access to modern technology. Commercial exchanges and technology transfers have multiplied the pathways to those technologies needed for ballistic missiles and weapons of mass destruction. These pathways reduce development times and costs, lowering both technical and budget obstacles to missile development and deployment.

Expanding world trade and the explosion in information technology have accelerated the global diffusion of scientific, technical and industrial information. The channels—both public and private, legal and illegal—through which technology, components and individual technicians can be moved among nations have increased exponentially.

5. Availability of Classified Information and Export-Controlled Technology

Trends in the commercial sector of a market-driven, global economy have been accompanied, and in many ways accelerated, by an increased availability of classified information as a result of:

—Lax enforcement of export controls.

—Relaxation of U.S. and Western export controls.

—Growth in dual-use technologies.

—Economic incentives to sell ballistic missile components and systems.

—Extensive declassification of materials related to ballistic missiles and weapons of mass destruction.

—Continued, intense espionage facilitated by security measures increasingly inadequate for the new environment.

—Extensive disclosure of classified information, including information compromising intelligence sources and methods. Damaging information appears almost daily in the national and international media and on the Internet.

E. Alternative Ballistic Missile Launch Modes

In evaluating present threats, it is misleading to use old patterns of development as guides. The history of U.S. and Soviet missile and WMD development has become irrelevant. Approaches that the U.S. considered and specifically rejected on grounds of safety, reliability, accuracy and requirements for high volume production are in many cases well-suited to nations less concerned about safety and able to meet their needs with only a few, less accurate, less reliable weapons. Analytical approaches the Intelligence Community could realistically rely on in the past need to be restudied and reevaluated in light of this newer model.

The Commission believes the U.S. needs to pay attention to the possibility that complete, long-range ballistic missile systems could be transferred from one nation to another, just as China transferred operational CSS-2s to Saudi Arabia in 1988. Such missiles could be equipped with weapons of mass destruction.

One nation's use of another nation's territory also needs to be considered. The U.S. did this during the Cold War, and the Soviet Union tried to do it in Cuba in the early 1960s. For example, if Iran were to deploy ballistic missiles in Libya, it could reduce the range required to threaten the U.S. as well as Europe. Given the existing patterns of cooperation the

Commission has already seen, both testing by one country on the territory of another and deriving data from other-country tests are also distinct possibilities.

Sea launch of shorter range ballistic missiles is another possibility. This could enable a country to pose a direct territorial threat to the U.S. sooner than it could by waiting to develop an ICBM for launch from its own territory. Sea launching could also permit it to target a larger area of the U.S. than would a missile fired from its home territory. India is working on a sea launch capability. Air launch is another possible mode of delivering a shorter range missile to U.S. territory.

The key importance of these approaches is that each would significantly shorten the warning time of deployment available to the United States.

F. Erosion of Warning

Precise forecasts of the growth in ballistic missile capabilities over the next two decades—tests by year, production rates, weapons deployed by year, weapon characteristics by system type and circular error probable (CEP)—cannot be provided with confidence. Deception and denial efforts are intense and often successful, and U.S. collection and analysis assets are limited. Together they create a high risk of continued surprise.

The question is not simply whether the U.S. will have warning of an emerging capability, but whether the nature and magnitude of a particular threat will be perceived with sufficient clarity in time to take appropriate action.

Concealment, denial and deception efforts by key target countries are intended to delay the discovery of strategically significant activities until well after they had been carried out successfully. The fact that some of these secret activities are discovered over time is to the credit of the U.S. Intelligence Community. However, the fact that there are delays in discovery of those activities provides a sharp warning that a great deal of activity goes undetected.

Both technical and human intelligence are inherently more difficult to collect in those countries where the U.S. has limited access, which include most of the ballistic missile countries of concern. The U.S. is not able to predict and anticipate with confidence the behavior and actions of emerging ballistic missile powers and their related political decision-making.

Their ballistic missile programs often do not follow a single, known pattern or model, and they use unexpected development patterns. These are not models of development the U.S. follows or that intelligence analysts expect to see. For example, Pakistan's test launch in April 1998 of its Ghauri MRBM—its version of the North Korean No Dong—could not be predicted on the basis of any known pattern of technical development either for MRBMs generally or Pakistan in particular. Similarly, North Korea's decision to deploy the No Dong after what is believed to be a single successful test flight is another example. Based on U.S. and Russian experience, the Intelligence Community had expected that a regular test series would be required to provide the confidence needed before any country would produce and deploy a ballistic missile system. Yet North Korea deployed the No Dong.

The Commission believes that the technical means of collection now employed will not meet emerging requirements, and considerable uncertainty persists whether planned collection and analysis systems will do so.

G. Methodology

In analyzing the ballistic missile threat, the Commission used an expanded methodology. We used it as a complement to the traditional analysis in which a country's known program status is used to establish estimates of its current missile capabilities. We believe this expanded approach provides insights into emerging threats that the prevailing approaches used by the Intelligence Community may not bring to the surface.

To guide our assessment of the ballistic missile threat to the United States, we posed three questions:

—What is known about the ballistic missile threat, including the domestic infrastructure of a ballistic missile power; the efforts of a power to acquire foreign technology, materials and expertise; and the scale, pace and progress of its programs?

—What is not known about the threat in each of those three categories?

—Can a power intent on posing a ballistic missile threat to any part of the United States, including the use of but not limited to ICBM-range missiles, use the open market, the black market and/or espionage to secure the needed technology and expertise and then carry out its program in ways that will minimize the interval between the time the U.S. becomes aware of the threat and the fielding of that capability?

In seeking answers to these questions, we familiarized ourselves with the current state of knowledge as well as the depth of analytic capability within the Intelligence Community related to ballistic missile and WMD threats. The Commission used its broad access to individuals, special compartmented intelligence and special access programs. We consulted with experts in the broader government and private analytic and policy communities. We reviewed the strengths, weaknesses and vulnerabilities of current and planned human and technical collection efforts and capabilities, especially in light of the increasingly sophisticated means and methods available to target countries to hide from U.S. intelligence collection. We reviewed with scientists, engineers and program managers from the public and private sectors the technical issues associated with the design, development and testing of ballistic missiles and the means and methods available to the emerging ballistic missile powers to meet the challenges associated with long-range ballistic missile development and testing.

The Commission analyzed the available information in order to develop an understanding of the threat from three perspectives:

—We examined the known size and quality of the deployed forces, the doctrine and the command and control systems that govern the forces and the availability of weapons of mass destruction to arm the forces. We reviewed the infrastructure supporting the programs and the extent of past and present foreign assistance available to those programs from Russia, China and other countries, including the West.

—We examined the ways in which the programs of emerging ballistic missile powers compared with one another. For example, we traced the development histories of the related programs of North Korea, Iran, Iraq and Pakistan and the relationships among them. This comparison helped in identifying the similarities between programs, the extent to which each had aided one another in overcoming critical development hurdles and, importantly, the pace at which a determined country can progress in its program development.

—We reviewed the resources ("inputs") available and the ways in which they provide indicators of the prospects for successful missile development.

By integrating these perspectives, we were able to partially bridge a significant number of intelligence gaps. Emphasizing inputs makes two important contributions to the analysis. Inputs include domestic opportunity costs, the foreign technology and expertise sought and obtained, the urgency with which facilities are constructed both above and below ground and the willingness to absorb cost and time penalties in order to hide activities from detection by U.S. intelligence. Attention to inputs across all elements of a program helps develop an understanding of the scale and scope of a program before traditional output indicators, such as testing and production rates, can be observed and evaluated. When combined with observed outputs and the application of engineering judgments, the understanding of the scale and scope of a program that this provided helped us to measure the probable pace and magnitude of a program and its potential products. We were then able to make what we believe to be reasonably confident estimates of what the various programs can achieve.

Rather than measuring how far a program had progressed from a known starting point, the Commission sought to measure how close a program might be to demonstrating the first flight of a long-range ballistic missile. This approach requires that analysts extrapolate a program's scope, scale, pace and direction beyond what the hard evidence at hand unequivocally supports. It is in sharp contrast to a narrow focus on the certain that obscures the almost-certain. The approach helps reduce the effects of denial and deception efforts. When strategically significant programs were assessed by narrowly focusing on what is known, the assessments lagged the actual state of the programs by two to eight years and in some cases completely missed significant programs.

We chose to focus on what is left to be accomplished in the programs of potentially threatening ballistic missile powers and alternative paths they can follow to attain their goals. We reviewed program histories and current activities, including foreign assistance, to determine whether a ballistic missile program acquired the means to overcome its identified problems. We considered the multiple pathways available for completing its development given the combination of expertise and technology available to it and the circumstances in which it is operating. This approach accepts as a basic premise that a power determined to possess a long-range missile, knowing that the U.S. is trying to track its every action but aware of U.S. intelligence methods and sources, will do its best to deny information and to deceive the U.S. about its actual progress.

Because of these options available to emerging ballistic missile powers, the Commission, unanimously recognizing that missile development and deployment now follows new models, strongly urges the use of an expanded approach to intelligence that assesses both inputs and outputs in other countries' ballistic missile programs. We believe this approach is needed in order to capture both sooner and more accurately the speed and magnitude of potential ballistic missile proliferation in the post–Cold War world and to assess, in time, the various threats this proliferation poses to the United States.

The Commission's key judgments are derived from applying this methodology and examining the evidence in light of the individual and collective experience of the nine Commissioners.

H. Summary

Ballistic missiles armed with WMD payloads pose a strategic threat to the United States. This is not a distant threat. Characterizing foreign assistance as a wild card is both incorrect and misleading. Foreign assistance is pervasive, enabling and often the preferred path to ballistic missile and WMD capability.

A new strategic environment now gives emerging ballistic missile powers the capacity, through a combination of domestic development and foreign assistance, to acquire the means to strike the U.S. within about five years of a decision to acquire such a capability (10 years in the case of Iraq). During several of those years, the U.S. might not be aware that such a decision had been made. Available alternative means of delivery can shorten the warning time of deployment nearly to zero.

The threat is exacerbated by the ability of both existing and emerging ballistic missile powers to hide their activities from the U.S. and to deceive the U.S. about the pace, scope and direction of their development and proliferation programs. Therefore, we unanimously recommend that U.S. analyses, practices and policies that depend on expectations of extended warning of deployment be reviewed and, as appropriate, revised to reflect the reality of an environment in which there may be little or no warning.

Notes

1. An unauthorized launch is one that has not received the required authorizations from senior political leaders and that might be conducted by elements within the General Staff or subordinate commanders. An inadvertent launch is one resulting from a mistaken assessment of sensor data, including from ballistic

missile early warning systems, or a misinterpretation of the strategic situation or some combination of the two, especially in times of crisis generated either by domestic or international events.

2. An ICBM has a range greater than 5,500 km.

3. An MRBM has a range of 1,000 to 3,000 km.

4. An SRBM has a range of less than 1,000 km.

5. An IRBM has a range of 3,000 to 5,500 km.

Excerpts from the
1999 National Intelligence Estimate

NATIONAL INTELLIGENCE COUNCIL
FOREIGN MISSILE DEVELOPMENTS AND THE
BALLISTIC MISSILE THREAT TO THE
UNITED STATES THROUGH 2015

September 1999

POTENTIAL ICBM THREATS TO THE UNITED STATES

We project that during the next 15 years the United States most likely will face ICBM threats from Russia, China, and North Korea, probably from Iran, and possibly from Iraq, although the threats will consist of dramatically fewer weapons than today because of significant reductions we expect in Russian strategic forces.

• The Russian threat will continue to be the most robust and lethal, considerably more so than that posed by China, and orders of magnitude more than that posed by the other three.

• Initial North Korean, Iranian, and Iraqi ICBMs would probably be fewer in number—a few to tens rather than hundreds or thousands, constrained to smaller payload capabilities, and less reliable and accurate than their Russian and Chinese counterparts.

- Countries with emerging ICBM capabilities are likely to view their relatively few ICBMs more as weapons of deterrence and coercive diplomacy than as weapons of war, recognizing that their use could bring devastating consequences. Thus, the emerging threats posed to the United States by these countries will be very different than the Cold War threat.

North Korea

After Russia and China, North Korea is the most likely to develop ICBMs capable of threatening the United States during the next 15 years.

- North Korea attempted to orbit a small satellite using the Taepo Dong-1 SLV in August 1998, but the third stage failed during powered flight; other aspects of the flight, including stage separation, appear to have been successful.

- If it had an operable third stage and a reentry vehicle capable of surviving ICBM flight, a converted Taepo Dong-1 SLV could deliver a light payload to the United States. In these cases, about two-thirds of the payload mass would be required for the reentry vehicle structure. The remaining mass is probably too light for an early generation nuclear weapon but could deliver biological or chemical (BW/CW) warfare agent.

- Most analysts believe that North Korea probably will test a Taepo Dong-2 this year, unless delayed for political reasons. A two-stage Taepo Dong-2 could deliver a several-hundred kilogram payload to Alaska and Hawaii, and a lighter payload to the western half of the United States. A three-stage Taepo Dong-2 could deliver a several-hundred kilogram payload anywhere in the United States.

- North Korea is much more likely to weaponize the more capable Taepo Dong-2 than the three-stage Taepo Dong-1 as an ICBM.

Iran

Iran is the next hostile country most capable of testing an ICBM capable of delivering a weapon to the United States during the next 15 years.

- Iran could test an ICBM that could deliver a several-hundred kilogram payload to many parts of the United States in the latter half of the next decade, using Russian technology and assistance.

- Iran could pursue a Taepo Dong-type ICBM. Most analysts believe it could test a three-stage ICBM patterned after the Taepo Dong-1 SLV or a three-stage Taepo Dong-2-type ICBM, possibly with North Korean assistance, in the next few years.

• Iran is likely to test an SLV by 2010 that—once developed—could be converted into an ICBM capable of delivering a several-hundred kilogram payload to the United States.

• Analysts differ on the likely timing of Iran's first flight test of an ICBM that could threaten the United States. Assessments include:

—likely before 2010 and very likely before 2015 (noting that an SLV with ICBM capabilities will probably be tested within the next few years);

—no more than an even chance by 2010 and a better than even chance by 2015;

—and less than an even chance by 2015.

Iraq

Although the Gulf war and subsequent United Nations activities destroyed much of Iraq's missile infrastructure, Iraq could test an ICBM capable of reaching the United States during the next 15 years.

• After observing North Korean activities, Iraq most likely would pursue a three-stage Taepo Dong-2 approach to an ICBM (or SLV), which could deliver a several-hundred kilogram payload to parts of the United States. If Iraq could buy a Taepo Dong-2 from North Korea, it could have a launch capability within months of the purchase; if it bought Taepo Dong engines, it could test an ICBM by the middle of the next decade. Iraq probably would take until the end of the next decade to develop the system domestically.

• Although much less likely, most analysts believe that if Iraq were to begin development today, it could test a much less capable ICBM in a few years using Scud components and based on its prior SLV experience or on the Taepo Dong-1.

• If it could acquire No Dongs from North Korea, Iraq could test a more capable ICBM along the same lines within a few years of the No Dong acquisition.

• Analysts differ on the likely timing of Iraq's first flight test of an ICBM that could threaten the United States. Assessments include unlikely before 2015; and likely before 2015, possibly before 2010—foreign assistance would affect the capability and timing.

Russia

Russia's strategic offensive forces are experiencing serious budget constraints but will remain the cornerstone of its military power. Russia expects its forces to deter both nuclear and conventional military threats and is prepared to conduct limited nuclear strikes to warn off an enemy or alter the course of a battle.

- Russia currently has about 1,000 strategic ballistic missiles with 4,500 warheads.

- Its strategic force will remain formidable through and beyond 2015, but the size of this force will decrease dramatically—well below arms control limits—primarily because of budget constraints.

- Russia will maintain as many strategic missiles and associated nuclear warheads as it believes it can afford, but well short of START I or II limitations.

    —If Russia ratifies START II, with its ban on multiple warheads on ICBMs, it would probably be able to maintain only about half of the weapons it could maintain without the ban.

- We judge that an unauthorized or accidental launch of a Russian strategic missile is highly unlikely so long as current technical and procedural safeguards are in place.

China

Chinese strategic nuclear doctrine calls for a survivable long-range missile force that can hold a significant portion of the US population at risk in a retaliatory strike.

- China's current force of about 20 CSS-4 ICBMs can reach targets in all of the United States.

- Beijing also is developing two new road-mobile, solid propellant ICBMs.

    —It conducted the first flight test of the mobile DF-31 ICBM in August 1999; we judge it will have a range of about 8,000 km and will be targeted primarily against Russia and Asia.

    —We expect a test of a longer range mobile ICBM within the next several years; it will be targeted primarily against the United States.

- China is developing the JL-2 SLBM, which we expect to be tested within the next decade. The JL-2 probably will be able to target the United States from launch areas near China.

- By 2015, China will likely have tens of missiles targeted against the United States, having added a few tens of more survivable land- and sea-based mobile missiles with smaller nuclear warheads—in part influenced by US technology gained through espionage.

- China has had the technical capability to develop multiple RV payloads for 20 years. If China needed a multiple-RV (MRV) capability in the near term, Beijing could use a DF-31-type RV to develop and deploy a simple MRV or multiple independently targetable reentry vehicle (MIRV)[1] for the CSS-4 in a few years. MIRVing a future mobile missile would be many years off.

- China is also significantly improving its theater missile capabilities and is increasing the size of its SRBM force deployed opposite Taiwan.

- We assess that an unauthorized launch of a Chinese strategic missile is highly unlikely. . . .

ALTERNATIVE THREATS TO THE UNITED STATES

Several other means to deliver WMD to the United States have probably been devised, some more reliable than ICBMs that have not completed rigorous testing and validation programs. The goal of an adversary would be to move the weapon within striking distance without a long-range ICBM. Most of these means, however, do not provide the same prestige and degree of deterrence or coercive diplomacy associated with long-range missiles, but they might be the means of choice for terrorists.

Forward-Based Threats

Several countries are technically capable of developing a missile-launch mechanism to use from forward-based ships or other platforms to launch SRBMs and MRBMs, or land-attack cruise missiles against the United States. Some countries may develop and deploy a forward-based system during the period of the next 15 years.

A short- or medium-range ballistic missile could be launched at the United States from a forward-based sea platform positioned within a few hundred kilometers of US territory. If the attacking country were willing to accept significantly reduced accuracy for the missile, forward-basing on a sea-based platform would not be a major technical hurdle. The reduced accuracy in such a case, however, would probably be better than that of some early ICBMs. The simplest method for launching a ship-borne ballistic missile would be to place a secured TEL onboard the ship and launch the missile from its TEL. If accuracy were a major concern, the missile and launcher would be placed on a stabilization platform to compensate for wave movement of the ocean, or the country would need to add satellite-aided navigation to the missile.

A concept similar to a sea-based ballistic missile launch system would be to launch cruise missiles from forward-based platforms. This method would enable a country to use cruise missiles acquired for regional purposes to attack targets in the United States.

• A country could launch cruise missiles from fighter, bomber, or commercial transport aircraft outside US airspace. US capability to detect planes approaching the coast, and the limited range of fighter and bomber aircraft of most countries, probably would preclude the choice of military aircraft for the attack. Using a commercial aircraft, however, would be feasible for staging a covert cruise missile attack, but it still would be difficult.

• A commercial surface vessel, covertly equipped to launch cruise missiles, would be a plausible alternative for a forward-based launch platform. This method would provide a large and potentially inconspicuous platform to launch a cruise missile while providing at least some cover for launch deniability.

• A submarine would have the advantage of being relatively covert. The technical sophistication required to launch a cruise missile from a submarine torpedo or missile tube most likely would require detailed assistance from the defense industry of a major naval power.

Non-Missile WMD Threats to the United States

Although non-missile means of delivering WMD do not provide the same prestige or degree of deterrence and coercive diplomacy associated with an ICBM, such options are of significant concern. Countries or non-state actors could pursue non-missile delivery options, most of which:

• Are less expensive than developing and producing ICBMs.

• Can be covertly developed and employed; the source of the weapon could be masked in an attempt to evade retaliation.

• Probably would be more reliable than ICBMs that have not completed rigorous testing and validation programs.

• Probably would be more accurate than emerging ICBMs over the next 15 years.

• Probably would be more effective for disseminating biological warfare agent than a ballistic missile.

• Would avoid missile defenses.

The requirements for missile delivery of WMD impose additional, stringent design requirements on the already difficult technical problem of designing such weapons. For example, initial indigenous nuclear weapon designs are likely to be too large and heavy for a modest-sized ballistic missile but still suitable for delivery by ship, truck, or even airplane. Furthermore, a country (or non-state actor) is likely to have only a few nuclear weapons, at least during the next 15 years. Reliability of delivery would be a critical factor; covert delivery methods could offer reliability advantages over a missile. Not only would a country want the warhead to reach its target, it would want to avoid an accident with a WMD warhead at the missile-launch area. On the other hand, a ship sailing into a port could provide secure delivery to limited locations, and a nuclear detonation, either in the ship or on the dock, could achieve the intended purpose. An airplane, either manned or unmanned, could also deliver a nuclear weapon before any local inspection, and perhaps before landing. Finally, a nuclear weapon might also be smuggled across a border or brought ashore covertly.

Foreign non-state actors, including some terrorist or extremist groups, have used, possessed, or are interested in weapons of mass destruction or the materials to build them. Most of these groups have threatened the United States or its interests. We cannot count on obtaining warning of all planned terrorist attacks, despite the high priority we assign to this goal.

Recent trends suggest the likelihood is increasing that a foreign group or individual will conduct a terrorist attack against US interests using chemical agents or toxic industrial chemicals in an attempt to produce a significant number of casualties, damage infrastructure, or create fear among a population. Past terrorist events, such as the World Trade Center bombing and the Aum Shinrikyo chemical attack on the Tokyo subway system, demonstrated the feasibility and willingness to undertake an attack capable of producing massive casualties.

Immediate Theater Missile Threats to US Interests and Allies

The proliferation of MRBMs—driven primarily by North Korean No Dong sales—has created an immediate, serious, and growing threat to US forces, interests, and allies in the Middle East and Asia, and has significantly altered the strategic balances in the regions.

- Iran's flight test of its Shahab-3, which is based on the No Dong, and Indian and Pakistani missile and nuclear tests may fuel additional interest in MRBMs.
- Pakistan has M-11 SRBMs from China and Ghauri MRBMs from North Korea; we assess both may have a nuclear role.
- India has Prithvi I SRBMs and recently began testing the Agni II MRBM; we assess both may have a nuclear role.

We judge that countries developing missiles view their regional concerns as one of the primary factors in tailoring their programs. They see their short- and medium-range missiles not only as deterrents but also as force-multiplying weapons of war, primarily with conventional weapons but with options for delivering biological, chemical, and eventually nuclear weapons.

Penetration Aids and Countermeasures

We assess that countries developing ballistic missiles would also develop various responses to US theater and national defenses. Russia and China each have developed numerous countermeasures and probably are willing to sell the requisite technologies.

- Many countries, such as North Korea, Iran, and Iraq probably would rely initially on readily available technology—including separating RVs, spin-stabilized RVs, RV reorientation, radar absorbing material (RAM), booster fragmentation, low-power jammers, chaff, and simple (balloon) decoys—to develop penetration aids and countermeasures.
- These countries could develop countermeasures based on these technologies by the time they flight test their missiles.

Foreign espionage and other collection efforts are likely to increase. China, for example, has been able to obtain significant nuclear weapons information from espionage, contact with scientists from the United States and other countries, publications and conferences, unauthorized media disclosures, and declassified US weapons information. We assess that China, Iran, and others are targeting US missile information as well.

NOTE

1. An MRV system releases multiple RVs along the missile's linear flight path, often at a single target; a MIRV system can maneuver to several different release points to provide targeting flexibility.

Notes

Chapter One

1. See "Remarks at Georgetown University," *Weekly Compilation of Presidential Documents,* vol. 26 (September 4, 2000), pp. 1988–93 (www.brookings.edu/defendingamerica); and Governor George W. Bush, "New Leadership on National Security," speech to the National Press Club, Washington, May 23, 2000 (www.georgewbush.com/News/speeches/052300_nsecurity.html [November 2000]).

2. See Ernest J. Yanarella, *The Missile Defense Controversy: Strategy, Technology, and Politics, 1955-1972* (University Press of Kentucky, 1977), pp. 3, 146–47.

3. John E. Pike, Bruce G. Blair, and Stephen I. Schwartz, "Defending against the Bomb," in Stephen I. Schwartz, ed., *Atomic Audit: The Costs and Consequences of U.S. Nuclear Weapons since 1940* (Brookings, 1998), p. 289.

4. See Frances Fitzgerald, *Way Out There in the Blue: Reagan, Star Wars and the End of the Cold War* (Simon and Schuster, 2000), pp. 147–209.

5. See, for example, Edwin Feulner, "An Immoral Treaty," *Heritage Commentary 2000,* June 1, 2000 (www.heritage.org/views/2000/ejf00-9.html [November 2000]). See the ABM Treaty and related documents in appendix A to this book.

6. For discussions of these efforts, see Mathew Bunn, *The Next Wave: Urgently Needed New Steps to Control Warheads and Fissile Material* (Washington: Carnegie Endowment for International Peace, 2000), pp. 29–74; and Jason Ellis, "Nunn-Lugar's Mid-Life Crisis," *Survival,* vol. 39 (Spring 1997), pp. 84–110.

7. Bruce G. Blair, "Trapped in the Nuclear Math," *New York Times,* June 12, 2000, p. A29.

8. Bush, "New Leadership on National Security."

9. National Intelligence Council, *Foreign Missile Developments and the Ballistic Missile Threat to the United States through 2015* (Central Intelligence Agency, September 1999), p. 16. (Hereafter, *1999 NIE.*) See also appendix D in

this book for excerpts from the council report and a complete report at www. brookings.edu/defendingamerica. A subsequent, still classified National Intelligence Council report on likely Russian and Chinese reactions to U.S. deployment of an NMD system is summarized in Bob Drogin and Tyler Marshall, "Missile Shield Analysis Warns of Arms Buildup," *Los Angeles Times,* May 19, 2000; and Steven Lee Myers, "Study Said to Find U.S. Missile Shield Might Incite China," *New York Times,* August 10, 2000, p. A1.

10. Clifford Gaddy and Michael O'Hanlon, "The Russian Submarine Disaster," *San Diego Union-Tribune,* August 27, 2000, p. G1.

11. Bush, "New Leadership on National Security." Emphasis in original.

12. See Joseph Cirincione, "Assessing the Assessment: The 1999 National Intelligence Estimate of the Ballistic Missile Threat," *Nonproliferation Review,* vol. 7 (Spring 2000), pp. 131–32.

13. *1999 NIE,* p. 1.

14. Ibid., p. 13.

15. Ibid., p. 4.

16. Michael R. Gordon and Steven Lee Myers, "Politics Mixes with Strategy in Plan for Antimissile System," *New York Times,* June 23, 2000, p. A1.

17. See *1999 NIE,* p. 8.

18. Hugh Pope, "Sanctions against Iraq Continue to Erode," *Wall Street Journal,* October 9, 2000, p. A24.

19. See Andrew M. Sessler and others, *Countermeasures: A Technical Evaluation of the Operational Effectiveness of the Planned U.S. National Missile Defense System* (Cambridge, Mass.: Union of Concerned Scientists, 2000), p. 27; and George N. Lewis, Theodore A. Postol, and John Pike, "Why National Missile Defense Won't Work," *Scientific American,* vol. 281 (August 1999), pp. 36–41.

20. See, for example, Walter B. Slocombe, remarks to the Center for Strategic and International Studies Statesmen's Forum, Washington, November 5, 1999 (www.csis.org/html/sf991105Slocombe.html [November 2000]).

21. See, for example, John Deutch, Harold Brown, and John P. White, "National Missile Defense: Is There Another Way?" *Foreign Policy,* vol. 119 (Summer 2000), pp. 91–100; and Richard L. Garwin, "A Defense That Will Not Defend," *Washington Quarterly,* vol. 23 (Summer 2000), pp. 109–24.

22. "Transcript of a Symposium On: National Missile Defense," sponsored by the Cato Institute, Council for a Livable World Education Fund, National Defense University Foundation, and the Jean and Samuel Zacher Foundation, Washington, June 27, 2000, p. 50.

23. Nonconventional means of attack have their own drawbacks. See Sydney J. Freedberg, Jr., "Bootleg A-Bombs," *National Journal,* July 8, 2000, pp. 2224–25; and K. Scott McMahon, "Unconventional Nuclear, Biological, and Chemical Weapons Delivery Methods: Whither the 'Smuggled Bomb,'" *Comparative Strategy,* vol. 15 (April 1996), pp. 123–34.

24. Preventive and preemptive attacks are closely related. The primary difference is one of timing and context. See Richard N. Haass, *Intervention: The Use of American Military Force in the Post–Cold War World* (Washington: Carnegie Endowment for International Peace, 1994), p. 52.

25. Quoted in Alison Mitchell, "Bush Debates Foreign Policy with Russian," *New York Times*, April 27, 2000, p. A10.

26. Sen. Thad Cochran, *Stubborn Things: A Decade of Facts about Ballistic Missile Defense* (U.S. Senate, 2000), pp. 29, 64–65 (www.senate.gov/~gov_affairs/Stubborn.htm [November 2000]).

27. See John Pomfret, "China Again Demands U.S. Drop Missile Defense Plan," *Washington Post*, July 12, 2000, p. A16.

28. The coverage of the defense depends on the speed of the interceptor missile, of course, as well as its reaction time. But for an interceptor with typical ICBM-like acceleration reaching a maximum speed of eight kilometers per second, Alaska and Hawaii can be covered from North Dakota, provided that the interceptor is fired within about three to five minutes of the ICBM launch (current early-warning satellites provide warning within about a minute of launch, so this should be eminently feasible). See Richard L. Garwin, "Boost-Phase Intercept: A Better Alternative," *Arms Control Today*, vol. 30 (September 2000), p. 9. For broader analysis about the coverage of this type of defense, see Melissa S. Ryan, "Study of Ballistic Missile Defense Systems," Department of Mechanical and Aerospace Engineering, Princeton University, May 2000, pp. 42–49. Others claim that Alaska and Hawaii could not be defended from North Dakota, but their calculations are not transparent. See David R. Tanks, *National Missile Defense: Policy Issues and Technological Capabilities* (Cambridge, Mass.: Institute for Foreign Policy Analysis, 2000), pp. 2-10–2-11. In terms of basic kinematics, North Dakota is considerably closer to populated parts of Alaska and Hawaii than North Korea is (by several hundred miles). So if an interceptor capable of traveling eight kilometers a second was launched within several minutes of an ICBM headed for a town in Hawaii or Alaska that was traveling at roughly seven kilometers a second, it should have time to intercept the ICBM.

29. Quoted in Sharon LaFraniere, "Putin Suggests Deeper Bilateral Weapons Cuts," *Washington Post*, November 14, 2000, p. A37.

30. Quoted by the ITAR-TASS press service, Moscow, November 13, 2000.

Chapter Two

1. David R. Tanks, *National Missile Defense: Policy Issues and Technological Capabilities* (Cambridge, Mass.: Institute for Foreign Policy Analysis, 2000), p. 3.3.

2. Curtis D. Cochran, Dennis M. Gorman, and Joseph D. Dumoulin, eds., *Space Handbook* (Maxwell Air Force Base, Alabama: Air University Press, 1985), pp. 3.27–30.

3. Thomas B. Cochran, William M. Arkin, and Milton M. Hoenig, *Nuclear Weapons Databook*, Volume I: *U.S. Nuclear Forces and Capabilities* (Ballinger Publishing, 1984), p. 107.

4. Tanks, *National Missile Defense*, p. 3.3.

5. See John Tirman, ed., *The Fallacy of Star Wars* (Vintage Books, 1984), pp. 52–65.

6. For more, see Stephen Weiner, "Systems and Technology," in Ashton B. Carter and David N. Schwartz, eds., *Ballistic Missile Defense* (Brookings, 1984), pp. 49–97; and Robert G. Nagler, *Ballistic Missile Proliferation: An Emerging Threat* (Arlington, Va.: System Planning Corporation, 1992), pp. 52–65.

7. See Stephen W. Young, *Pushing the Limits: The Decision on National Missile Defense* (Washington: Coalition to Reduce Nuclear Dangers and Council for a Livable World Education Fund, 2000), p. 9 (www.clw.org/pub/clw/coalition/libbmd.htm [November 2000]).

8. For more, see David B. H. Denoon, *Ballistic Missile Defense in the Post–Cold War Era* (Westview Press, 1995), chaps. 3–5; and Department of Defense, "The Strategic Defense Initiative: Defense Technologies Study," reprinted in Steven E. Miller and Stephen Van Evera, eds., *The Star Wars Controversy* (Princeton University Press, 1986), pp. 291–322.

9. For more information, see the Federation of American Scientists' website at (www.fas.org/spp/starwars/program [November 2000]).

10. Chapter 4 discusses this concept further.

11. See J. C. Toomay, *Radar Principles for the Non-Specialist* (Mendham, N.J.: SciTech Publishing, 1998), pp. 1–64.

12. See chapter 4 for more detail.

13. David Mosher and Michael O'Hanlon, *The START Treaty and Beyond* (Congressional Budget Office, 1991), p. 148.

14. Mosher and O'Hanlon, *The START Treaty and Beyond*, pp. 167–71.

15. George N. Lewis and Theodore A. Postol, "Future Challenges to Ballistic Missile Defense," *IEEE Spectrum*, vol. 34 (September 1997), pp. 60–68.

16. The then–Martin-Marietta Corporation proposed fast-burn boosters back in the early 1980s; see Tirman, ed., *The Fallacy of Star Wars*, pp. 60–62.

17. See Andrew M. Sessler and others, *Countermeasures: A Technical Evaluation of the Operational Effectiveness of the Planned US National Missile Defense System* (Cambridge, Mass.: Union of Concerned Scientists, April 2000), p. 42; and Gen. Larry Welch (ret.), chairman, and others, *Report of the Panel on Reducing Risk in Ballistic Missile Defense Flight Test Programs* (Department of Defense, February 27, 1998), p. 56 (www.fas.org/spp/starwars/program/welch/index.htm/ [November 2000]).

18. See the testimony of Richard L. Garwin and David C. Wright, *Ballistic Missiles: Threat and Response*, Hearings before the Senate Committee on Foreign Relations, 106 Cong. 1 sess. (Government Printing Office, 2000), pp. 74–90.

Chapter Three

1. See Joseph Cirincione, "Assessing the Assessment: The 1999 National Intelligence Estimate of the Ballistic Missile Threat," *Nonproliferation Review*, vol. 7 (Spring 2000), p. 131.

2. Stephen W. Young, *Pushing the Limits: The Decision on National Missile Defense* (Washington: Coalition to Reduce Nuclear Dangers and Council for a Livable World Education Fund, 2000), p. 32.

3. Governor George Bush, "New Leadership on National Security," speech to the National Press Club, Washington, May 23, 2000 (www.georgewbush.com/News/speeches/052300_nsecurity.html [November 2000]).

4. "A Look at . . . Missile Defense," *Washington Post*, June 11, 2000, p. B3.

5. Arkady Ostrovsky, "Russia 'Unable' to Afford Nuclear Arsenal," *Financial Times* (London), October 7, 1998, p. 2; and Ronald E. Powaski, "Russia: The Nuclear Menace Within," *Current History*, vol. 98 (October 1999), p. 340.

6. Bruce Blair and Clifford Gaddy, "Russia's Aging War Machine: Economic Weakness and the Nuclear Threat," *Brookings Review*, vol. 17 (Summer 1999), p. 11; and Cliff Gaddy and Michael O'Hanlon, "The Russian Submarine Disaster," *San Diego Union-Tribune*, August 27, 2000, p. G1.

7. See, for example, John Diamond, "Russia Says Missiles May Revive Cold War," *Chicago Tribune*, May 3, 2000, p. N1.

8. National Intelligence Council, "Foreign Missile Developments and the Ballistic Missile Threat to the United States through 2015" (September 1999), p. 9 (Hereafter, *1999 NIE*); Andrew M. Sessler and others, *Countermeasures: A Technical Evaluation of the Operational Effectiveness of the Planned US National Missile Defense System* (Cambridge, Mass.: Union of Concerned Scientists, April 2000), pp. 10–11; Paul Podvig, "The Russian Strategic Forces: Uncertain Futures," *Breakthroughs*, vol. 7 (Spring 1998), pp. 11–21; and Dean A. Wilkening, *The Evolution of Russia's Strategic Nuclear Force*, Center for International Security and Cooperation Report (Stanford University, July 1998), pp. 42–43.

9. *1999 NIE*, p. 16.

10. David Hoffman, "New Life for 'Star Wars' Response," *Washington Post*, November 22, 1999, p. A18.

11. David R. Tanks, *National Missile Defense: Policy Issues and Technological Capabilities* (Cambridge, Mass.: Institute for Foreign Policy Analysis, 2000), p. 3.4.

12. Quoted in David Hoffman, "Russian Rocket Called Invincible," *Washington Post*, February 25, 1999, p. A20. See also David Hoffman, "Moscow Warns U.S. on Missile Defense," *Washington Post*, October 26, 1999, p. A19.

13. Accidental launches refer to attacks that begin because equipment breaks or malfunctions. Unauthorized launches refer to attacks deliberately initiated by individuals acting without the permission of the appropriate government officials. Erroneous or inadvertent launches refer to attacks initiated in the mistaken belief that the enemy has already fired its weapons.

14. Powaski, "Russia: The Nuclear Menace Within," p. 340.

15. Sonni Efron, "'Missile Attack' on Russia Was Just a Scientific Probe," *Los Angeles Times*, January 26, 1995, p. A1; Geoffrey Forden, Pavel Podvig, and Theodore A. Postol, "False Alarm, Nuclear Danger," *IEEE Spectrum*, vol. 37 (March 2000), pp. 31–32, 34; and Alessandra Stanley, "Strains of Chechnya War Setting Russians on Edge," *New York Times*, January 29, 1995, p. 1.

16. Forden, Podvig, and Postol, "False Alarm, Nuclear Danger," p. 32. See also David Hoffman, "Russia 'Blind' to Attack by U.S. Missiles," *Washington*

Post, June 1, 2000, p. A1; and David Hoffman, "Russia's Missile Defenses Eroding," *Washington Post*, February 10, 1999, p. A1.

17. *1999 NIE*, p. 11. See also Bill Gertz, "Russian Renegades Pose Nuke Danger," *Washington Times*, October 22, 1996, p. A1.

18. On the question of accidental nuclear war, see Bruce Blair, *The Logic of Accidental Nuclear War* (Brookings, 1993).

19. See Sessler and others, *Countermeasures*, pp. 5–7; Forden, Podvig, and Postol, "False Alarm, Nuclear Danger," p. 34; and Dean Wilkening, "Ballistic-Missile Defence and Strategic Stability," *Adelphi Paper* 334 (London: International Institute for Strategic Studies, 2000), pp. 14, 89.

20. For quick overviews of Chinese nuclear forces, see "Chinese Nuclear Forces, 2000," *Bulletin of the Atomic Scientists*, vol. 56 (May–June 2000), pp. 78–79; and Ming Zhang, "What Threat?" *Bulletin of the Atomic Scientists*, vol. 55 (September–October 1999), pp. 52–57.

21. Bates Gill, James Mulvenon, and Mark Stokes, "The Chinese Second Artillery Corps: Transition to Credible Deterrence," in James Mulvenon and Andrew Yang, eds., *The People's Liberation Army as Organization* (Santa Monica, Calif.: Rand Corporation, forthcoming), pp. 13–21; and John Wilson Lewis and Xue Litai, *China Builds the Bomb* (Stanford University Press, 1988), pp. 210–18.

22. Gill, Mulvenon, and Stokes, "Chinese Second Artillery Corps," pp. 46–52; and Jane Perlez, "China Likely to Modernize Nuclear Arms, U.S. Believes," *New York Times*, May 12, 2000, p. A11.

23. See *Report of the United States House of Representatives Select Committee on U.S. National Security and Military Commercial Concerns with the People's Republic of China*, H. Rept. 59, 106 Cong. 1 sess. (Government Printing Office, 1999). For criticisms of the Cox Report see, Alastair Iain Johnston and others, *The Cox Committee Report: An Assessment* (Stanford University, Center for International Security and Arms Control, December 1999), pp. 5–62; Jonathan Pollack, "The Cox Report's Dirty Little Secret," *Arms Control Today*, vol. 29 (April–May 1999), pp. 26–27; and John M. Spratt, Jr., "Keep the Facts of the Cox Report in Perspective," *Arms Control Today*, vol. 29 (April–May 1999), pp. 24–25.

24. For a quick overview of the U.S. modernization programs, see Robert S. Norris and William M. Arkin, "U.S. Nuclear Forces, 2000," *Bulletin of the Atomic Scientists*, vol. 56 (May–June 2000), pp. 69–71. See also Walter Pincus, "U.S. Nuclear Stockpile Plans Draw Scrutiny," *Washington Post*, April 24, 2000, p. A2.

25. *1999 NIE*, p. 11.

26. Erik Eckholm, "China Arms Expert Warns U.S. Shield May Force Buildup," *New York Times*, May 11, 2000, p. A1. See also Charles Ferguson, "Sparking a Buildup: U.S. Missile Defense and China's Nuclear Arsenal," *Arms Control Today*, vol. 30 (March 2000), pp. 13–18.

27. *1999 NIE*, p. 16.

28. Bill Gertz, "Chinese Decoy Warhead Designed to Beat Defenses," *Washington Times*, September 16, 1999, p. A1.

29. The 1995 NIE called the prospect of an unauthorized Chinese missile launch "remote"; the 1999 NIE called it "highly unlikely." DCI National Intelligence Estimate, President's Summary, "Emerging Missile Threats to North America during the Next 15 Years," November 1995, PS/NIE 95-19 (Hereafter, *1995 NIE*); and *1999 NIE*, p. 11. See appendixes B and D in this book and also www.brookings.edu/defendingamerica, which includes the complete 1999 *NIE* and excerpts from the *1995 NIE*.

30. Walter Pincus, "U.S., China May Retarget Nuclear Weapons," *Washington Post*, June 16, 1998, p. A10; and Zhang, "What Threat?" p. 53.

31. Sessler and others, *Countermeasures*, p. 9.

32. *1995 NIE*.

33. *Commission to Assess the Ballistic Missile Threat to the United States*, Executive Summary of Report to Congress (GPO, July 15, 1998), p. 1.

34. For discussions of the North Korean missile program, see Joseph S. Bermudez, Jr., "A History of Ballistic Missile Development in the DPRK," Occasional Paper 2 (Monterey, Calif.: Monterey Institute of International Studies, Center for Nonproliferation Studies, November 1999); and Scott Snyder, "Pyongyang's Pressure," *Washington Quarterly*, vol. 23 (Summer 2000), pp. 163–70.

35. Kongdan Oh and Ralph C. Hassig, *North Korea through the Looking Glass* (Brookings, 2000), p. 113; and Tanks, *National Missile Defense*, p. 1.15.

36. *1995 NIE*.

37. A General Accounting Office report charged the November 1995 NIE with having "overstated" its evidence. See General Accounting Office, "Foreign Missile Threats: Analytic Soundness of Certain National Intelligence Estimates," August 1996, GAO/NSIAD-96-225, p. 3 (www.fas.org/spp/starwars/gao/nsi96225.htm [November 2000]). Another congressionally mandated panel concluded that the NIE's conclusions were "based on a stronger evidentiary and technical case than was presented in the estimate." See Central Intelligence Agency, "NIE 95-19: Independent Panel Review Of 'Emerging Missile Threats to North America during the Next 15 Years,'" OCA-1908, December 26, 1996 (www.fas.org/irp/threat/missile/oca961908.htm [November 2000]).

38. See Cirincione, "Assessing the Assessment," p. 126; and *Commission to Assess the Ballistic Missile Threat*, pp. 22–25.

39. *Commission to Assess the Ballistic Missile Threat*, pp. 5–6.

40. Quoted in Kathryn Tolbert, "North Korea Confirms It Will Not Test Missile," *Washington Post*, September 25, 1999, p. A22. See also William J. Perry, *Review of United States Policy toward North Korea: Findings and Recommendations* (Department of State, Office of the North Korea Policy Coordinator, October 12, 1999).

41. Secretary of Defense William Cohen, quoted in Gopal Ratnam, "Deadline May Postpone NMD," *Defense News*, August 7, 2000, p. 52.

42. *Commission to Assess the Ballistic Missile Threat*, p. 25.

43. *1999 NIE*, p. 9.

44. "Four components are vital to the success of a ballistic missile development program. In descending order of complexity, they are the guidance system, the

reentry vehicle, the propulsion system, and the warhead." Janne Nolan, *Trappings of Power: Ballistic Missiles in the Third World* (Brookings, 1991), p. 32.

45. Ibid., p. 33.

46. Ibid., pp. 34–35.

47. *1999 NIE*, p. 4.

48. Ibid., p. 9.

49. Sessler and others, *Countermeasures*, p. 11; and Li Bin, "Nuclear Missile Delivery Capabilities in Emerging Nuclear States," *Science and Global Security*, vol. 6 (1996), pp. 311–32.

50. For the text of the Agreed Framework, see Leon D. Sigal, *Disarming Strangers: Nuclear Diplomacy with North Korea* (Princeton University Press, 1998), pp. 262–64.

51. James Risen, "Ferreting Out North Korea's Nuclear Secrets: U.S. Intelligence Experts at Odds," *New York Times*, August 5, 2000, p. A4.

52. "IAEA Concerned over NK Nuke Program," *Korea Times*, September 25, 2000.

53. *Commission to Assess the Ballistic Missile Threat*, p. 12.

54. Ibid.

55. Steve Fetter, "Ballistic Missiles and Weapons of Mass Destruction," *International Security*, vol. 16 (Summer 1991), pp. 5–42.

56. K. Scott McMahon, Stanley Orman, and Richard Speier, "Countermeasure Doubletalk: UCS Overstates Ease of Defeating Missile Defense," *Defense News*, June 19, 2000, p. 19; and K. Scott McMahon, Stanley Orman, and Richard Speier, "NMD Rebuttal," *Defense News*, July 24, 2000, p. 36.

57. Sessler and others, *Countermeasures*, p. 39.

58. *1999 NIE*, p. 16.

59. See McMahon, Orman, and Speier, "Countermeasure Doubletalk," p. 19.

60. Sessler and others, *Countermeasures*, p. 96.

61. *1999 NIE*, p. 16.

62. See Steven Lee Myers, "Pentagon Says North Korea Is Still a Dangerous Missile Threat," *New York Times*, September 22, 2000, p. A12.

63. Quoted in Doug Struck and Joohee Cho, "N. Korean Dismisses Missile Idea," *Washington Post*, August 15, 2000, p. A1.

64. For a discussion of Iran's ballistic missile policies, see Anoushiravan Ehteshami, "Teheran's Tocsin," *Washington Quarterly*, vol. 23 (Summer 2000), pp. 171–76.

65. Bill Gertz, "Iran Missile Test Fails after Takeoff," *Washington Times*, September 22, 2000, p. A5; "Iranian Missile Trial Successful," *Washington Post*, July 16, 2000, p. A21; and "Iranian Shabab-3 Missile Test Sparks Pentagon Concern," *Aerospace Daily*, July 19, 2000, p. 84.

66. Joseph Cirincione, *Demystifying the Ballistic Missile Threat* (Washington: Carnegie Endowment for International Peace, 2000), p. 4.

67. *Commission to Assess the Ballistic Missile Threat*, p. 12.

68. *1999 NIE*, p.10. Emphasis in original.

69. Ibid.

70. Rodney W. Jones and Mark G. McDonough, *Tracking Nuclear Proliferation: A Guide in Maps and Charts, 1998* (Washington: Carnegie Endowment for International Peace, 1998), p. 169.

71. Quoted in Walter Pincus, "CIA Not Ruling Out 'Possibility' Iran Can Build Nuclear Bomb," *Washington Post*, January 18, 2000, p. A8.

72. Ibid.

73. Seth Carus, "Iran and Weapons of Mass Destruction," pre-publication copy prepared for the American Jewish Committee annual meeting, May 2000, p. 2; and Pincus, "CIA Not Ruling Out 'Possibility' Iran Can Build Nuclear Bomb," p. A8.

74. *Commission to Assess the Ballistic Missile Threat*, p. 13.

75. Carus, "Iran and Weapons of Mass Destruction," p. 3.

76. Ibid., p. 5.

77. Michael Dobbs, "Soviet-Era Work on Bioweapons Still Worrisome," *Washington Post*, September 12, 2000, p. A1; and Judith Miller and William J. Broad, "Bio-Weapons in Mind, Iranians Lure Needy Ex-Soviet Scientists," *New York Times*, December 8, 1998, p. A1.

78. Quoted in Carus, "Iran and Weapons of Mass Destruction," p. 5.

79. See, for example, Carus, "Iran and Weapons of Mass Destruction," pp. 1–2; and *Worldwide Threats*, statement of Director of Central Intelligence George J. Tenet, Hearings before the Senate Committee on Armed Services, 106 Cong. 1 sess. (GPO,1999), p. 13.

80. The Federation of American Scientists maintains a detailed history of the UN inspection regime (http://sun00781.dn.net/nuke/guide/iraq/index.html [November 2000]).

81. Steven Lee Myers, "Flight Tests by Iraq Show Progress of Missile Program," *New York Times*, July 1, 2000, p. A1; and "German Agency Confirms Discovery of Missile Factory," *Chicago Tribune*, August 26, 2000, p. 12.

82. Michael Evans, "Saddam Seeks Russian Missile Deal," *London Times*, August 14, 2000, p. 12.

83. *1999 NIE*, p. 10.

84. Ibid.

85. Ibid.

86. David Albright and Khidhir Hamza, "Iraq's Reconstitution of Its Nuclear Weapons Program," *Arms Control Today*, vol. 28 (October 1998), p. 12; and *Commission to Assess the Ballistic Missile Threat*, p. 14.

87. Albright and Hamza, "Iraq's Reconstitution of Its Nuclear Weapons Program," p. 11.

88. See Fetter, "Ballistic Missiles," pp. 9–15.

89. Steven Mufson, "Threat of 'Rogue' States: Is It Reality or Rhetoric?" *Washington Post*, May 29, 2000, p. A1. Other major American political figures hold views similar to Berger's. See, for example, "Interview with Condoleeza Rice," Fox News Network, June 8, 2000, Transcript 060802cb.254; Saul Singer, "Views of a 'Visionary,'" *Jerusalem Post*, August 17, 1999, p. 9; and Sen. Thad Cochran, "Remarks to the National Press Club," Washington, March 8, 2000. See also the contributions in Peter Lavoy, Scott D. Sagan, and James J. Wirtz, eds.,

Planning the Unthinkable: How New Powers Will Use Nuclear, Chemical, and Biological Weapons (Cornell University Press, 2000).

90. For a discussion of the Indian and Pakistani missile programs, see Ben Sheppard, "South Asia Nears Nuclear Boiling Point," *Jane's Intelligence Review*, vol. 11 (April 1999), pp. 33–35.

91. *1999 NIE*, p. 15.

92. Sydney J. Freedberg, Jr., "Bootleg A-Bombs," *National Journal*, July 8, 2000, p. 2224.

93. Robert D. Walpole, "Statement for the Record to the Senate Subcommittee on International Security, Proliferation, and Federal Services on the Ballistic Missile Threat to the United States," February 9, 2000 (www.clw.org/coalition/walpole020900.htm [November 2000]).

94. See K. Scott McMahon, "Unconventional Nuclear, Biological, and Chemical Weapons Delivery Methods: Whither the 'Smuggled Bomb,'" *Comparative Strategy*, vol. 15 (April 1996), pp. 123–34.

95. William J. Broad, "How Japan Germ Terror Alerted World," *New York Times*, May 26, 1998, p. A1.

96. In fiscal year 2000, authorities seized an estimated 10 percent of all cocaine headed for U.S. borders—much of it in smaller shipments than would be required for a nuclear device. See Donna Leinwand, "Coast Guard Cocaine Seizures Set Record," *USA Today*, September 28, 2000, p. 3. Modern technology may allow some improvements in such figures in the years ahead. For example, ideas are now being proposed to improve the performance of Customs by making greater use of electronic monitoring of most trade traffic—which could help officials concentrate most physical inspections on cargo associated with suspicious individuals or companies. See Stephen E. Flynn, "Beyond Border Control," *Foreign Affairs*, vol. 79 (November–December 2000), pp. 57–68.

97. Freedberg, "Bootleg A-Bombs," p. 2225.

98. *1999 NIE*, p. 15.

99. See Lachlan Forrow and others, "Accidental Nuclear War—A Post–Cold War Assessment," *New England Journal of Medicine*, April 30, 1998, pp. 1328–29.

100. Fetter, "Ballistic Missiles," p. 27. Personal communication from Steve Fetter, July 27, 2000.

Chapter Four

1. Roberto Suro, "Key Missile Defense Radar Planned for Remote Island," *Washington Post*, May 7, 2000, p. A6.

2. Andrew M. Sessler and others, *Countermeasures: A Technical Evaluation of the Operational Effectiveness of the Planned US National Missile Defense System* (Cambridge, Mass.: Union of Concerned Scientists, April 2000), pp. 20–28.

3. William S. Cohen, "FY 2000 Defense Budget," briefing slides, Department of Defense, February 1999 (www.defenselink.mil/news/Feb1999/602011999_b+032-99.html [November 2000]).

4. See Gopal Ratnam, "BMDO Deployment Pace Rests on $1 Billion Bonus," *Defense News*, March 20, 2000, pp. 1, 36.

5. David R. Tanks, *National Missile Defense: Policy Issues and Technological Capabilities* (Cambridge, Mass.: Institute for Foreign Policy Analysis, 2000), pp. 2.11, 4.18–4.22; Sen. Thad Cochran, *Stubborn Things: A Decade of Facts about Ballistic Missile Defense* (U.S. Senate, 2000), p. 40; and e-mail communications with Harold Feiveson and David Wright, September 2000.

6. *U.S. National Missile Defense Policy and the Anti-Ballistic Missile Treaty*, testimony of Undersecretary of Defense for Policy Walter B. Slocombe before the House Committee on Armed Services, 106 Cong. 1 sess. (Government Printing Office, 1999).

7. Steven Lee Myers, "Washington Split Deepens in Debate over Missile Plan," *New York Times*, August 30, 2000, p. A1.

8. Roberto Suro, "Missile Sensor Failed in Test's Final Seconds, Data Indicate," *Washington Post*, January 20, 2000, p. A4.

9. Geoffrey Forden, *Budgetary and Technical Implications of the Administration's Plan for National Missile Defense* (Congressional Budget Office, April 2000), p. 10. The administration and CBO cost estimates differ by only about $3.9 billion, or roughly 20 percent.

10. Tony Capaccio, "National Missile Defense Cost Estimate Rises Nearly 20 Percent," *Defense Week*, September 11, 2000, p. 2.

11. Forden, *Budgetary and Technical Implications*, p. 10.

12. Ibid., pp. 5–17; and briefing by the Honorable Walter B. Slocombe, undersecretary of defense for policy, "U.S. Limited National Missile Defense Program," Harvard-CSIS Ballistic Missile Defense Conference, Cambridge, Mass., May 2000.

13. See Michael O'Hanlon, "Defense and Foreign Policy: Time to End the Budget Cuts," in Henry J. Aaron and Robert D. Reischauer, eds., *Setting National Priorities: The 2000 Election and Beyond* (Brookings, 1999), pp. 37–72.

14. Richard W. Stevenson, "Debating Detailed Plans for Hypothetical Money," *New York Times*, September 7, 2000, p. A24.

15. "Report of the National Missile Defense Independent Review Team," *Arms Control Today*, vol. 30 (July–August 2000), p. 37; Robert Burns, "Pentagon Uncertain on ABMs by 2005," *Associated Press*, July 25, 2000; Paul Mann, "Next President Faces Missile Defense Knot," *Aviation Week and Space Technology*, September 18, 2000, pp. 27–28; and Christopher Marquis, "Cohen Says Missile Defense System Requires Support of Allies," *New York Times*, July 26, 2000, p. A3.

16. Elaine Sciolino, "Key Missile Parts Are Left Untested as Booster Fails," *New York Times*, July 9, 2000, p. 1.1; and Roberto Suro, "Failure of Booster Foiled Missile Test," *Washington Post*, July 9, 2000, p. A1.

17. Suro, "Missile Sensor Failed in Test's Final Seconds, Data Indicate," p. A4; Bradley Graham, "U.S. Anti-Missile Test Marks a Measured Step," *Washington Post*, October 4, 1999, p. A1; and Richard L. Garwin, "A Defense That Will Not Defend," *Washington Quarterly*, vol. 23 (Summer 2000), pp. 114–18.

18. Gen. Larry Welch (ret.), chairman, *Report of the Panel on Reducing Risk in Ballistic Missile Defense Flight Test Programs* (Department of Defense, February 27, 1998), p. 10 (www.fas.org/spp/starwars/program/welch/index.html [November 2000]). See also Gen. Larry Welch (ret.), chairman, *National Missile Defense Review* (Department of Defense, November 1999) (www.fas.org/spp/starwars/program/welsh.pdf [November 2000]).

19. Statement of Lt. Gen. Ronald T. Kadish, director, Ballistic Missile Defense Organization, before the Senate Armed Services Committee, February 28, 2000, p. 6 (www.fas.org/spp/starwars/congress/2000-h/kadish28feb00.htm [January 2001]).

20. Tony Capaccio, "Pentagon's Top Tester Warns on Missile Defense Time Line," *Defense Week*, June 5, 2000, p. 1.

21. See Kerry Gildea, "NMD Deployment in 2005 Not Most Likely Date, Welch Reports," *Defense Daily*, June 30, 2000, p. 1.

22. Statement of Kadish before the Senate Armed Services Committee, p. 5; and Forden, *Budgetary and Technical Implications*, p. 25.

23. Michael C. Sirak, "NMD Booster Schedule Delayed; First Flight May Be Pushed to Mid-2001," *Inside the Pentagon*, June 22, 2000, pp. 3–4; Bruce A. Smith, "NMD Test Failure Seen as Small Slip in Large Program," *Aviation Week and Space Technology*, July 17, 2000, p. 31; and Roberto Suro, "Missile Defense System May Face Delay," *Washington Post*, August 9, 2000, p. A4.

24. William J. Broad, "A Missile Defense with Limits: The ABC's of the Clinton Plan," *New York Times*, June 30, 2000, p. A1.

25. Tanks, *National Missile Defense*, p. 3.4.

26. See Lt. Gen. Ron Kadish, "Clearing the Fog: Eliminating Misconceptions in the Debate about Deploying a Limited National Missile Defense System," *Armed Forces Journal International*, vol. 137 (June 2000), p. 59.

27. See Sessler and others, *Countermeasures*, pp. 169–70.

28. Ibid., pp. 145–48.

29. Sciolino, "Key Missile Parts Are Left Untested," p. 1.1; and Suro, "Failure of Booster Foiled Missile Test," p. A1.

30. See Robert Wall, "NMD Flight Testing Slows; Boost-Phase Intercept Bolstered," *Aviation Week and Space Technology*, August 28, 2000, pp. 50–51.

31. William J. Broad, "Pentagon Has Been Rigging Antimissile Tests, Critics Maintain," *New York Times*, June 9, 2000, p. A1.

32. William J. Broad, "Ex-Employee Says Contractor Faked Results of Missile Tests," *New York Times*, March 7, 2000, p. 1.

33. Defense Science Board 1998 Summer Study Task Force, *Joint Operations Superiority in the 21st Century* (Department of Defense, 1998), pp. 97–100; Congress, Office of Technology Assessment, *Proliferation of Weapons of Mass Destruction* (GPO, 1993), p. 52.

34. Bob Drogin and Tyler Marshall, "Missile Shield Analysis Warns of Arms Buildup," *Los Angeles Times*, May 19, 2000, p. A1.

35. Lt. Gen. John Costello, Army Space and Missile Defense Command, "National and Theater Missile Defense," briefing slides presented at the Associa-

tion of the U.S. Army, Arlington, Va., May 17, 1999 (www.smdc.army.mil [November 2000]).

36. Forden, *Budgetary and Technical Implications*, p. 10.

37. Lisbeth Gronlund, letter to the editor, "Taking a Close Look at the 'Demarcation' Agreements," *Arms Control Today*, vol. 28 (June–July 1998), p. 36; and John Pike, "Ballistic Missile Defense: Is the U.S. Rushing to Failure?" *Arms Control Today*, vol. 28 (April 1998), p. 10.

38. Tanks, *National Missile Defense*, pp. 5.6–5.7.

39. See Harold A. Feiveson, ed., *The Nuclear Turning Point* (Brookings, 1999), pp. 86–89.

40. Amb. Henry Cooper and the Heritage Foundation's Commission on Missile Defense, *Defending America: A Plan to Meet the Urgent Missile Threat* (Washington: Heritage Foundation, 1999), pp. 36–58.

41. See Rodney W. Jones, *Taking National Missile Defense to Sea: A Critique of Sea-Based and Boost-Phase Proposals* (Washington: Council for a Livable World, 2000), p. 19.

42. Walter Pincus, "Estimate Skyrockets for Expanding Navy's Ship-Based Missile Defense," *Washington Post*, March 5, 1999, p. A4; and statement of Lt. Gen. Lester Lyles, director, Ballistic Missile Defense Organization, Hearings before the Subcommittee on Strategic Forces of the Senate Committee on Armed Services, February 24, 1999, 106 Cong. 1 sess., pp. 11–14.

43. See Ballistic Missile Defense Organization, "Summary of Report to Congress on Utility of Sea-Based Assets to National Missile Defense" (Department of Defense, June 1, 1999), pp. 1–23.

44. The Pentagon appears to agree; see Roberto Suro, "Sea-Based Missile Defenses Supported," *Washington Post*, May 27, 2000, p. A1.

45. Robert Holzer, "DoD Weighs Navy Interceptor Options," *Defense News*, July 24, 2000, p. 1.

46. See David Mosher and Raymond Hall, *Costs of Alternative Approaches to SDI* (Congressional Budget Office, 1992), p. 9.

47. The authors thank George Lewis and David Wright for help with some of these ideas.

48. Theodore A. Postol, "A Russian-US Boost-Phase Defense to Defend Russia and the U.S. from Postulated Rogue-State ICBMs," Massachusetts Institute of Technology, briefing paper presented at Carnegie Endowment for International Peace, Washington, October 12, 1999.

49. See Richard L. Garwin, "The Wrong Plan," *Bulletin of the Atomic Scientists*, vol. 56 (March–April 2000), pp. 36–41; and Garwin, "A Defense That Will Not Defend," pp. 121–22. Garwin estimates the weight of such a boost-phase interceptor, which need not carry a heavy payload, at fourteen tons; by contrast, existing U.S. ICBMs and SLBMs generally weigh thirty to one hundred tons.

50. Theodore Postol, "Hitting Them Where It Works," *Foreign Policy*, no. 117 (Winter 1999–2000), p. 132.

51. Presentation by Richard Garwin, Harvard-CSIS Ballistic Missile Defense Conference, Cambridge, Mass., May 11, 2000.

52. See, for example, Thomas B. Cochran, William M. Arkin, and Milton M. Hoenig, *Nuclear Weapons Databook*, Volume I: *U.S. Nuclear Forces and Capabilities* (Ballinger Publishing, 1984), p. 145.

53. The Martin-Marietta Corporation (now part of Lockheed Martin) prepared such a study for the Fletcher Panel, an official advisory group evaluating technologies for national missile defense for the Pentagon. See John Tirman, ed., *The Fallacy of Star Wars* (Vintage Books, 1984), p. 62.

54. Postol, "Hitting Them Where It Works," pp. 132–33.

55. David Mosher and Michael O'Hanlon, *The START Treaty and Beyond* (Congressional Budget Office, 1991), p. 139; and Forden, *Budgetary and Technical Implications*, p. 12.

56. Forden, *Budgetary and Technical Implications*, p. 10.

57. Richard L. Garwin, "Effectiveness of Proposed National Missile Defense against ICBMs from North Korea," March 17, 1999 (www.fas.org/rlg [November 2000]).

58. See Dean Wilkening, "Airborne Boost-Phase Ballistic Missile Defense," briefing slides, Stanford University, Center for International Security and Cooperation, May 9, 2000.

59. Kerry Gildea, "Theater Missile Defense Programs in Trouble, Top Pentagon Official Warns," *Aerospace Daily*, May 25, 1999, p. 39; Geoffrey E. Forden, "The Airborne Laser," *IEEE Spectrum*, vol. 34 (September 1997), pp. 40–49; and John Donnelly, "Basis for Pentagon Approval of Airborne Laser 'Questionable,'" *Defense Week*, March 15, 1999, p. 1.

60. General Accounting Office, *Defense Acquisitions: DoD Efforts to Develop Laser Weapons for Theater Defense*, GAO/NSIAD-99-50 (March 1999).

61. The space-based laser program is probably two decades in the future; ibid., p. 20.

62. Tanks, *National Missile Defense*, pp. 5.14–5.15.

63. Terry M. Neal, "Bush Backs Wider Missile Defenses," *Washington Post*, May 24, 2000, p. A1; and Alison Mitchell, "Bush Says U.S. Should Reduce Nuclear Arms," *New York Times*, May 24, 2000, p. A1.

64. Mosher and O'Hanlon, *The START Treaty and Beyond*, pp. 69–70, 167–71.

65. R. James Woolsey, "The Way to Missile Defense," *National Review*, June 19, 2000, pp. 36-41.

66. Tirman, *Fallacy of Star Wars*, pp. 102–04.

67. Chapter 6 develops this proposal more fully.

Chapter Five

1. See Steven Lee Myers and Jane Perlez, "Documents Detail U.S. Plan to Alter '72 Missile Treaty," *New York Times*, April 28, 2000, p. A1; "Proposal on ABM: 'Ready to Work with Russia,'" *New York Times*, April 28, 2000, p. A10.

2. Bill Gertz, "Joint Chiefs Oppose Russian Plan to Cut 1,000 U.S. Warheads," *Washington Times*, May 11, 2000, p. A1; Bill Gertz and David Sands, "President Sticks to 2,000 Limit for Nuclear Arms Cuts," *Washington Times*, May 12, 2000,

p. A10; and Walter Pincus and Roberto Suro, "How Low Should Nuclear Arsenal Go?" *Washington Post*, May 12, 2000, p. A4.

3. Quoted in "Putin: 'We've Established Now . . . Personal Relations,'" *Washington Post*, June 5, 2000, p. A11. For a compendium of remarks by Russian officials on missile defense and the ABM Treaty, see Sen. Thad Cochran, *Stubborn Things: A Decade of Facts about Ballistic Missile Defense* (U.S. Senate, 2000), appendix B (www.senate.gov/~gov_affairs/Stubborn.htm [November 2000]).

4. See David Sands, "Putin Missile Plan Covers All Europe," *Washington Times*, June 7, 2000, p. A11.

5. Michael R. Gordon, "Putin Seeks Allies in Quest to Fight U.S. Missile Plan," *New York Times*, June 11, 2000, p. 1.6; Michael R. Gordon, "Russian Officials Flesh Out Alternative Antimissile Proposal," *New York Times*, June 14, 2000, p. A12; and Daniel Williams, "Russia Wants Political Shield," *Washington Post*, June 14, 2000, p. A34.

6. Quoted in Martin Nesirky, "Interview—Russian General Slams U.S. on Missile Plan," *Reuters*, February 14, 2000.

7. David Hoffman, "Russian Generals Diverge from Putin-Clinton Stance on Missile Threat," *Washington Post*, June 30, 2000, p. A27.

8. David Hoffman, "Moscow Warns U.S. on Missile Defense," *Washington Post*, October 26, 1999, p. A19; David Hoffman, "New Life for 'Star Wars' Response," *Washington Post*, November 22, 1999, p. A18; and David Hoffman, "Russian Rocket Called Invincible," *Washington Post*, February 25, 1999, p. A20.

9. David Mosher and Michael O'Hanlon, *The START Treaty and Beyond* (Congressional Budget Office, 1991), p. 148.

10. "Interview with Security Council Secretary Sergei Ivanov on the New Military Doctrine of Russia (Vremya Ort Program 21:00, April 24, 2000), translated by Federal News Service.

11. Igor Ivanov, "The Missile-Defense Mistake," *Foreign Affairs*, vol. 79 (September–October 2000), pp. 16–17.

12. Quoted in Fred Weir, "Putin Tries Big Shift in Military Strategy," *Christian Science Monitor*, August 2, 2000, p. 1.

13. Quoted in Michael R. Gordon, "Putin Wins Vote in Parliament on Treaty to Cut Nuclear Arms," *New York Times*, April 15, 2000, p. A1.

14. Sharon LaFraniere, "Russian Threatens Action over U.S. Missile Plan," *Washington Post*, June 23, 2000, p. A21.

15. See Clifford Gaddy and Michael O'Hanlon, "The Russian Submarine Disaster," *San Diego Union-Tribune*, August 27, 2000, p. G1; and Michael Dobbs, "Soviet-Era Work on Bioweapons Still Worrisome," *Washington Post*, September 12, 2000, p. A1.

16. We discuss this question more fully in chapter 6.

17. See Michael McDevitt, "Beijing's Bind," *Washington Quarterly*, vol. 23 (Summer 2000), pp. 177–86.

18. Quoted in John Pomfret, "China Warns of New Arms Race," *Washington Post*, November 11, 1999, p. A1.

19. Barbara Crossette, "At U.N., Russia Hardens Line on Changes to Missile Treaty," *New York Times*, April 26, 2000, p. A10.

20. Quoted in Ted Plafker, "China Joins Russia in Warning U.S. on Shield," *Washington Post*, July 29, 2000, p. A1.

21. John Pomfret, "China Threatens Arms Control Collapse," *Washington Post*, July 14, 2000, p. A1.

22. Erik Eckholm, "What America Calls a Defense China Calls an Offense," *New York Times*, July 2, 2000, p. 4.3.

23. Quoted in "Why China Hates NMD," *Wall Street Journal*, July 11, 2000, p. A26.

24. See Gideon Long and Charles Aldinger, "China Hits Missile Plan as Meddling in Taiwan," *Washington Times*, July 7, 2000, p. A1; and Walter Pincus, "U.S. Weighs Possible Foreign Reaction to Missile Defense," *Washington Post*, July 7, 2000, p. A13.

25. See Eric McVadon, "PRC Exercises, Doctrine and Tactics toward Taiwan: The Naval Dimension," in James R. Lilley and Chuck Downs, eds., *Crisis in the Taiwan Strait* (Washington: National Defense University Press, 1997), pp. 248–76; and Michael O'Hanlon, "Why China Can't Conquer Taiwan," *International Security*, vol. 25 (Fall 2000), pp. 51–86.

26. Bill Gertz, "Admiral Says Taiwan Invasion Would Fail," *Washington Times*, March 8, 2000, p. A5; and Steven Mufson and Thomas E. Ricks, "Pentagon Won't Back Taiwan Deal," *Washington Post*, April 17, 2000, p. A1.

27. Brad Roberts, Robert A. Manning, and Ronald N. Montaperto, "China: The Forgotten Nuclear Power," *Foreign Affairs*, vol. 79 (July–August 2000), p. 56.

28. John Pomfret, "China Again Demands U.S. Drop Missile Defense," *Washington Post*, July 12, 2000, p. A16.

29. See Michael D. Swaine, *Taiwan's National Security, Defense Policy, and Weapons Procurement Processes* (Santa Monica, Calif.: Rand Corporation, 1999).

30. "The Missile Misses," *Washington Post*, July 9, 2000, p. B6.

31. Ibid.

32. Roberto Suro, "Study Sees Possible China Nuclear Buildup," *Washington Post*, August 10, 2000, p. A2.

33. Central Intelligence Agency, *Unclassified Report to Congress on the Acquisition of Technology Relating to Weapons of Mass Destruction and Advanced Munitions, 1 July through 31 December 1999* (www.cia.gov/cia/publications/bian/bian_aug2000.htm [November 2000]); Bill Gertz, "Pakistan Gets More Chinese Weapons," *Washington Times*, August 9, 2000, p. A1; David E. Sanger and Eric Schmitt, "Reports Say China Is Aiding Pakistan on Missile Project," *New York Times*, July 2, 2000, p. 1.1; and Roberto Suro, "Study Sees Possible China Nuclear Buildup," *Washington Post*, August 10, 2000, p. A2.

34. Pomfret, "China Threatens Arms Control Collapse," p. A1.

35. Quoted in Pomfret, "China Threatens Arms Control Collapse," p. A1.

36. Among others, see Stephen Cambone and others, *European Views of National Missile Defense* (Washington: Atlantic Council of the United States, September 2000), pp. 4–5 (www.acus.org/Publications/policypapers/TransatlanticRelations/EuropeNMD.pdf [accessed November 2000]); *Foreign*

Affairs—Eighth Report, House of Commons, United Kingdom (www. publications.parliament.uk/pa/cm1999900/cmselect/cmfaff/407/40702.htm [November 2000]); and Xavier de Villepin, "La defense antimissiles du territoire (NMD) aux Etats-Unis," Rapport d'information no. 417, June 14, 2000.

37. In one poll, 77 percent of the Canadians polled agreed that Canada should help the United States build a missile defense for all of North America. David - Pugliese, "Canada Gets Closer to U.S. NMD Effort," *Defense News*, March 27, 2000, p. 18.

38. Camille Grand, "Missile Defense: The View from the Other Side of the Atlantic," *Arms Control Today*, vol. 30 (September 2000), pp. 12–14.

39. See Cambone and others, *European Views of National Missile Defense*, pp. 18–19.

40. David Cracknell, "'Star Wars' Missile Shield Threatens to Split the Cabinet," *London Sunday Telegraph*, July 2, 2000, p. 9.

41. George Jones, "We'll Back Star Wars, Says Hague," *London Daily Telegraph*, January 12, 2001, p. 1.

42. Keith J. Costa, "Study Group Calls on Britain to Take Up Ballistic Missile Defenses," *Inside the Pentagon*, June 8, 2000, p. 14.

43. Charles Grant, "Europe and Missile Defence," *Centre for European Reform Bulletin*, no. 11 (April–May 2000), p. 6.

44. See Bruno Tertrais, "Future Shock? Assessing the Impact of NMD on International Security," paper prepared for the PIR Center for Policy Studies, Moscow, September 4, 2000. Tertrais also offers useful advice on how the United States might better handle the NMD issue.

45. Some European analysts acknowledge this even as they criticize U.S. NMD plans on other grounds. Francois Heisbourg, "Brussels's Burden," *Washington Quarterly*, vol. 23 (Summer 2000), p. 129.

46. Quoted in Grand, "Missile Defense," p. 12.

47. For a good discussion of this issue, see Grand, "Missile Defense: The View from the Other Side of the Atlantic," pp. 16–17.

48. Quoted in Christopher Marquis, "Cohen Says Missile Defense System Requires Support of Allies," *New York Times*, July 26, 2000, p. A3.

49. Gopal Ratnam and Amy Svitak, "Pentagon Eyes Naval Deployment of NMD Radar," *Defense News*, August 21, 2000, p. 1.

50. *Foreign Affairs—Eighth Report*.

51. Quoted in Ratnam and Svitak, "Pentagon Eyes Naval Deployment of NMD Radar," p. 20.

52. Quoted in "U.S. Delegation to Brief Greenland on Anti-Missile Scheme," Agence France Presse, August 21, 2000.

53. Ivo H. Daalder and Philip H. Gordon, "Watch for Missile Defense to Become a European Conundrum," *International Herald Tribune*, February 23, 2000, p. 8.

54. Philip H. Gordon, "Their Own Army?" *Foreign Affairs*, vol. 79 (July–August 2000), pp. 12–17; and Charles A. Kupchan, "In Defence of European Defence: An American Perspective," *Survival*, vol. 42 (Fall 2000), pp. 16–32.

55. Heisbourg, "Brussels's Burden," pp. 127–33.

56. Michael Evans, "Star Wars Dispute Hangs over G8 Agenda," *London Times*, July 21, 2000, p. 17.

57. Victor D. Cha, "Engaging North Korea Credibly," *Survival*, vol. 42 (Summer 2000), p. 150.

58. Bernard Lagan, "Spy Bases Ready for U.S. Missile Shield," *Sydney Morning Herald*, July 18, 2000, p. 5; and Michael Richardson, "Missile Shield Stirs Up Dissent in Australia," *International Herald Tribune*, July 19, 2000, p. 7.

59. "Labor Slates Missile Defence," *Canberra Times*, July 18, 2000, p. 1; and Malcolm Fraser, "Missile Defense?" *International Herald Tribune*, July 28, 2000, p. 10.

60. Judith Miller and James Risen, "A Nuclear War Feared Possible over Kashmir," *New York Times*, August 8, 2000, p. A8.

61. "Remarks to the One America Meeting," *Public Papers of the President*, doc. 506, March 9, 2000, p. 2.

62. George Perkovich, *India's Nuclear Bomb* (University of California Press, 1999), pp. 404–43; on the Kargil war, see Praveen Swami, *The Kargil War* (New Delhi: Leftword Books, 1999); and Pamela Constable, "Selective Truths," in an unedited collection of essays, *Guns and Yellow Roses: Essays on the Kargil War* (New Delhi: HarperCollins, 1999), pp. 35–61.

63. See, for example, Brahma Chellaney, "New Delhi's Dilemma," *Washington Quarterly*, vol. 23 (Summer 2000), pp. 147–49; Joseph Cirincione, "The Asian Nuclear Reaction Chain," *Foreign Policy*, vol. 118 (Spring 2000), pp. 120–36; Bob Drogin and Tyler Marshall, "Missile Shield Analysis Warns of Arms Buildup," *Los Angeles Times*, May 19, 2000, p. A1; Gaurav Kampani and Peter Saracino, "National Missile Defense Threatens Stability in South Asia," *Defense News*, July 10, 2000, p. 15; George Lewis, Lisbeth Gronlund, and David Wright, "National Missile Defense: An Indefensible System," *Foreign Policy*, vol. 117 (Winter 1999–2000), p. 135; and Michael R. Gordon and Steven Lee Myers, "Risk of Arms Race Seen in U.S. Design of Missile Defense," *New York Times*, May 28, 2000, p. 11.

64. Perkovich, *India's Nuclear Bomb*, pp. 444–68.

65. See Kanti Bajpai, "India's Nuclear Posture after Pokhran II," *International Studies* (New Delhi), vol. 37 (October–December 2000), pp. 267–301.

66. Richard Perle, "A Better Way to Build Missile Defense," *New York Times*, July 13, 2000, p. A29.

67. See, for example, Stephen W. Young, *Pushing the Limits: The Decision on National Missile Defense* (Washington: Coalition to Reduce Nuclear Dangers and Council for a Livable World Education Fund, April 2000), pp. 24–25.

68. See Ivo H. Daalder, James M. Goldgeier, and James M. Lindsay, "Deploying NMD: Not Whether, But How," *Survival*, vol. 42 (Spring 2000), pp. 19–21; and Charles V. Pena, "Arms Control and Missile Defense: Not Mutually Exclusive," *Policy Analysis*, July 26, 2000.

69. Quoted in Jack Mendelsohn, "Box 5c: The Effect of NMD on Proliferation," in Lawyers Alliance for World Security, *White Paper on National Missile Defense* (Washington, 2000), p. 38.

Chapter Six

1. Although the Rumsfeld Commission's discussion of the potential ICBM threat attracted the most media attention, the commission also highlighted the potential threat that shorter-range ballistic and cruise missiles pose. See *Commission to Assess the Ballistic Missile Threat to the United States*, executive summary of report to Congress (Government Printing Office, July 15, 1998), pp. 20–21. See appendix C to this volume, and for the entire report see www.brookings.edu/defendingamerica.

2. In this book we do not investigate the details of what a defense against the shorter-range missile threat might entail, though it would no doubt be an expensive proposition, given the length of America's coastline and the difficulty of detecting cruise missiles. But a combination of balloon aerostats, existing air defenses, selectively located surface-to-air missile batteries for air defense, and TMD could do a reasonable job. Technologies are presently being developed that could perform these various tasks. But the pace of research is perhaps too slow, with a target date of roughly 2010 for even completing a master plan on cruise missile defense for overseas battlefields. Cruise missile defense research efforts should probably grow to at least the cost of individual TMD programs—perhaps $100 million to $300 million a year above current levels. The costs of deployment would be much more significant. Consider just the missiles. Spacing a battery of Patriot PAC-3 interceptors every sixty miles or so along the U.S. border might cost several billion dollars. This price tag is both too large to ignore, in thinking about longer-term homeland defense requirements, and not so large as to make the effort entirely prohibitive. This back-of-the-envelope analysis is obviously preliminary in nature but goes to underscore the importance of avoiding a fixation with NMD systems at the expense of cruise missile defense.

3. For a proposal along similar lines, see Jan Lodal, *The Price of Dominance* (New York: Council on Foreign Relations Press, 2001), chap. 3.

4. Dean Wilkening, *Ballistic-Missile Defence and Strategic Stability*, Adelphi Paper 334 (London: International Institute for Strategic Studies, 2000), p. 67.

5. On Shemya's short construction season, see Roberto Suro, "Key Missile Defense Radar Planned for Remote Island," *Washington Post*, May 7, 2000, p. A6.

6. Michael R. Gordon and Steven Lee Myers, "Politics Mixes with Strategy in Plan for Antimissile System," *New York Times*, June 23, 2000, p. A1.

7. See Dean A. Wilkening, "Amending the ABM Treaty," *Survival*, vol. 42 (Spring 2000), pp. 41–42.

8. In February 2001 President Putin gave NATO Secretary General Lord Robertson a proposal for a joint Russian-European missile defense that conspicuously made no mention of boost-phase interceptors. See Michael R. Gordon, "Moscow Signaling a Change of Tone on Missile Defense," *New York Times*, February 22, 2001, p. A1.

9. See David Mosher and Michael O'Hanlon, *The START Treaty and Beyond* (Congressional Budget Office, 1991), pp. 18–26.

10. Walter Pincus and Roberto Suro, "How Low Should Nuclear Arsenal Go?" *Washington Post*, May 12, 2000, p. A4.

11. Philipp C. Bleek, "Russia Ready to Reduce to 1,500 Warheads, Addressing Dispute over Strategic Forces' Fate," *Arms Control Today*, vol. 30 (September 2000), p. 22.

12. See Michael O'Hanlon, *Technological Change and the Future of Warfare* (Brookings, 2000), pp. 160–66.

13. See, for example, Carla Anne Robbins, "Bipartisan Thinkers Look Past Traditional Arms Control," *Wall Street Journal*, May 18, 2000, p. A28.

14. See Michael McDevitt, "Beijing's Bind," *Washington Quarterly*, vol. 23 (Summer 2000), pp. 177–86.

15. Governor George W. Bush, "New Leadership on National Security," speech to the National Press Club, Washington, May 23, 2000 (www.georgew-bush.com/News/speeches/052300_nsecurity.html [November 2000]).

16. See Roberto Suro, "Bush on Defense: Details to Come," *Washington Post*, September 21, 2000, p. A1.

17. See "Presidential Election Forum: The Candidates on Arms Control," *Arms Control Today*, vol. 30 (September 2000), p. 4.

18. "Presidential Election Forum," p. 3.

19. Bush, "New Leadership on National Security"; "Presidential Election Forum," pp. 5–6.

20. P. L. 106-38.

21. Chris Chambers, "Majority of Americans Continue to Support Nuclear Missile Defense System," *Gallup Poll Monthly*, no. 418 (July 2000), p. 66; and Pew Research Center for the People and the Press, "Voter Preferences Vacillate," May 14, 2000, p. 13 (www.people-press.org/may00que2.htm [November 2000]).

22. Pew Research Center, "Voter Preferences Vacillate," pp. 11, 32. Gallup has found similar results. Chambers, "Majority of Americans Continue to Support Nuclear Missile Defense," p. 66.

23. The argument draws on the one laid out in Ivo H. Daalder, James M. Goldgeier, and James M. Lindsay, "Deploying NMD: Not Whether, But How," *Survival*, vol. 42 (Spring 2000), pp. 23–25.

24. Eric Schmitt, "Senate Kills Test Ban Treaty in Crushing Loss for Clinton; Evokes Versailles Pact Defeat," *New York Times*, October 14, 1999, p. A1.

25. See Richard Lowry, "Test-Ban Ban: How the Treaty Went Down," *National Review*, November 8, 1999, pp. 20–22; and Matthew Rees, "The Right Thing for Our Country," *Weekly Standard*, October 25, 1999, pp. 24–26.

26. CNN, Late Edition with Wolf Blitzer, October 17, 1999, Transcript 99101700V47.

27. James M. Goldgeier, *Not Whether But When: The U.S. Decision to Enlarge NATO* (Brookings, 1999), pp. 125–27. More generally, see James M. Lindsay, *Congress and the Politics of U.S. Foreign Policy* (Johns Hopkins University Press, 1994), pp. 122–26.

Index

Missiles—other specific: Chinese
CSS–4, 221, 222; Chinese DF-31,
221, 222; Chinese JL-2, 221;
Chinese M11, 207, 225; Indian
Agni, 37, 206–07, 225; Indian
Prithvi, 206–07, 225; Indian
Sagarika, 207; Iranian Shahab, 37,
65, 204–05, 225; Iraqi Al Abbas,
206; Iraqi Al Hussein, 206;
Minuteman, 37; MX, 37, 93, 109;
North Korean No Dong, 37, 59,
136, 207–08, 213, 220, 225; North
Korean Taepo Dong, 60, 61, 62,
69, 107, 135, 136, 164, 193,
203–04, 219, 220; Navy theater-
wide, 42; Pakistani Ghauri,
207–08, 213, 225; Pakistani
Tarmuk, 207; Scud, 3–4, 37, 51,
59, 7, 89, 117, 135, 202–08; Soviet
SS-18, 30, 37, 53, 54, 94; Soviet
SS-25, 37; Standard, 101, 102;
Tomahawk, 93; Trident, 108
Missile Technology Control Regime
(MTCR), 17, 194–95
Monitoring. See Verification and
monitoring
Moscow summit (2000), 118
MTCR. See Missile Technology
Control Regime
Multiple independently targetable
reentry vehicles (MIRVs): defense
against, 46; Russia and, 121–22;
technology of, 48, 95; use of, 31.
See also Reentry vehicles
Mutual assured destruction (MAD).
See Mutual vulnerability
Mutual vulnerability, 5. See also
Deterrence
MX missile, 93

Nagasaki, 80
National Intelligence Council (U.S.),
11
National Intelligence Estimate (NIE):
ballistic missile threat, 74;
countermeasure development, 63;

excerpts from, 193–96, 218–26;
Iraqi missiles, 69; North Korean
missiles, 59, 60, 61; Russian
countermeasures, 54
National Missile Defense (NMD,
U.S.): Anti-Ballistic Missile Treaty
and, 90–91, 108, 109, 114, 117,
144, 145, 156–62; arguments for
and against, 142–45, 147; arms
race, arms reductions, and arms
control, 139–41, 158, 161, 167;
Bush, George W. and, 1, 20, 91,
152, 162–64; China and, 123–30,
140, 144; Clinton Capability 1, 2,
and 3, 82–83, 86–91, 99–101, 118,
119, 120, 152; compared with
theater missile defenses, 37–40;
costs of, 28, 91–92, 100, 102,
108–09, 111, 115, 163–64; effects
of, 1–2, 13, 19–20, 28, 98, 119,
130, 141, 144; Europeans and, 133;
evolution and missions, 8, 14, 37;
India and Pakistan, 137–39;
international politics of, 116–41,
145, 151; layered and space-based
systems, 111–15, 144–67; missile
speeds, 101–02, 108; mutual
assured destruction and, 7; NATO
and, 116–17, 130, 131–34;
post–cold war views of, 7, 119;
proposals for, 22–28, 82–83,
86–87, 89–115, 144–67; Russia
and, 102, 117–23, 140, 144, 146,
158; sales and proliferation of
technology, 75; schedule and
deployment, 92–94, 107, 110, 152,
153–54; sensible and limited
defense, 20–22; space-based, 111;
testing, 93; threats to the U.S. and,
50, 78, 106–07; two-tiered,
145–67; types of, 43–46; use of
prevention, preemption, and
deterrence, 17–20; U.S. friends and
allies, 130–39, 145, 153–54,
161–62; U.S. views of, 1–2, 7. See
also Clinton (Bill) administration—